Virtual exchange in the Asia-Pacific: research and practice

Edited by Eric Hagley and Yi'an Wang

Published by Research-publishing.net, a not-for-profit association
Contact: info@research-publishing.net

© 2020 by Editors (collective work)
© 2020 by Authors (individual work)

Virtual exchange in the Asia-Pacific: research and practice
Edited by Eric Hagley and Yi'an Wang

Publication date: 2020/12/21

Rights: the whole volume is published under the Attribution-NonCommercial-NoDerivatives International (CC BY-NC-ND) licence; **individual articles may have a different licence**. Under the CC BY-NC-ND licence, the volume is freely available online (https://doi.org/10.14705/rpnet.2020.47.9782490057788) for anybody to read, download, copy, and redistribute provided that the author(s), editorial team, and publisher are properly cited. Commercial use and derivative works are, however, not permitted.

Disclaimer: Research-publishing.net does not take any responsibility for the content of the pages written by the authors of this book. The authors have recognised that the work described was not published before, or that it was not under consideration for publication elsewhere. While the information in this book is believed to be true and accurate on the date of its going to press, neither the editorial team nor the publisher can accept any legal responsibility for any errors or omissions. The publisher makes no warranty, expressed or implied, with respect to the material contained herein. While Research-publishing.net is committed to publishing works of integrity, the words are the authors' alone.

Trademark notice: product or corporate names may be trademarks or registered trademarks, and are used only for identification and explanation without intent to infringe.

Copyrighted material: every effort has been made by the editorial team to trace copyright holders and to obtain their permission for the use of copyrighted material in this book. In the event of errors or omissions, please notify the publisher of any corrections that will need to be incorporated in future editions of this book.

Typeset by Research-publishing.net
Cover theme by © 2020 iStockphoto.com/amtitus
Cover layout by © 2020 Raphaël Savina (raphael@savina.net)

ISBN13: 978-2-490057-78-8 (Ebook, PDF, colour)
ISBN13: 978-2-490057-79-5 (Ebook, EPUB, colour)
ISBN13: 978-2-490057-77-1 (Paperback - Print on demand, black and white)
Print on demand technology is a high-quality, innovative and ecological printing method; with which the book is never 'out of stock' or 'out of print'.

British Library Cataloguing-in-Publication Data.
A cataloguing record for this book is available from the British Library.

Legal deposit, France: Bibliothèque Nationale de France - Dépôt légal: décembre 2020.

Table of contents

v   Notes on contributors

xi   Acknowledgments

xiii Foreword
     Darla K. Deardorff

1   Introduction and overview
     Eric Hagley and Yi'an Wang

Section 1.
Bringing virtual exchange in the Asia-Pacific region into focus: research, roadmaps and reaction

11   Ethnographic approaches to developing intercultural competence through intercultural interactions in the higher education context in China
     Yi'an Wang and Liyang Miao

37   What do we exchange in virtual exchange? Reflections on virtual exchange as intercultural dialogue
     Jan Van Maele

61   Tackling international controversies in virtual exchange
     Masahito Watanabe

77   ICC cultivation in a multiform course mode
     Ran Liu and Yi'an Wang

Section 2.
Virtual exchange in the language and intercultural studies classroom

105 Collaborative tasks in telecollaboration: their challenges and potentials
     Hisae Matsui

Table of contents

125 The practical realities of virtual exchange
Sandra Healy and Olivia Kennedy

145 The affordances of wikis for virtual exchange
Thomas Kaufmann

165 The role virtual exchange could play in helping prepare students for real-life study abroad
Andrew Ryan

179 Improving interactions between teachers and students in virtual exchanges – a case of mentor/learner relationships in MOOCs
Richard Draeger Jr and Steve J. Kulich

201 Project Ibunka – a web-based virtual exchange project
Masahito Watanabe

231 Musings on virtual exchange in the Asia-Pacific and beyond
Eric Hagley

241 Author index

Notes on contributors

Editors

Eric Hagley is a research fellow at Hosei University in Japan. He created the International Virtual Exchange Project (IVEProject) which has had over 23,000 students from 18 countries participating in Virtual Exchange (VE) over the last 5 years. The IVEProject continues to expand and is one of many VE that are changing the way communicative language teaching is being taught around the world. He has written and presented on VE extensively. He is the co-chair and president of the Asia Pacific Virtual Exchange Association (APVEA) and was vice-president of PacCALL from 2009 to 2018.

Yi'an Wang is Professor and Vice Dean of the School of Foreign Languages and Literature at Hangzhou Dianzi University in PR China. He got his MA in Intercultural Communication at the University of Sydney and holds a PhD in Intercultural Communication from Shanghai International Studies University in China. His research interest focuses on intercultural competence development and assessment and its application in different contexts, intercultural adjustment, and intercultural training. He is one of the coordinators of ERASMUS+ project "Resources for interculturality in Chinese Higher Education/RICH-Ed" in China.

Invited author

Darla K. Deardorff is Executive Director of the Association of International Education Administrators (AIEA), a research scholar at Duke University, and holds faculty positions at universities in several countries including Nelson Mandela University (S. Africa), Meiji University (Japan), Shanghai International Studies University (China), York University (Canada), and North Carolina State University, and Harvard University's Global Education Think Tank. Author/editor of 8 books and over 60 book chapters/articles, she is Founding President of the World Council on Intercultural and Global Competence, and regularly gives invited talks, trainings and workshops around the world. She can be reached through LinkedIn and at d.deardorff@duke.edu.

Notes on contributors

Authors

Chapter 1

Yi'an Wang, see Editors' section.

Liyang Miao is Associate Professor of the School of Foreign Languages and Literature at Hang Dianzi University in PR China. She got her MA in TESOL at the University of New South Wales in Australia. She has been teaching the course Intercultural Communication for over six years. Her research interest focuses on intercultural competence development and assessment, intercultural training, IC teaching and learning in Chinese higher education. She is a member of the core team of ERASMUS+ project "Resources for interculturality in Chinese Higher Education/ RICH-ED" in China. She is the Main Educator of the HDU Gold Online/ Virtual Reality Course Intercultural Communication.

Chapter 2

Jan Van Maele teaches and researches communication at the Faculty of Engineering Technology, KU Leuven, Belgium. He holds a PhD in language assessment from UCL, Belgium. His main interests are intercultural interaction, international education, and language assessment. He has conducted various projects in these fields with partners in Europe, Asia, and Latin America. Currently he coordinates the Erasmus+ RICH-Ed project on interculturality in Chinese higher education. In recent years he has been a visiting research scholar in the UK, Japan, and China.

Chapter 3

Masahito Watanabe is Professor of Yokohama National University, Japan, teaching general English courses and linguistics for university students and coordinating English instructors. Linguistics and pedagogical grammar are the major fields of the study. A translator of Grammar in Use Intermediate Third Edition (CUP), Language Arts: Product and Assessment for Diverse Classroom Fifth Edition (Waveland Pr. Inc.), etc.

Notes on contributors

Chapter 4

Ran Liu is a freelance researcher. She got her MA in Intercultural Communication at Hangzhou Dianzi University, the study experience motivated her to experience different culture, then she got her MA in Heritage Management at University of Kent and volunteered in museum projects in Athens, Greece. Her interests are in online education, virtual museum construction and intercultural training. She also participated in constructions aid programmes held by African Development Bank in Kenya.

Yi'an Wang, see Editors' section.

Chapter 5

Hisae Matsui is Lecturer in the Department of East Asian Studies at Princeton University. She received her Ed.D. in Technology Education and MA in TESOL/Linguistics from West Virginia University (USA). At Princeton University, she has been teaching Japanese language from elementary to advanced levels. Her scholarly interests are various forms of integrations of technology in foreign language pedagogy.

Chapter 6

Sandra Healy is Associate Professor of Applied Linguistics at Kyoto Institute of Technology in Japan. She has taught graduate and undergraduate courses for more than twenty years in Japanese universities. Her research focuses on the use of technology in second language education, and issues concerning language and identity, particularly gender and culture.

Olivia Kennedy runs the Foreign Languages program at Nagahama Institute of Bioscience and Technology, and also teaches at Kyoto Institute of Technology. She is passionate about improving learner experiences and outcomes in the L2 classroom. Her research focuses on overcoming barriers to the meaningful integration of technology into the learning space.

Notes on contributors

Chapter 7

Thomas Kaufmann M.Ed. is a graduate student of Learning Design and Leadership at the University of Illinois Champaign-Urbana. He's also an Instructor of English for the University of Indianapolis in their China program in Shaoxing, China at Zhejiang Yuexiu University. Most recently due to the pandemic, he's delivered his courses (Technical Writing, Professional Writing, Business Communications, and Research Writing) through virtual exchange.

Chapter 8

Andrew Ryan teaches at the Hokkaido University of Education in Japan and is also their Global Education Leadership Advisor. His particular fields of interest are how to prepare students for overseas study both in terms of language and life and how to assist students on their return from study abroad to maintain their language levels and global outlook.

Chapter 9

Dr Richard Draeger Jr (PhD in Intercultural Communication, University of Wisconsin, Milwaukee) is a faculty member with the School of Finance and Economics at Shanghai International Studies University (SISU). His research interests lie at the intersection of education and development of intercultural communicative competence.

Dr Steve J. Kulich (PhD in Intercultural Communication/Education, Humboldt Univ. of Berlin, Germany) is Founder/Director of the SISU Intercultural Institute (SII) and Distinguished Professor at Shanghai International Studies University (resident since 1993), and Lead Educator of the SISU-FutureLearn "Intercultural Communication" MOOC (run since 2015). Awarded for contributions to Shanghai and the IC field in China, he is also President of the International Academy of Intercultural Research (IAIR). His research interests focus on the cultivation of own-cultural awareness and intercultural competence through education and training, the history of intercultural studies, and Chinese values and identity research.

Chapter 10

Masahito Watanabe, see Author's chapter 3

Chapter 11

Eric Hagley, see Editors' section.

Reviewers

David Campbell is Assistant Professor in the Department of Human Sciences at Obihiro University of Agriculture and Veterinary Medicine in Obihiro, Hokkaido, Japan. His current research interests are Moodle and virtual exchanges. He has created three self-paced listening courses in Moodle and helped improve the Moodle forum module through grants from the Moodle Association of Japan. His newest project is to revamp and enhance the Moodle database module.

William Green is Professor at Sapporo University, Japan. He was educated in the UK, and holds a PhD from Lancaster University. In addition to virtual exchange, his research interests include literary linguistics and language teacher cognition. In his most recent research he has focused on elementary school teachers who, despite not being language specialists, are asked to teach a foreign language. When he is not teaching, reading or writing, he spends his time exploring the delights of Hokkaido with his golden retriever, Olive.

Eric Hagley, see Editors' section.

Weiwei Vivian Shen (沈维维) is Associate Professor in School of Foreign Languages and Literatures of Hangzhou Dianzi University and PhD in English Language and Literature at Shanghai International Studies University and PhD

Notes on contributors

in English studies at the University of Bayreuth. Her academic research focuses mainly on Intercultural studies and Asian American literature. She is on her way to exploring and contributing an innovative perspective to the combination of Intercultural Communication and Literary Studies. Her recent publications include monographs "Critical Interviews" (forthcoming), "Critical Negotiations: New Perspectives on Asian American Women's Ficiton (2019)," "The Third Space in Nie Huangling's Mulberry and Peach and Bharati Muhkerjee's Jasmine" (2015), and "Differences and Analogies: Chinese Diasporic Literature" (forthcoming). She lives now in Hangzhou, P.R. China

Dr Wei Sun is a Fulbright Specialist in Communications/Journalism. Her research interests include intercultural communication, new media studies, and health communication. She is Associate Professor and Director of Graduate Studies in the Department of Communication, Culture and Media Studies at Howard University located in Washington, DC. Her publications have appeared in the Journal of Qualitative Research Reports in Communication, Journal of Faculty Development, The Howard Journal of Communications, Intercultural Communication Studies, and World Communication. Her scholarly works on health communication, social media, and intercultural communication have been included in many academic books.

Yi'an Wang, see Editors' section.

Acknowledgments

This work was supported by the Zhejiang Provincial gold Online Course Project (Intercultural Communication) in 2020, Zhejiang Provincial 'Thirteen-Five-Year Plan' Experimental Virtual Simulation Teaching Project in 2019 and 2020, Zhejiang Provincial University-Industry Collaborative Education Program in 2020, and Graduate Education Teaching Reform Project of Hangzhou Dianzi University in 2020.

We would also like to thank the contributors who have been patient and worked hard to ensure the publication could be completed. We are also particularly grateful to Sylvie Thouësny and her team at Research-publishing.net. Their assistance and dedication have been marvelous and we are truly grateful.

To the team at Hangzhou Dianzi University who ensured the conference went so smoothly – our sincere appreciation. We know how much work went in.

Finally, to you the reader, thank you for your interest in virtual exchange. We hope that your passion will ensure that it becomes a regular part of second/foreign language education around the world.

Eric Hagley and Yi'an Wang

Foreword

Darla K. Deardorff[1]

This publication on virtual exchange is incredibly timely, coming as it does during the pandemic, when universities are increasingly turning to virtual exchange as a viable tool for intercultural learning, particularly when travel and physical exchange are challenging to nearly impossible. The chapters in this publication provide useful and vetted insights into how to implement virtual exchange in practical and concrete ways, from using wikis in online learning to developing mentor/learner relationships in Massive Open Online Courses (MOOCs) to a web-based virtual exchange project. This kind of practical information, grounded in research, is needed now more than ever as universities turn to virtual exchange and online learning as a way forward even in the post-pandemic world. Moreover, given that so much of the intercultural literature is published in the Global North, these chapters provide much-needed insights from uniquely Asia-Pacific perspectives.

In reading through these chapters, some key themes emerge. First, intercultural learning must be intentionally addressed in the online environment. It is not sufficient to expect that simply bringing students together from different places in the world will naturally result in intercultural learning. Such intentionality, in fact, is key to effective virtual exchange. Second is the overall goal of intercultural understanding within virtual exchange, even within challenging international conflicts and sensitive topics (Chapter 3). Indeed, given careful construction of online experiences, intercultural understanding is a realistic goal to achieve. The third theme that emerges is that of connection and collaboration, which is at the heart of virtual exchange. The pandemic has mightily illustrated the need for connections, including more meaningful and deeper connections which are often difficult to achieve through online interactions. However, as discussed in Chapter 1, it is possible to engage in

1. Duke University, Durham, North Carolina, United States; d.deardorff@duke.edu

How to cite: Deardorff, D. K. (2020). Foreword. In E. Hagley & Y. Wang (Eds), *Virtual exchange in the Asia-Pacific: research and practice* (pp. xiii-xiv). Research-publishing.net. https://doi.org/10.14705/rpnet.2020.47.1142

© 2020 Darla K. Deardorff (CC BY)

Foreword

such meaningful connections. In fact, UNESCO has implemented virtual Story Circles[2] in 2020, training United Nations (UN) staff in such countries as Brazil and Cameroon on intercultural competence development, using virtual Story Circles. At the end of one such experience, one UN staff member commented that the virtual Story Circles experience was the most amazing and meaningful experience she had had in all the months of lockdown in her country.

The themes from this publication point toward a bigger picture of the power of human connection in working together to find our common humanity despite our differences. Working together across what may divide us as humans, we are capable and resilient in embracing each other and the oneness of our humanity and in so doing, build a more peaceful world together.

---

2. See open access manual in 5 languages at https://unesdoc.unesco.org/ark:/48223/pf0000370336

Introduction and overview

Eric Hagley[1] and Yi'an Wang[2]

1. Background

The year 2020 will more than likely go down in history as a year many terrible things happened. Yet in the field of education it will also go down as a year in which educators had to overcome enormous hurdles, which they did emphatically. Though never going to take the place of educators, technology came to the fore in the field in 2020 and assisted educators to carry on the incredible work they do. Schools were closed due to the pandemic so education had to go online. It was due to this that Virtual Exchange (VE) started to come of age too. When study abroad programs were so badly affected by the pandemic, other options had to be entertained. When language classes had to go online, teachers started to look outside of their normal boxes. It was then they discovered VE was an option too. As more people who had not seen it before saw that technology could be beneficial to education, the options available showed themselves and the ones that were truly useful flourished. VE was a chief one among them. It is timely then, that this volume appears now.

Due to the incredible work of the UniCollaboration group and the Steven's Initiative, there is now little to add regarding what VE is and its history. In Europe and North America it is bringing people together and helping people to understand and appreciate the wonderful variety of cultures that exist on our planet. However, in Asia and many other parts of the world, VE is still in its infancy and wanting to grow. This volume was born from the third

1. Hosei University, Tokyo, Japan; apveachair@gmail.com; https://orcid.org/0000-0002-4795-8043

2. Hangzhou Dianzi University, Hangzhou, China; wangyian2003@hotmail.com

How to cite: Hagley, E., & Wang, Y. (2020). Introduction and overview. In E. Hagley & Y. Wang (Eds), *Virtual exchange in the Asia-Pacific: research and practice* (pp. 1-7). Research-publishing.net. https://doi.org/10.14705/rpnet.2020.47.1143

Asia-Pacific VE Association's (APVEA) conference in Hangzhou, China. The first biennial conference was held in Muroran, Japan, where just 15 or so passionate proponents of VE in the Asia-Pacific gathered. The second conference at Princeton University expanded on the first exchange and the third conference was where it became obvious that VE was not going to be a 'flash in the pan' movement in Asia. Over 100 educators and researchers from throughout the Asia-Pacific region and beyond participated in fruitful discussion and promotion of VE. The work from that conference appears here and shows that VE is growing in the region.

This volume concentrates on VE in the foreign language and intercultural classroom contexts. The authors herein note that VE has a broad reach within these contexts. It is a shame that there is not more research included here on VE in other contexts such as has been done in Europe. There is still a lot of room to expand! Nevertheless, there is much in this book that will assist the development of VE in Asia and the Pacific and the aim of this book is to offer ideas, assistance, and support to researchers and practitioners in the region.

2. Book organisation

2.1. Bringing virtual exchange in the Asia-Pacific region into focus: research, roadmaps and reaction

The book's first section begins with a chapter by **Yi'an Wang** and **Liyang Miao** who note the importance of research in general and how our students can become a part of this by taking on the role of the ethnographer. Ethnography is an essential element in research of VE but Wang and Miao explore the way students use the researcher role in a multiform VE course to expand on and deepen their understanding of culture and from this develop their Intercultural Communicative Competence (ICC). The chapter speaks to the essence of what can be gained from engagement in intercultural exchange and VE in particular. Though most ethnographic research projects to date have involved people in physical exchanges, the model proposed by Wang and Miao and the methods used in the study will no doubt lead to ethnography becoming an essential component of many VE in the future.

In the second chapter of this section, **Jan Van Maele** brings the focus of VE back to the messages that are shared therein. Often the technology aspect of VE can get in the way of communication, thus it is important to have a grounding of what practitioners and participants alike should be aiming to gain from VE. Van Maele brings the expertise of others into his argument that true dialogue, and all that that term encapsulates, is crucial for any VE to be considered successful. Through dialogue relationships are born. When the dialogue is between people from different cultural backgrounds, a number of challenges present themselves but the relationships that develop can be richer and more complex. Van Maele notes ways for developing these, particularly through the use of story circles, and offers that VE "holds a promise of transformation for the participants: what we get back in the exchange is us, ourselves, our interconnected selves". This is an important point to remember – that participation in VE is a powerful way of not only understanding the 'other' but also of developing our own 'self'.

VE can assist students in many ways and it can also be the medium in which participants build their conceptions of controversy. In chapter three, **Masahito Watanabe** offers a framework on which we can develop our students' preparedness to engage in topics that they may often shy away from. Such topics need to be engaged with rather than put to one side but require a greater level of awareness of both the 'self' and the 'other'. With this, participation in conflict resolution can occur and the participants can carry out said resolution with more confidence. What Watanabe asks his students to bring to such engagements is a 'naïve sentiment' and he offers ways of developing this. It is a powerful tool which all who participate in in-depth exchanges should carry. This chapter will no doubt become a roadmap for many instructors on how to approach controversial topics in not only VE but everyday life.

In the final chapter in this section, **Ran Liu** and **Yi'an Wang** outline the results of a very large study on the effects of participation in VE on Chinese university students' ICC. Few studies have involved such large numbers of students and though, as the authors note, there were some limitations to the study, the results show students do indeed improve their ICC. The multiform manner of instruction was unique and offers another roadmap for instructors to have their students participate in VE and develop their students' ICC. The authors believe that VE needs to be 'popularized' as the benefits are many with students' interest in and ability to interact with other cultures increased. They note that, as with many parts of the Asia-Pacific, students rarely have the opportunity to interact with foreign cultures if they do not have access to VE. They note that making VE standard in foreign language classes would be difficult but very beneficial.

2.2. Virtual exchange in the language and intercultural studies classroom

The second section of the book mainly reports on research and practice in more specific settings. **Hisae Matsui** begins this section by focusing on the collaborative aspect of VE. Certainly if individuals do not collaborate well the possibilities that are available become more limited. This is even more the case when teams of students are meant to be working with each other. Tasks will not be completed and the chances of conflict arising increase if collaboration is not carried out well. This aspect of VE is therefore crucial for effective implementation and to ensure positive outcomes. Understanding how students collaborate is therefore vital and this chapter offers some clear guidelines for improving the prospects of goal attainment for groups participating in VE. It also notes a number of pitfalls that practitioners need to be aware of when organizing team projects in VE. The particular VE researched here was a dual-language VE or eTandem but the core content applies to all international exchanges and is an important addition to the field.

Sandra Healy and **Olivia Kennedy** then explore three different types of VE they have been associated with in their classrooms. Their comprehensive observations of the different models are particularly useful to teachers thinking about beginning a VE as they give detailed descriptions of the benefits and drawbacks of the different models. All instructors involved in VE should be cognizant of the numerous issues they also cover to ensure the best outcome for all concerned. Choice of model, language use within the exchange and between teachers, cross-cultural and intercultural problems, time-management, expectations, and technology are all issues that are covered. An understanding of each of these will assist VE teachers making this chapter a 'must-read' for any budding VE practitioner.

When thinking about VE, one of the first choices teachers have to make is what platform they will use to conduct the VE. There have been many different platforms used in VE to date, but one that has not received as much attention as perhaps it should is the wiki. **Thomas Kaufmann** makes a compelling case for using wikis in VE in this chapter as the wiki affords teachers and students numerous opportunities for more focused collaboration, development of metacognitive skills and the ability to participate more deeply in the creative process of document building. From the researcher and pedagogue's point of view, the wiki allows researchers to see in greater detail the processes that take place and teachers can ensure students' writing includes recursive elements ensuring a deeper understanding of said process. Other features of wikis such as 'track changes' allow teachers to assess writing from both a summative and formative aspect, something traditional writing tools do not allow.

Lee and Song (2019) showed that VE can be as useful as study abroad with relation to improving students' "affective and behavioral aspects of ICC" (p. 192) but obviously did not go so far as to say study abroad was not a worthwhile pursuit. Obviously physical travel abroad, for those that can afford it, offers incredible opportunities. Considering the costs involved, it would be ideal if students who do travel abroad can gain every opportunity that presents itself. In the next chapter, **Andrew Ryan** points out that VE can be used as a preparation course for students. Prior to their travel they become accustomed to difference and train to be adept at seizing communication opportunities and overcoming shyness and other anxieties that travel abroad inevitably produces. With a gentle introduction to foreign culture via a VE, students may be better prepared to 'hit the ground running' when they do arrive at their destination and therefore be better able to attain all the benefits that the travel abroad experience will offer.

Introduction and overview

Richard Draeger Jr and **Steve J. Kulich** look at another aspect of online interaction that is not only related to VE. The chapter looks at a particular element of how a Massive Open Online Course (MOOC) is carried out, that being what interactions occur between the mentors helping facilitate the course and the participants. The particular MOOC the research here was carried out in involved intercultural exchange on a large scale and the results apply equally to facilitators in any VE. The type of feedback facilitators give to VE/MOOC participants can often result in the exchange prospering or withering. Mentors, teachers and/or facilitators require training in giving quality feedback to assist participants in their attainment of the goals of the VE in which they are engaging. This chapter looked at how Communication Accommodation Theory can be utilized to improve understanding and ensure the interactions that take place are both meaningful and helpful.

In the penultimate chapter in this section we revisit **Masahito Watanabe**'s 'Project Ibunka', one of the earliest and largest VE in Asia. Its birth and development in addition to the reasons for its ongoing success are outlined. What we learn from this chapter is that VE is a powerful force for bringing people together to explore cultures and seek to better understand each other. We also see that those that coordinate and lead the project are passionate about doing so. They have specific goals that their students should attain and sequences of which participants should follow. With the assistance of dedicated and well-trained facilitators the objectives of the VE are obtained. What is also shown in this case-study are the clear benefits to students of participation in VE: improved learner centeredness; an increase (often for the first time) in real intercultural communication, and finally qualitative change in the way students write. All are powerful reasons to incorporate VE into language classes.

The final chapter is more of a loose bookend. It is written in a less academic way and simply offers some reflections on what **Eric Hagley** sees are issues that, if overcome, would help in the development and implementation of VE to a broader audience. The goal should be that VE becomes a part of all second language and cultural courses throughout the world. To attain that goal much has to be done and the musings in this final chapter delve into this.

3. Conclusion

In the history of second language education, a number of developments have had a huge effect – corpus linguistics and the resulting understanding of lexis which led to the development of graded readers and extensive reading; the communicative approach and how it moved people away from rote learning; these are two of the major developments that have truly changed the way second language learning is carried out. In years to come I have no doubt that VE will be considered as influential as these or more so when it comes to how second and foreign languages are taught. The benefits of VE are numerous yet still there are too many barriers to implement it systematically. This book will hopefully be a useful resource to expand the understanding of VE, be useful for future practitioners to learn how to employ VE in their classrooms, and be a catalyst to ensure VE becomes a part of language courses the world over.

Reference

Lee, J., & Song, J. (2019). Developing intercultural competence through study abroad, telecollaboration, and on-campus language study. *Language Learning & Technology, 23*(3), 178-198. http://hdl.handle.net/10125/44702

Section 1.

Bringing virtual exchange in the Asia-Pacific region into focus: research, roadmaps and reaction

1. Ethnographic approaches to developing intercultural competence through intercultural interactions in the higher education context in China

Yi'an Wang[1] and Liyang Miao[2]

Abstract

With the recent developing trend of redefining 'culture' across disciplines in intercultural and foreign language education (Corbett, 2003; Shaules, 2007; Spencer-Oatey & Franklin, 2010), it is widely agreed that culture requires a broader definition to improve the teaching and learning of it. Wilkinson (2012) suggests "a redefinition of culture in anthropological rather than aesthetic terms" (p. 302) to ensure that intercultural and language learning leads to Intercultural Competence (IC). Others (Buttjes, 1991; Risager, 2006) also note the importance of anthropological conceptualization when culture is taught in foreign and/or second language classrooms, because motivation to learn the language is increased. Byram (1991) similarly emphasized the need to include active 'cultural experience' in the foreign language classroom, and provided examples including cooking and geography lessons, in which students learn about the food and geography of the country whose language they are studying. A crucial element in research within the anthropology field is ethnography. Thus, to achieve a fuller understanding of culture "as the full gauntlet of social experience that students of foreign languages both learn and participate in" (Wilkinson, 2012, p. 302), including Holliday's (2004) concept of 'small culture', students should take on the role of

1. Hangzhou Dianzi University, Hangzhou, China; wangyian2003@hotmail.com

2. Hangzhou Dianzi University, Hangzhou, China; elenamiaomiao@126.com

How to cite: Wang, Y., & Miao, L. (2020). Ethnographic approaches to developing intercultural competence through intercultural interactions in the higher education context in China. In E. Hagley & Y. Wang (Eds), *Virtual exchange in the Asia-Pacific: research and practice* (pp. 11-36). Research-publishing.net. https://doi.org/10.14705/rpnet.2020.47.1144

Chapter 1

ethnographer too; ethnography practices, in a variety of forms, have become central to intercultural approaches to culture and language teaching and learning (Corbett, 2003).

Keywords: ethnographic approach, intercultural competence, virtual intercultural exchange, MOOC course.

1. Ethnography in language and intercultural education

Brewer (2000) defines ethnography as follows:

> "[e]thnography is the study of people in naturally occurring settings or 'fields' by means of methods which capture their social meanings and ordinary activities, involving the researcher participating directly in the setting, if not also the activities, in order to collect data in a systematic manner but without meaning being imposed on them externally" (p. 9).

Ethnography usually involves an extended period of fieldwork, during which the anthropologist-ethnographer immerses herself within the target culture or society and collects data through participation, observation, interviews and analysis of detailed records of everyone and everything observed (Jackson, 2006; Wilkinson, 2012). However, over the past few decades, ethnography has gained currency beyond the discipline of anthropology. Ethnographic methodologies and techniques have been widely adopted and modified in the relatively newer disciplines of cultural studies, media research and intercultural language education (Corbett, 2003). Though it is clear that the construction of ethnographic accounts of culture demand professional researchers with highly qualified training and dedication, many scholars argue that some training in ethnographic techniques, both in the intercultural classroom and during periods of residence abroad, can benefit learners in classes where intercultural events take place to develop their language proficiency and IC (e.g. Corbett, 2003; Du,

2008; Jackson, 2006, 2010, 2011, 2012; Risager, 2006; Roberts et al., 2001; Wilkinson, 2012).

1.1. Ethnography and language education

Corbett (2003) emphasized the important role of ethnography in language education by illustrating how ethnography influences curriculum planners and materials designers, particularly in English as a Second or Foreign Language (ESL/EFL) teaching. As Corbett (2003) claimed, the adoption of intercultural approaches in the language classroom "demands a new way of thinking about how language works and a new set of goals for the [learners] to achieve" (p. 102), which has led to some forms of teacher development and curricular change. Corbett (2003) further points out that "at this level of language education, ethnography can support more effective innovation" (p. 102). However, Corbett (2003) also warned that any innovation of curriculum which involves a period of ethnographic exploration must "take into consideration the way in which established practices accord status to members of the educational community" (p. 103).

Some practical researchers also show that the adoption of ethnographic activities in ESL/EFL education and training is both doable and desirable if adequate resources are available. For example, Corbett (2003, pp. 105-113) reported that some ethnographic activities (e.g. concept training, cultural associations, negative etiquette, critical incidents) are designed to deepen learners' understanding of cultural acquisition in language classrooms; he made a general distinction between two types of ethnographic activities in terms of learning aims:

> "those [designed to] promote observations and understanding of the target culture with intercultural mediation as a goal, and those activities [designed to] encourage learners to 'think' [ethnographically] like those in the target culture, and to reproduce their cultural behavior" (p. 106).

However, Corbett (2003) also warned that we must be cautious about 'decentring' home cultures when the latter type activities are undertaken because "they are not meant to deny or substitute [counterparts] of home culture or to imply that one way of thinking is better than the other" (p. 107). One example is that of the 'critical incident', which is increasingly used in intercultural classrooms to train learners "to think ethnographically, to 'decentre' from their everyday habits of thought, and to realize that the ordinary is culturally constructed" (Corbett, 2003, p. 113). Close-ended critical incident exercises were the more commonly used activities to culturally assimilate or sensitize students, but Albert (1995) and Snow (2015) developed a more open-ended critical incident exercise, which they called the 'encounter exercise'. These were, according to Snow (2015, p. 287), particularly useful for building four aspects of IC: (1) awareness of problematic situations and the habit of switching to more conscious thinking modes; (2) considering multiple interpretations; (3) awareness of actors which may negatively impact the interpretation process; and (4) awareness of the benefit-of-the-doubt choice. An example of where this was shown to be beneficial was reported by Roberts, Davies, and Jupp (1992). Workers new to the UK were given training to assist them in finding and keeping work, and during this training students were involved in data collection, interviews, and other tasks that were similar in many ways to ethnography. Indeed, the UK's industrial language training service viewed these kinds of tasks as essential for the effective training of and improving opportunities for the migrant workers.

1.2. Developing IC in ethnographic pedagogy

In addition to language proficiency, more and more researchers find that the use of ethnography clearly benefits the development of core capacities related to IC, such as empathy, sensitivity, awareness, and critical reflection. Roberts et al. (2001) suggested that ethnography involves "putting yourselves in someone else's shoes", which does not "make you that other person, but [is] a constant reminder to you that the experience, however temporary and unlike you, has become a part of you" (p. 38). Jackson (2006) proposed that the primary goal of ethnography in intercultural education is to develop in learners a deeper understanding of target cultures from the perspective of an insider. Damen (1987) claimed that ethnography in cultural learning provides learners with the dual perspective of understanding a target culture, through one's own cultural lens and from inside the target culture. To sum up, the 'understanding' that learners gain from their ethnographic experiences leads to an important capacity related to IC – empathy, which does not "imply a compassion for others' plight" like sympathy, but does "indicate the ability to understand the other, to apprehend their point of view and their felt experiences" (Roberts et al., 2001, p. 39). Empathy usually involves a process of social interaction and dialogue, through which learners develop the ability to look at the world from others' perspectives, understanding and apprehending the differences apart from their own, and developing critical reflections on both the target culture and their own.

Du (2008) also summarized two major characteristics, derived from the principles of ethnography, which may promote learners' IC. First, ethnography requires learners to be more sensitive through participatory observation, collecting data inductively rather than deductively in a cross-cultural context. The inductive approach encourages learners to be more cautious and objective, in order to avoid ethnocentric and judgmental views of target cultures. Secondly, ethnography requires researchers to build up "thick, rich description" (Geertz, 1973, p. 125), which not only applies to data collection, but also to data analysis and interpretation. Compared to thin description, a researcher using thick description does not simply focus on describing and interpreting the event itself, but relates the true meaning of the event to its context. In this sense, ethnography can be viewed as "a holistic research method" (Du, 2008, p. 82) through which researchers are intended to increase their sensitivity to and awareness of different contexts through the processes of data collection, analysis, and interpretation. The relationship between ethnography and context may lead to some further questions; for example, about power. Agar (1994) noted:

> "[e]thnography always deals with context and meaning [...]. But the last fifteen years have taught us to ask another question – what systems of power hold those contexts and meanings in place? [...]. You look at local context and meaning just like we always have, but then you ask why are things this way? What power, what interests wrap this local world so that it feels like the natural order of things to its inhabitants?" (p. 28).

Moreover, much recent research has shown links between the theories of 'experiential learning' – particularly Kolb's (1984) learning cycle – with the adoption of ethnography in intercultural education. Kolb's (1984) model suggests a recurring circularity in which experience, reflection, and learning reinforce each other. Although Kolb's (1984) model is not a typical cultural learning theory and has been criticized for its Western assumptions of selfhood (Tennant, 1997), the model is widely applied in different intercultural education and training contexts. For example, Kohonen, Jaatinen, Kaikkonen, and Lehtovaara (2001) expand Kolb's (1984) cycle by including experience, conceptualization, reflection, and application as the central elements that constitute experiential learning in foreign language education. Roberts et al. (2001) claimed that Kolb's (1984) three elements of experience, reflection and learning may also be integrated in any component of an ethnographic program – i.e. the Ealing Ethnography Program (EEP) – in which language learners are trained as ethnographers.

Holmes and O'Neill (2012) noted the importance of links between theory and practice in intercultural education and training by combining three key approaches – experiential learning, ethnographic inquiry and praxis – in her business-management classroom. Based on experiential learning theories and the ethnographic inquiry approach, Holmes and O'Neill (2012) demonstrated the notion of 'praxis' in the global business and management education. Praxis refers to "the need for self-conscious and ethical actions where individuals question their past behavior as well as future possibilities" (Holmes & O'Neill, 2012, p. 474). In practice, students are encouraged to "reframe past behavior, which they have performed and examined in their intercultural encounters within the context of their research tasks" (Holmes & O'Neill, 2012, p. 474).

To sum up, linking ethnography with intercultural pedagogy has been shown to contribute to learners' understanding of these social and intercultural experiences with otherness conceptually, analytically, and emotionally (Roberts, 2003). To this end, ethnography is proposed "as a teaching and learning method" in intercultural education (Wilkinson, 2012, p. 303). Intercultural researchers and practitioners have designed and undertaken small or large-scale projects as effective interventions in different intercultural education contexts.

1.3. Devising ethnographic projects in language and intercultural education

An increasing volume of literature on the intercultural approach encourages learners to undertake larger or small-scale ethnographic projects of various types to explore target cultures (Corbett, 2003; Damen, 1987; Holmes & O'Neill, 2012; Jackson, 2008, 2010, 2011; Roberts et al., 2001). Looking more closely at the example of Roberts et al. (2001), we see a detailed description of the EEP project conducted at Thames Valley University. Language students in this program were trained to be ethnographers over three years in three distinct stages (Roberts et al., 2001, pp. 12-14). Stage one was an introduction to ethnography during their second year of their BA program. Stage two was an ethnographic study conducted during their year abroad, and the final stage was a written report of their ethnographic projects after they had returned to their home university. The first stage involved acquiring ethnographic skills (e.g. participant observation, from data collection to analysis) as well as anthropological and sociolinguistic concepts (e.g. national identities and local boundaries, belief and action) in the expectation that such skills would transfer to investigation of the target cultures when they were abroad. In the second stage, students went to two different countries, each for a period of four or five months. They were required to design and undertake an ethnographic study in one of these countries. In the last year, students were required to write a report based on their ethnographic studies, which were integrated into the curriculum, including assessment of the ethnographic project as part of the final degree award. Roberts (2003) concluded that, for learners,

> "the ethnographic experience provides an intellectual framework, a set of methods and a new orientation to learning from the everyday things of life which should enhance their period of residence abroad and develop a new consciousness for their future work and learning" (p. 128).

More recently, other researchers have conducted comparatively small-scale ethnographic projects in the context of education abroad. Taking an

Chapter 1

ethnographic approach, Jackson (2008, 2010, 2011, 2012) did a series of investigations on the language and (inter)cultural development and self-identities of Hong Kong Chinese university students who participated in various faculty-led exchange programs (short-term, semester- or year-long sojourns) in England. She collected qualitative data from semi-structured interviews, surveys, reflection journals, diaries and field notes, and a language use log. The Intercultural Development Inventory (IDI) (Hammer & Bennett, 2002) was used to assess students' development of intercultural sensitivity. What she found was that many factors influenced the outcomes, such as how hosts interacted with students, how much effort was put into language development, students' personalities, the amount of socio-emotional support available, and an array of other considerations. Jackson (2012) suggested that experiential activities related to ethnographic tasks or projects should be integral in the design of study abroad programs, in order to help students sustain intercultural contact with host nationals, through which the sojourners can develop "a sense of belonging in the host environment, thereby facilitating both language and intercultural learning and adjustment" (p. 458). In addition, mixed-method studies, which combine qualitative data (e.g. semi-structured interviews, field notes from participant observation) and quantitative data (e.g. IDI), were recommended to be applied in such programs.

Another example was Holmes and O'Neill (2012), who investigated how 35 international students in New Zealand, guided by an ethnographic approach, developed and evaluated their IC over a six-week immersion period with a previously unknown cultural other. The student researchers conducted an ethnographic field work assignment which aimed at "identifying a cultural informant – a cultural other – and participating in the life world of this informant through dialogue and action" (Holmes & O'Neill, 2012, p. 710). The ethnographic field assignments had two key objectives: (1) to help students gain a better understanding of someone from another culture; and (2) through that engagement, develop and evaluate their IC (Holmes & O'Neill, 2012, p. 709). Guided by the Preparing, Engaging, Evaluating, and Reflecting (PEER) model developed by Holmes and O'Neill (2012), the student researchers had to acknowledge many things in the data collection process, such as stereotyping, confusion, and fear when it came to interacting with others, but through this, and with guidance, they were able to develop IC.

2. Developing IC through interviews as intercultural interactions in domestic contexts

As mentioned in Wang and Kulich (2015), intercultural encounters, interaction, and experience are crucial for the development of IC (Corbett, 2003), with Stier (2003, 2006) stating that the processual character is often hidden behind the word 'encounter'. Stier (2003, 2006) set IC into two categories: content-competencies (or *knowing that* competencies) and processual competencies (or *knowing how* competencies including the interactional context in which intercultural communication takes place). Alred, Byram, and Fleming (2003) affirmed that, "it is in the interaction with others that we develop" (p. 3) because human beings are social and cultural entities.

However, an encounter with otherness alone does not automatically lead to being 'intercultural'. Alred et al. (2003) distinguish between 'intercultural experience' and 'being intercultural'. The former is "simply a statement of fact", but the latter implies "a more qualitative judgment about the nature of such an encounter" and requires "the awareness of experiencing otherness and the ability to analyze the experience and act upon the insights into self and other which the analysis brings" (Alred et al., 2003, p. 4). Indeed, an international experience alone does not guarantee the acquirement of IC if there are no well-designed interventions before, during, or after a sojourn. A number of studies on both study abroad and intercultural education have shown that immersion in a different culture is not sufficient (even though it is perhaps a necessary) condition to nurture IC (Jackson, 2011, 2012; Paige, Hegeman, & Jon, 2006). In addition to experience, there must also be reflection, analysis, and action. This implies that experience of any kind of otherness can be viewed as intercultural experience if it illustrates the potential for transformation through reflection, analysis, and action (Alred et al., 2003; Jackson, 2010; Vande Berg, Connor-Linton, & Paige, 2009). Program designs that seek to cultivate 'ethnographic awareness' can facilitate the requisite engagement, analytical, and reflective processes needed to benefit from these intercultural encounters (Wang & Kulich, 2015).

A key part of this method has historically been the interviewing of informants. Intercultural application of 'ethnographic interviewing' (Spradley, 1979; Roberts et al., 2001) is recommended where fieldwork or participatory observation opportunities are not readily available. Corbett (2003) showed that such an ethnographic theme could be furthered developed by focusing on the key tool of 'interview' as a means of exchanging information and collecting data for ethnographic projects. Many others, as listed in Wang and Kulich (2015), have advocated employing 'ethnographic interview' techniques as a culture learning tool in many contexts, such as in study abroad programs (Barro, Jordan, & Roberts, 1998; Jurasek, 1995; Lam, 2006; Roberts et al., 2001), teacher training (Allen, 2000; Byram & Duffy, 1996), and classrooms (Bateman, 2002; Du, 2008; Robinson & Nocon, 1996).

For example, Du (2008) adopted the ethnographic interview approach in a Chinese as a foreign language classroom in the United States to create real cross-cultural contacts with native speakers of the target culture:

> "[s]tudents were first trained in the skills of ethnographic interview techniques, and then arrangements were made for them to conduct two ethnographic interviews on their desired topics over the time frame of fifteen weeks within a single semester. A concurrent mixed methods research design was employed to capture the [development of learners' IC]. The intercultural developmental inventory [...] and a custom-designed survey were used [to collect] quantitative data, [while the qualitative data were collected from four sources:] a custom-designed survey, students' reflective papers, final essays, and focus-group interviews" (p. 83).

Lam (2006) designed an ethnographic interview approach for a group of mainland Chinese students in an undergraduate program in a university in Hong

Kong in order to display the in-depth picture of the underlying adjustment difficulties encountered by the first batch of these mainland Chinese students. Two rounds of formal ethnographic interviews were conducted among these mainland informants and their local counterparts in Hong Kong from 1999 to 2000. The findings revealed that, rather than the commonly addressed difficulties such as diet, language, and environment, the mainland students experienced more significant difficulties when they tried "to immerse themselves into the local Hong Kong network where they met major setbacks due to their social and cultural diversity, and most importantly, the different perception of their identity" (Lam, 2006, p. 93).

The ethnographic interview is still a developing field in China. China has developed greatly in the past few decades and an influx of people from countries outside China has meant some cities have pockets of "multicultural and multilingual fields" for leaning (Jordon, 2002, p. 208). This is one area where work could be done, but with the advent of Virtual Exchange (VE), there are many other options available.

3. Challenges of ethnographic approaches to intercultural teaching

The constraints of ethnographic approaches in intercultural teaching, such as intensive labor and the higher costs of such programs, are significant. Learner training to develop "student ethnographers", attaining "others" to carry out the ethnography with, and being able to reproduce the research if required are all part of these difficulties. In response to these challenges, a distinction between 'real' or 'pure' and 'applied' or 'pragmatic' ethnography has been noted in some intercultural ethnographic approach literature (Barro et al., 1998; Corbett, 2003; Hymes, 1980; Roberts et al., 1992).

Hymes (1980) believes we are born ethnographers but we lose the habit of being so. He further suggests that learners can use ethnography to pursue particular interests and careers instead of struggling to become professional ethnographers.

He views ethnography as a continuum, with two poles and an 'in-between' category:

> "as a general possession, although differentially cultivated. At one pole would be a certain number of people trained in ethnography as a profession. At the other pole would be the general population, respected [...] as having a knowledge of their worlds, intricate and subtle in many ways [...] and as having come to this knowledge by a process ethnographic in character. In between [...] would be those able to combine some disciplined understanding of ethnographic inquiry with the pursuit of their vocation whatever that might be" (Hymes, 1980, p. 99)

Though the UK's industrial language training service (Roberts et al., 1992, pp. 171-244) provides an exemplary extensive ethnographic model, even their research team, which included Holliday (1994), was careful to distinguish between 'practical' or 'applied ethnography' and 'full' or 'pure ethnographic' research (cf. Corbett, 2003, p. 104). According to Corbett (2003), applied ethnographers are different from full or pure ethnographers because they intend to: (1) seek an account of a part of a cultural group or community rather than a comprehensive one; (2) submit their data for more applied discourse analysis than real professional ethnographers; (3) have a practical outcome rather than an academic one.

As noted above, the EEP conducted by Roberts et al. (2001) at Thames Valley University benefited from academic integration, legitimacy, and funding. Though the EEP was elaborated carefully and integrated fully into the degree program over three years, the course team distinguished it from 'real' ethnographic research:

> "[t]he students are not intending to become specialists in social anthropology. They are language students who, we hope, will become even better language students as a result of living the ethnographic life [...] They need the cultural tools for making sense of new intercultural contacts and experiences rather than positivistic facts about other

countries, structures and systems which are, despite the text-books' attempts to freeze-dry them and turn them into fresh-looking, digestible items of information, constantly in a process of contestation and change (Barro et al., 1998, p. 97).

It is with this in mind that the research outlined here was proposed. Application of ethnography was a goal, but it is understood that it could not be done as a specialist would do it. Nevertheless, it is useful in strengthening students' intercultural awareness, understanding and, through that, competence.

4. Adoption, design, and details of the ethnographic interview training approach in a higher education context in China

4.1. The IC course at Hangzhou Dianzi University (HDU)

The research took place at a mid-size university on the east coast of China. Each year, hundreds of foreign students and teachers come to the university, and over a thousand home students and teachers study abroad. Therefore, with the recent trend of internationalization and globalization, the IC courses at the university have rapidly developed in the last two decades and have gradually been taken up by students of various levels: undergraduate, postgraduate, and international.

The first intercultural communication course was offered in 2004 to English majors in the School of Foreign Languages, and has been conducted continuously as a compulsory course for more than 10 years. Since 2009, the intercultural communication course has been offered as an important part of the selective English course and has become one of the largest courses (based on intake) for domestic students, attracting more than 1,500 students annually. Meanwhile, with the increase in the number of international students, the intercultural communication course has been offered as a compulsory course for all the international students, such that 500 students take it annually.

Chapter 1

The first Master's Degrees (MA) intercultural communication course at the university was established in 2007 and offered to a group of English postgraduates in the College of Foreign Languages. It has since become a compulsory course in the MA program. A well-trained teaching team has been established, including a full professor, four associate professors, and more than ten lecturers, who are making great efforts to conduct and improve IC teaching and education. It is therefore very apparent that the research outlined here was carried out in an environment that is well developed.

4.2. IC research and projects at HDU

As reported in Wang and Kulich (2015), in the last decade, increased global flows of people, information, and high technologies have made some students' "home cultures" into "multicultural and multilingual fields" for learning (Jordon, 2002, p. 208). Whenever national or 'foreign' boundaries become less clear-cut, home-based learners may more readily encounter 'difference' without having to leave home (Kramsch & Whiteside, 2008; Risager, 2006; Wilkinson, 2012). Furthermore, the rise of the internet as a tool for communication and self-expression also increased language learners' interaction with partners from the other cultures through online intercultural exchange (O'Dowd, 2007). On the other hand, we are aware of the fact that there are many students in the mainland of China who face constraints (e.g. limited funding, inadequate study abroad opportunities, less international exposure domestically) to experiences in intercultural diversity. Therefore, the IC team launched a broader program of research, initiated in Chinese contexts, that seeks to develop learners' IC through small, locally-based interview projects that make use of cultural groups or products that are available 'at home' (Wang, 2016; Wang, Deardorff, & Kulich, 2017; Wang & Kulich, 2015).

With the awareness that younger generations are more familiar with e-life, some scholars suggest that intercultural understanding can happen not only in the obvious cross-cultural interactions abroad, but also 'at home', through virtual online intercultural exchange (O'Dowd, 2007; Merryfield, 2007). The IC team made great efforts to develop the MOOC Course and a blended learning online platform for the IC course (Miao & Wang, 2014). Since the fall of 2016, the intercultural communication course has been active on the Zhejiang Institutions of Higher Learning Online Open Course Sharing Platform[3] every semester, a platform which includes most of the top online courses from universities and colleges in the Zhejiang province of China. The intercultural communication course provides various resources for students, such as short video lectures, case studies, discussion forums, and intercultural practices and activities. As of October 2020, the course has run eight times and attracted more than 5,000 students from over 50 different universities and colleges all over China. The course was nominated as a Gold Online Course in Zhejiang province in 2019.

The IC research teams has also made great efforts in cooperating with partners from different countries through international projects including RICH-Ed[4] and other international VE projects. The RICH-Ed program aims at supporting Chinese universities in creating learning environments that empower students and staff for global engagement. To this end, the project sets out to define a pedagogical approach for intercultural learning, and to develop learning resources for students and support staff that will be tested at five Chinese partner universities and elsewhere in the Yangtze River Delta and North-east China[5]. As one of the Chinese Coordinators, our IC team took on a leadership role in the first working package, 'preparatory analysis and training', and worked closely with partners on the other seven working packages to provide rich resources for interculturality in Chinese higher education. This shows that the team involved in this research was well qualified to carry it out.

4.3. Procedures

In a previous paper, Wang and Kulich (2015) outlined in detail how we adopted and designed our ethnographic interview training approach. In brief, we wanted students to have intercultural encounters with "others" from a different

---

3. https://www.zjooc.cn/ucenter/teacher/course/build/mooc

4. Resources for Interculturality in Chinese Higher Education is an Erasmus+ CBHE Project (2017-2020).

5. http://www.rich-ed.com/riched/index.php?s=/home/index/index.html

culture. We encouraged students to develop ethnographic awareness and deeper understanding of the relationships between 'self' and 'others'. The procedure we asked students to follow was:

- reflect on and write up one's "Own culture story";
- choose a target cultural group and informant(s) representing that group;
- do library or Internet research on the groups to prepare interview topics;
- establish and extend relationships by sharing "Own cultural stories";
- carry out "friendly conversations";
- write reflective journal entries;
- conduct formal interviews; and
- review the process and write up a final development report.

As noted, the details of this procedure can be found in Wang and Kulich (2015), but needless to say, there is much involved in ensuring this process is successful.

4.4. The training process

To assist students to successfully conduct the project, ten training sessions were included, and the total training time was more than 350 minutes. The training sessions were organized by the researcher and his teaching assistants, and took place during or after class. The objectives of the training sessions were to (1) acquaint students with the project and ethnographic approaches to intercultural communication; (2) provide students with an overview of the practices and attitudes of the "ethnographic interview approach" and how to apply them in their own project; (3) guide students to conduct their own project as the procedures suggest (e.g. how to write 'My cultural story', select self-representative pictures, find 'Other culture' partners, make preparations for interviews, and structure observational and reflective thoughts in the post-interview journal and final report writing); and (4) cultivate a degree of 'ethnographic awareness' that would improve learners' IC. The training materials were carefully selected from IC textbooks, training guide books, and IC academic papers written by renowned IC and ethnographic scholars such as Corbett, Holliday, Pederson, Holmes, LeCompte, and Schensul.

There were six themes in the ten training sessions: (1) Introducing the project and training sessions, (2) My own culture story writing, (3) The Ethnographic approach to intercultural research, (4) Finding an e-partner for online interviews, (5) Face-to-face communication, and (6) Designing and conducting an intercultural interview. The training session details follow.

A 30-minute in-class instructional training session was arranged in week one to ice-break and introduce the objectives and procedures of the project, and the arrangement of the training sessions as a whole. Course syllabus, project instructions, and the proposed session plan were stated clearly and distributed to students at the very beginning of the course program.

In weeks 2 and 3, two 30-min training sessions were offered after class each week to discuss how to organize and write the first assignment of the project – 'My own-culture story'. In the training session in week 2, students were instructed to overview the 'My own-culture story' and finish one reading chapter, *The story of the self,* which was selected from the textbook *Intercultural communication: an advanced resource book for students,* written by Holliday, Hyde, and Kullman (2010). The chapter includes some short reading passages about personal stories and identity construction. Holliday et al. (2010) also designed three intercultural communication research tasks in their chapter, to "develop reflection and strategies for action which will increase learners' awareness about how they may approach intercultural communication" (Holliday et al., 2010, p. 229). Under the teacher's guidance, students were required to accomplish "Exploring age", "Interpersonal factors" and "Interview as cultural interaction" respectively in the training session. In week 3, another chapter from the Holliday et al.'s (2010) book *Becoming the self by defining the other* was assigned to students with three intercultural communication tasks ("Contrasting yourself with others", "Signaling my characteristics" and "How you manage your identity"). Students were encouraged to understand deeply how culture shapes personal identity by contrasting themselves with others. These intercultural communication tasks were ethnographic in approach through which students were expected to (1) be critically aware of how culture shapes their personal identities; (2) increase their ethnographic interview knowledge and skills as an intercultural communicator; and (3) understand the etic and emic levels of cultural analysis through contrasting themselves with others.

Two training sessions were conducted in weeks 4 and 5 to introduce the ethnographic approach to intercultural communication. In week 4, one 90-minute training session was arranged to help students become familiar with what ethnography is and how an ethnographic project can be designed in intercultural communication. Before the training session, students were asked to read two book chapters (Chapter 1: *What is ethnography,* and Chapter 5: *Choosing and designing an ethnographic research project*) in LeCompte and Schensul's (1999) book *Designing and conducting ethnographic research.* The key points in these chapters were highlighted in the training session. In addition, the case study outlined by Holmes and O'Neill (2012) above to demonstrate how an ethnographic approach was applied to develop learners' IC was given as a further reading. The PEER model developed by Holmes and O'Neill (2012) was also introduced to students in preparation for the future data collection process.

In week 5, another 30-minute training session was arranged for the second part of "The ethnographic approach to intercultural communication". This training session focused on how to collect and analyze ethnographic data. Chapter 6 (*Collecting ethnographic data*) and Chapter 7 (*Data analysis: how ethnographers make sense of their data*) from LeCompte and Schensul's (1999) book were selected as the reading materials. Students were organized to discuss how they applied what they learned in the training sessions to their projects. Students' first-hand feedback and suggestions were taken into consideration for further discussion.

In order to guide students to select their interview partners and build successful relations, two 30-minute training sessions were organized in weeks 6 and 7. The training materials from these two sessions were selected from Corbett's (2010) IC textbook *Intercultural language activities.* The training session in week 6 was designed to give practical advice on setting up computer-mediated intercultural exchange, finding an e-partner for the interview project, and developing online discussions. Students were instructed to read the chapter *Setting up an online community* (Corbett, 2010) and finish three specially-designed activities in the chapter: (1) *setting up an online intercultural exchange* teaches learners how to organize an online collaboration with appropriate e-partners elsewhere; (2) *describing an e-partner* helps learners establish relationships with their e-partners; and (3) *starting and developing an online discussion* offers practical suggestions on how to start and develop successful online discussions. In addition, the websites and technological platforms for online exchanges were introduced to students to help them locate an e-partner located in another country.

Different to the topics on online exchanges, the training session in week 7 focused on face-to-face communication to help students establish and extend relationships by sharing 'own cultural stories' and carrying out 'friendly conversations'. Three activities from Corbett's (2010) chapter *Face-to-face* were included in this session: (1) *sharing stories in conversation* focuses on sharing their selected pictures and own culture story highlights as an aid to getting started, opening up, and eliciting reciprocal responses; (2) *supporting talk* is designed to raise awareness of verbal communication – "the impression that the learners are giving to other speakers through their management of support talk" (Corbett, 2010, p. 88), such as 'back-channelling'; and (3) *exploring non-verbal communication* is designed to raise awareness of non-verbal communication such as eye contact, body language, and gestures.

To ensure that the interview project was appropriately conducted, three important training sessions were arranged from week 8 to 10. They served to introduce what ethnographic interview skills are and how these techniques can help learners better understand perspectives from different cultures, as well as providing guidance on selecting interview topics. In week 8, a 45-minute in-class training session included a general introduction to ethnographic interviews and two practical activities from Corbett's (2010) book chapter *Interviewing – developing interview questions* and *Following interview questions*. Students were asked to practice two important ethnographic interview skills: developing interview questions, and eliciting information by asking follow-up questions. In addition, a list of questions (more than 100 questions from nine topics) designed by Pederson (2004) was distributed to students as a guided resource for their interview project. The list includes topics such as social customs, family life, housing, clothing and food, class structure, political patterns, religion and folk beliefs, economic institutions, arts, and value systems. Although these questions were much more than any interview could cover, they provided potential interview topics and the structure for a comprehensive interview.

In weeks 9 and 10, two more 20-minute in-class review sessions were carried out, with practical activities to help students become more familiar with ethnographic interview techniques. *Exploring assumptions* was arranged in week 9 to focus on how learners might interpret their interviewees' unspoken assumptions. *Preparing an online interview* was arranged in week 10 for the students who were arranging an online interview. Students were again guided on how to best proceed and respond to this type of online interview interaction, through practical training. In addition to the face-to-face training sessions in and after the class, an online environment was created to offer resources and interaction between the teachers and students.

4.5. Online environment for teacher-student interaction

The online environment consists of two main tools for accessing materials, participating in activities, and processing training for the course project; they are the course blog and the discussion forum.

The course blog is a space on the web where teachers can write and publish (post) about a topic or topics. Different from traditional websites, blogs provide instant 'type-n-click' communications, which can be done anywhere, anytime and from any browser (Dooly, 2007). Obviously, blogs encourage teacher-student discussion and interaction as they allow for comments to be posted.

The course blog is on the most popular blog platform in China – Sina Micro blog[6], which functions as Twitter does in the West. One important function of the course blog is to collect and share case studies of intercultural communication

---

6. http://weibo.com/u/2421784760

between teachers and learners. Learners were required to collect at least one case related to intercultural communication from the media or their own experiences and offer their feedback and analysis of the case. After communicating with learners and examining the appropriateness of the cases, the teacher sends the cases to all the course learners though the micro blog.

There are now more than 360 active micro blog fans, most of whom were course students who had been enrolled within the last five years (since 2015), and about 460 IC case studies have been recorded in this online IC course community. Distance students who do not meet face-to-face have been communicating about their experiences in the course, and they comment on the new case studies every semester. The blog has been an "intercultural home community" for all the enrolled students in the course.

Like blogs, online discussion forums can promote discussion and reflection between students and their teachers. The discussion forum of the course was established through a QQ group, a very popular online instant messaging/chat system for the young generations in China, which is often used as a means for complementary interaction between students and teachers for posting materials, clarifying, and further explaining the lecture points, mentioning deadlines or items in the class agenda, or organizing online discussions.

Since the launch of the course in 2016, most of the online interactions have been included in the platform. On the platform, participants could read or download all the requisite materials (course syllabus, training plan, reading materials, appendix, etc.) and a weekly overview of the lectures and training sessions, provided by the teachers and their assistants. In addition, the forum hosted online discussions that took place as part of the training activities during the course's 16-week duration. The online discussions were used to guide the learners to organize and conduct the course project, where teachers and students could communicate, discuss, and coordinate the relevant projects. A final point to make is that student feedback on this was very positive – indeed, another whole chapter could be given over to cover this, but suffice it to say that students enjoyed the activity greatly.

5. Conclusion

The chapter highlights the value of a descriptive and reflective intercultural ethnographic interview approach as an intervention and means of developing IC, which is particularly effective in the higher education context in China. In recent decades, more intercultural researchers and practitioners have come to believe that the use of ethnography has clear benefits to the development of core capacities related to IC, such as empathy, sensitivities, awareness, and critical reflection (e.g. Corbett, 2003; Du, 2008; Jackson, 2006, 2012; Roberts et al., 2001; Wilkinson, 2012). Though there have been some criticisms of time-limited curricula's ability to implement procedures that are adequately 'ethnographic', the training process in the course outlined here was designed carefully with the aim of cultivating 'ethnographic awareness' in order to facilitate the requisite engagement, analytical, and reflective processes needed to gain full benefit from the intercultural encounters. Corbett (2003) suggests that learners should be encouraged to "live the ethnographic life" (p. 116). Even for those learners who have limited access to native speakers and target cultural products, the basic materials for 'pragmatic ethnography' (someone to talk to and some events to observe) are available to some degree (i.e. via technology). The trainers can develop learners' ethnography skills through 'decentering' activities that analyse the home culture, and make imaginative use of the available cultural resources (Corbett, 2003, p. 116).

References

Agar, M. (1994). The intercultural frame. *Intercultural Journal of Intercultural Relations, 18*(2), 221-237. https://doi.org/10.1016/0147-1767(94)90029-9

Albert, R. (1995). The intercultural sensitizer/ culture assimilator as a cross-cultural training method. In S. Fowler & M. Mumford (Eds), *Intercultural sourcebook* (vol. 1, pp. 157-167). Intercultural Press.

Allen, L. (2000). Culture and the ethnographic interview in foreign language teacher development. *Foreign Language Annuals, 31*(1), 51-57.

Alred, G., Byram, M., & Fleming, M. (2003). *Intercultural experience and education.* Multilingual Matters.

Barro, A., Jordan, S., & Roberts, C. (1998). Cultural practice in everyday life: the language learner as ethnographer. In M. Byram & M. Fleming (Eds), *Language learning in intercultural perspective: approaches through drama and ethnography* (pp. 76-93). Cambridge University Press.

Bateman, B. (2002). Promoting openness toward culture learning: ethnographic interviews for students of Spanish. *The Modern Language Journal, 86,* 318-331.

Brewer, J. D. (2000). *Ethnography.* Open University Press.

Buttjes, D. (1991). Mediating language and cultures: the social and intercultural dimension restored. In D. Buttjes & M. Byram (Eds), *Mediating languages and cultures: towards an inventory theory of foreign language education* (pp. 3-16). Multilingual Matters.

Byram, M. (1991). Teaching language and culture: towards an integrated model. In D. Buttjes & M. Byram (Eds), *Mediating languages and cultures: towards an inventory theory of foreign language education* (pp. 17-30). Multilingual Matters.

Byram, M., & Duffy, S. (1996). The ethnographic interview as a personal journal. *Language Culture and Curriculum, 9*(1), 3-18.

Corbett, J. (2003). *An intercultural approach to English language teaching.* Multilingual Matters.

Corbett, J. (2010). *Intercultural language activities.* Cambridge University Press.

Damen, L. (1987). *Culture learning: the fifth dimension in the language classroom.* Addison-Wesley.

Dooly. M. (2007). Choosing the appropriate communication tools for an online exchange. In R. O' Dowd (Ed.), *Online intercultural exchange: an introduction for foreign language teachers.* Multilingual Matters. https://doi.org/10.21832/9781847690104-012

Du, W. H. (2008). *Integrating culture learning into foreign language curricula: an examination of the ethnographic interview approach in a Chinese as a foreign language classroom.* Unpublished Doctoral Dissertation. The University of Wisconsin, Milwaukee, U.S.A.

Geertz, C. (1973). *The interpretation of cultures.* Basic Books.

Hammer, M., & Bennett, M. J. (2002). *Intercultural development inventory manual.* The Intercultural Communication Institute.

Holliday, A. (1994). *Appropriate methodology and social context.* Cambridge University Press.

Holliday, A. (2004). Small cultures. In A. Holliday, A. Hyde & J. Kull (Eds), *Intercultural communication: an advanced resource book* (pp. 62-64). Routledge.

Holliday, A., Hyde, M., & Kullman, J. (2010). *Intercultural communication: an advanced resource book for students*. Routledge.

Holmes, P., & O'Neill, G. (2012). Developing and evaluating intercultural competence: ethnographies of intercultural encounters. *International Journal of Intercultural Relations, 36*(5), 707-718. https://doi.org/10.1016/j.ijintrel.2012.04.010

Hymes, D. (1980). *Language in education: ethnolinguistic essays*. Centre for Applied Linguistics.

Jackson, J. (2006). Ethnographic pedagogy and evaluation in short-term study abroad. In M. Byram & A. W. Feng (Eds), *Living and studying abroad: research and practice* (pp. 134-156). Multilingual Matters. https://doi.org/10.21832/9781853599125-009

Jackson, J. (2008). *Language, identity, and study abroad: sociocultural perspective*. Equinox.

Jackson, J. (2010). *Intercultural journeys: from study to residence abroad*. Palgrave Macmillan.

Jackson, J. (2011). Assessing the impact of a semester abroad using the IDI and semi-structured interviews. [Distinguished paper award]. In *Proceedings of the 2nd Intercultural Development Inventory conference, Minneapolis, MN, USA*.

Jackson, J. (2012). Education abroad. In J. Jackson (Ed.), *The Routledge handbook of language and intercultural communication* (pp. 449-463). Routledge.

Jordon, S. (2002). Ethnographic encounters: the processes of cultural translation. *Language and Intercultural Communication, 2*(2), 96-110. https://doi.org/10.1080/14708470208668079

Jurasek, R. (1995). Using ethnography to bridge the gap between study abroad and the on-campus language and culture curriculum. In C. Kramsch (Ed.), *Redifining the boundaries of language study* 221-251. Heinle & Heinle.

Kohonen, V., Jaatinen, R., Kaikkonen, P., & Lehtovaara, J. (2001). *Experiential learning in foreign language education*. Pearson. https://doi.org/10.4324/9781315840505

Kolb, D. (1984). *Experiential learning*. Prentice-Hall.

Kramsch, C., & Whiteside, A. (2008). Language ecology in multilingual settings: towards a theory of symbolic competence. *Applied Linguistics, 29*(4), 645-671. https://doi.org/10.1093/applin/amn022

Lam, M.-H. (2006). Reciprocal adjustment by host and sojourning groups: mainland Chinese students in Hong Kong. In M. Byram & A. W. Feng (Eds), *Living and studying abroad: research and practice* (pp. 91-107). Multilingual Matters. https://doi.org/10.21832/9781853599125-007

LeCompte, M. D., & Schensul, J. J. (1999). *Designing and conducting ethnographic research.* Altamira Press.

Merryfield, M. M. (2007). The web and teachers' decision-making in global education. *Theory and Research in Social Education, 35*(2), 256-275. https://doi.org/10.1080/00933104.2007.10473335

Miao, L. Y., & Wang, Y. A. (2014). A model of intercultural competence development based on web. *Journal of Hangzhou Dianzi University (Social Sciences), 9*(4), 68-72.

O'Dowd, R. (2007). *Online intercultural exchange: an introduction for foreign language teachers.* Multilingual Matters.

Paige, R. M., Hegeman, R., & Jon. J.-E. (2006). *Georgetown University research report.* Unpublished manuscript. University of Minnesota, Minneapolis, MN.

Pederson, P. B. (2004). *110 experiences for multicultural learning.* American Psychological Association.

Risager, K. (2006). *Language and culture: global flows and local complexity.* Multilingual Matters.

Roberts, C. (2003). Ethnography and cultural practice: ways of learning during residence abroad. In G. Alred, M. Byram & M. Fleming (Eds), *Intercultural experience and education* (pp. 114-130). Multilingual Matters. https://doi.org/10.21832/9781853596087-011

Roberts, C., Byram, M., Barro, A., Jordan, S., & Street, B. (2001). *Language learners as ethnographers.* Multilingual Matters. https://doi.org/10.21832/9781853596810

Roberts, C., Davies, E., & Jupp, T. (1992). *Language and discrimination: a study of communication in multi-ethnic workplaces.* Longman.

Robinson, G., & Nocon, H. (1996). Second culture acquisition: ethnography in the foreign language classroom. *The Modern Language Journal, 80*, 431-449.

Shaules, J. (2007). *Deep culture: the hidden challenges of global living.* Multilingual Matters.

Snow, D. (2015). English teaching, intercutlural competence, and critical incident exercises. *Language and Intercultural Communication, 15*(2), 285-299. https://doi.org/10.1080/14708477.2014.980746

Spencer-Oatey, H., & Franklin, P. (2010). *Intercultural interaction: a multidisciplinary approach to intercultural communication.* Foreign Language Teaching and Research Press.

Spradley, J. (1979). *The ethnographic interview.* Holt, Rinehart & Winston.

Stier, J. (2003). Internationalization, ethnic diversity and the acquisition of intercultural competencies. *Journal of Intercultural Education, 14*(1), 77-91. https://doi.org/10.1080/1467598032000044674

Stier, J. (2006). Internationalisation, intercultural communication and intercultural competence. *Journal of Intercultural Communication, 11*(1), 1-12.

Tennant, M. (1997). Psychology and adult learning (2nd ed.). Routledge.

Vande Berg, M., Connor-Linton, J., & Paige, R. M. (2009). The Georgetown Consortium project: intervening in student learning abroad. *Frontiers: The Interdisciplinary Journal of Study Abroad, 18*(1), 1-75. https://doi.org/10.36366/frontiers.v18i1.251

Wang, Y. A. (2016). *Exploring model-based approaches to cultivate and assess intercultural competence through a domestic interview-based course design in China.* Unpublished Doctoral Dissertation. Shanghai International Studies University, Shanghai, China.

Wang, Y. A., Deardorff, D., & Kulich, S. (2017). Chinese perspectives on intercultural competence in international higher education (pp. 95-108). In D. Deardorff & L. A. Arasaratnam-Smith (Eds), *Intercultural competence in international higher education.* Routledge. https://doi.org/10.4324/9781315529257-9

Wang, Y. A., & Kulich, S. J. (2015). Does context count? Developing and assessing intercultural competencethrough an interview- and model-based domestic course design in China. *International Journal of InterculturalRelations, 48*, 38-57. https://doi.org/10.1016/j.ijintrel.2015.03.013

Wilkinson, J. (2012). The intercultural speaker and the acquisition of intercultural/ global competence. In J. Jackson (Ed.), *The Routledge handbook of language and intercultural communication* (pp. 296-309). Routledge. https://doi.org/10.4324/9780203805640.ch18

2. What do we exchange in virtual exchange? Reflections on virtual exchange as intercultural dialogue

Jan Van Maele[1]

Abstract

On its website, APVEA reminds us that "virtual exchanges are technology-enabled, sustained, people-to-people education programs". This chapter addresses the question of what we exchange when we engage in virtual exchange by exploring the meaning and value of virtual exchange as intercultural dialogue, and by considering the impact of the technological medium on the process. A small group of expert practitioners (N=6) were consulted for their views on virtual exchange. Their responses sketch a picture in which virtual exchange stretches beyond transaction into interaction among and transformation of the participants. The expert practitioners value virtual exchange for enhancing employability and foremost for its dialogic qualities. Next, the chapter explores the meaning of dialogue more deeply from a Bohmian perspective and considers applications in organizational development (Isaacs, 1999), restorative justice (Pranis, 2005), and intercultural competence development (Deardorff, 2020). When the intercultural dimension is made salient, this creates additional chances for realizing the dialogue principles of participation, coherence, awareness, and unfolding. The chapter then illustrates how intercultural dialogue is reshaped in a virtual environment as it is mediated by the technological context in which it is conducted. Specific attention is paid to the circle, the talking piece, and the facilitator. The chapter concludes by stating that, although

---

1. KU Leuven, Leuven, Belgium; jan.vanmaele@kuleuven.be; https://orcid.org/0000-0002-7778-1787

How to cite: Van Maele, J. (2020). What do we exchange in virtual exchange? Reflections on virtual exchange as intercultural dialogue. In E. Hagley & Y. Wang (Eds), *Virtual exchange in the Asia-Pacific: research and practice* (pp. 37-59). Research-publishing.net. https://doi.org/10.14705/rpnet.2020.47.1145

intercultural dialogue will always be mediated by technology in virtual exchange settings, it makes good sense to speak of 'virtual dialogue' in situations that take the core principles, practices, and structural components of dialogue as outlined in this chapter as a starting point for designing online intercultural dialogue activities.

Keywords: virtual exchange, dialogue, intercultural competence, virtual intercultural dialogue.

1. Introduction

What is the role of educators in a world that is characterized by increasing diversity, even super-diversity (Vertovec, 2017), while discourses of polarization and acts of discrimination remain widely spread? The nearly ubiquitous availability of the internet provides a powerful platform for fostering knowledge, understanding, and friendships across borders yet it has also shown another face as a terrifying tool for invading privacy, spreading fake news, and fueling hatred. Nevertheless, in the face of such threats, educators across the world have sought and often realized new chances for development of foreign language proficiency, cultural knowledge of the other, intercultural understanding, teamwork skills, or all of the above, through what has become known as virtual exchange. What is more, the corona pandemic that struck the world in 2020 served as a forceful reminder that there may be times and situations when virtual is the only available mode for exchange.

When one takes the beginner's course on the Erasmus+ Virtual Exchange platform[2], one learns that "[v]irtual exchange combines the deep impact of intercultural dialogue and exchange with the broad reach of digital technology" (Erasmus+ Virtual Exchange, 2019, n.p.). This is no small feat given the high complexity of setting up, maintaining, and leveraging virtual

---

2. https://europa.eu/youth/erasmusvirtual_en

exchange in educational contexts, as any reader who has personally engaged in it will attest. Aside from the organizational and technological challenges, McLuhan's (1964) old dictum – 'the medium is the message' – is as relevant as ever when it comes to the impact of the characteristics of digital media on the nature and the meaning of communication in virtual exchange. Yet, it seems that the learning processes and outcomes that educators are seeking are affected by the digital context in which they are realized in ways that have not sufficiently been recognized. In her extensive review of published studies, Avgousti (2018) points out the impact of specific (multi-) modalities in online intercultural exchanges, particularly in the context of L2 learning. In his overview of the emerging field of intercultural new media studies, Shuter (2012) draws attention to the fact that intercultural communication knowledge and theory are still largely rooted in a twentieth-century paradigm of face-to-face interaction and that it hence remains unclear to what extent existing definitions of notions such as 'cultural identity', 'intercultural competence', or 'intercultural dialogue' are applicable to the virtual world. After examining the available research, he concludes that while factors from the physical world may also impinge on outcomes in the virtual world, intercultural dialogue, for example, "may be governed by different processes in virtual communities than organic ones [and that therefore, it] may be necessary to utilize multiple new media platforms to achieve intercultural dialogue" in a virtual world (Shuter, 2012, p. 226).

Fortunately, educators who are considering engaging in virtual exchange can increasingly rely on formal and informal support networks, including dedicated associations like the Asia-Pacific Virtual Exchange Association[3], and can benefit from (online) training such as that offered by Erasmus+ Virtual Exchange. The latter program targets young adults from Europe and the Southern Mediterranean "to have a meaningful intercultural experience by engaging in online facilitated dialogue as part of their formal or non-formal education" (Erasmus+ Virtual Exchange, 2019, n.p.). This educational purpose is intrinsically linked to the wider socio-political calls for the promotion of the values of tolerance and

---

3. https://apvea.org/

non-discrimination that followed brutal terrorist attacks in several European capitals during the preceding years (e.g. European Union Education Ministers, 2015). The Soliya Connect program (2007-2020) provides another example in which educators bring together university students from the 'Western' and the 'predominantly Muslim' societies in online dialogue groups to explore global themes and increase intercultural understanding. These examples demonstrate that it would be too restrictive to study and write about virtual exchange as purely a trend in educational technology. Viewed from a broader societal perspective, new communication technologies can be seen to serve exchange and dialogue in that they allow more immediate connections between learners who are located across geographical and cultural fault lines than might otherwise be possible. From an institutional point of view, virtual exchange can hence be mobilized as a means to implement 'internationalization at home' policies[4]. At a deeper level, it can be welcomed as an antidote to the rather grim conclusion that "the age of instant communication is also an age of instant miscommunication and instant conflict or even worse" (Jia, 2019, p.7).

Starting from these observations, the present chapter addresses the question of what we exchange when we engage in virtual exchange by exploring successively the key components of the earlier cited definition on the Erasmus+ Virtual Exchange platform: the notion of virtual exchange, the notion of intercultural dialogue, and the impact of digital technology on intercultural dialogue.

2. Virtual exchange

2.1. The object and value of virtual exchange

On its homepage, quoting INTENT, APVEA reminds us that "virtual exchanges are technology-enabled, sustained, people-to-people education programs"[5]. Virtual exchange is used here in a generic sense, comprising practices such

---

4. https://research.ncl.ac.uk/atiah/about/

5. https://apvea.org/

as e-tandem, teletandem, e-twinning, telecollaboration, collaborative online international learning, and open virtual mobility (see e.g. O'Dowd, 2020; Rajagopal et al., 2020). While this definition states the context in which the exchange takes place ('education') and refers to its medium ('technology-enabled'), duration ('sustained'), and actors ('people-to-people'), it omits any information about what exactly is exchanged in virtual exchanges. Neither does it indicate what is deemed of value to the participants in these exchanges. In order to formulate an answer, six expert practitioners of virtual exchange (Table 1) were presented with this widespread definition of virtual exchange and the following complementary questions: (1) what exactly is exchanged in virtual exchange, and (2) what do you value most about virtual exchange as you have experienced it?

Table 1. Profile of the Respondents (R)

	R1	R2	R3	R4	R5	R6
Gender	F	F	M	F	F	F
Residence	Belgium	Belgium	Belgium	UK	Netherlands	Italy
Response	written	written	written	written	written	oral online (transcribed)
Status	All respondents work at a university with over ten years' experience in online education as educators and as researchers in this domain.					

2.1.1. What exactly is exchanged in virtual exchange?

The responses about the nature of the object of exchange can be arranged in the following approximate order from low to high complexity: "bits, clustered in data, representing information and presented as text, audio, and/or video" (R3); "messages" (R4); "materials, artifacts" (R5); "knowledge" (R1, R4, R6); "expertise" (R4); "ideas" (R3, R5); "opinions" (R4, R6); "views on life and society" (R1); and "insights into different perspectives" (R1, R4).

The named objects of exchange can be seen to cover different stages of what Pine and Gilmore (1999) refer to as "the progression of valuable intelligence" (pp. 188-189). At the bottom there is *noise*, 'bits', an abundance of unorganized observations with little or no meaning. When observations are codified, they become *data*. When these data are delivered to others as 'messages' within a common frame of reference, we speak of *information*. On the next rung of the ladder, we find *knowledge*, which is intelligence that is gained from and applied through experiences. Several respondents also draw attention to the fact that what is shared in virtual exchange often did not exist before the experience, referring to "ideas generated in the process of the interaction" (R4) and "exchanges that can be typified as knowledge co-construction" (R5). At the top, Pine and Gilmore (1999) put the *wisdom* that is gained through (at times painful) experience and is required for transformation. The offering at this ultimate stage "is not, however, the wisdom itself; that is only a means. The offering is the changed individual" (Pine & Gilmore, 1999, p. 191).

Seen as a transformation activity, virtual exchange goes beyond the sort of transaction that its name seems to imply: *you have something that is of value to me more than it is to you, and I have something that can be of value to you, so let us swap, thereby adding value to each other in the transaction.* Instead, as the respondents recognize, what is at stake is jointly constructed in the interaction and consequently, in virtual exchange activities, relational work has to be a constant focus alongside the task at hand. For instance,

> "When teams start to work together, they are advised to take the time to get to know each other, for the reason that when conflict occurs there is a basis of trust to make it easier to work through it. In this case, we could ask rather what didn't they exchange?" (R4).

The fact that transformative learning requires effort and can be painful is echoed by the respondents through the recurrent mentioning of obstacles and borders that need to be crossed: e.g. "the aim […] is to bridge gaps or cross borders between countries (regions, continents) and cultures" (R3); "working together [a]cross many borders (physical and virtual, real and artificial) and experiencing and reflecting on what it means and what it takes" (R5). The value of virtual exchange is here seen to reside in the transformation that takes place in each learner. As one respondent puts it:

"becoming a [virtual exchange] facilitator is extremely engaging; I wish I could facilitate more. I have seen the budding of the transformation; people start thinking about things they haven't thought about before. They say at the end: I hadn't realized how prejudiced I was" (R6).

2.1.2. What do you value most about virtual exchange as you have experienced it?

In line with their view of virtual exchange as an activity of joint creation, the expert practitioners put forward the following values: openness, inclusiveness, respect, trust, safety, and authenticity. With respect to authenticity, R6 clarifies that when designing a virtual exchange project, educators have to make sure they create a genuine need for communicating with the cultural other: "why bother having an exchange if they can learn it from you"? Other examples include: "create more authentic person-to-person connections" (R1); "inclusive and participatory communication" (R4); "openness and respect" (R3); "the trusted environment" (R1); "familiarity and trust" (R2); and "a safe and low-stakes situation" (R4).

As will become clear in next section, these are the same values that characterize dialogue. In this respect it is not surprising that in some occasions on their website Erasmus+ Virtual Exchange replaces the reference to 'education programs' used in the INTENT definition with the term 'dialogues': "technology-enabled, people-to-people *dialogues* sustained over a period of time" (https://europa.eu/youth/node/54451_en; emphasis added).

2.2. Virtual exchange and employability

If one enrolls for the introductory course to dialogue facilitation on Erasmus+ Virtual Exchange , one learns that virtual exchange has another aim besides enabling people to have a meaningful intercultural experience. Virtual exchange, it is stated, "also fosters the development of what have been recognized as employability skills such as digital competence […] foreign language competence, communication skills, media literacy and the ability to work in a diverse cultural context"[6]. Such skills can be referred to as employability skills because they "relate to generic personal and interpersonal qualities which are independent of the field of study [... and are] transferable" (Jones, 2013, p. 96) in the sense that they represent "a set of achievements – skills, understandings and personal attributes – that makes graduates more likely to gain employment and be successful in their chosen occupations" (Yorke, 2006, p. 8).

Interestingly, most respondents mention one or more employability skills in their answers to the question about what they value most in virtual exchange. Their responses cover language and communication skills – e.g. "listening to each other" (R6); "improve everyone's use of English as a lingua franca, particularly those for whom it's a L1" (R4) – and e-media literacy – e.g. "educating good digital citizens of the Web" (R1). One respondent (R2) illustrates the employability factor with reference to a specific task: "video recording yourself prior to e.g. online job interview will raise the awareness of the context of interaction, the quality of the message and the efficiency". This task is featured on the open online platform for assessing intercultural communicative competence that was developed within the CEFcult project (2009-2011, EU Lifelong Learning Program; see Van Maele, Baten, Beaven, & Rajagopal, 2013). After recording themselves with the webcam while they practice for a virtual job screening interviews, learners can offer these recordings for language and cultural assessment to assessors of their choice, including peers, experts, and themselves (self-assessment). As mentioned in Van Maele et al. (2013, pp. 250-252), they are allowed to record themselves as often as they want, and maintain full control over which performance they submit for assessment or export to their portfolios. CEFcult follows the pedagogy underlying the use of personal learning environments: networked learners, in control of their learning, use the technological tools to support and create their own environment for learning, for connecting and interacting with resources and people (Drexler, 2010). The authenticity of the task and the criteria was validated by collaborating with managers from internationally operating companies. As such, CEFcult presents an illustration of how virtual

---

6. https://evolve-erasmus.eu/about-evolve/what-is-virtual-exchange/

exchange can be explicitly leveraged for employability of participating students.

2.3. Dialogue

As the discussion above makes clear, virtual exchange is valued for and defined in terms of its dialogic qualities. This raises the question of how dialogue should be understood in this context. In search for an answer, we will first go to the etymological roots and turn to Bohm's (1999) perspective on dialogue. Further insights into the notion will be gleaned from dialogue applications in organization development and restorative justice, and in intercultural competence development.

2.3.1. The meaning of dialogue

Although it is sometimes used in a looser sense, its etymology clearly sets dialogue apart from practices such as debate (Latin *battere*: to fight), discussion (Latin *dis-quatere*: to shake apart), or conversation (Indo-European *vertere*: to turn around, to bend) (Harper, 2001-2020). For instance, in the introductory course for facilitators offered through Erasmus+ Virtual Exchange (2019), dialogue is explicitly distinguished from debate. In a debate, participants are focused on beating the opponent; they listen to form counterarguments and defend their assumptions as truth. Dialogue, by contrast, is a joint search for community understanding; participants listen to find meaning in what others say and they re-evaluate their assumptions. Its meaning can be traced back to the classic Greek roots *dia* (through, among, between) and *logos* (word):

> "[t]he picture or image that this derivation suggests is of a *stream of meaning* flowing among and through us and between us. This will make possible a flow of meaning in the whole group, out of which may emerge some new understanding" (Bohm, 1999, p. 6; italics in original).

This etymological gloss on dialogue suggests that the transformation that is valued in virtual exchange does not result from external pressure (as would be the case in debates, discussions, and conversations) but stems from suspending our assumptions, attending to our thoughts behind the assumptions that perceive the world in a fragmentary way, widening our attention, listening to find shared meanings, and working toward coherence. This is the approach to dialogue that was articulated by David Bohm (1999), the famous 20th century physicist, who arguably wrote one of the most profound reflections on the topic. The principles of Bohmian dialogue have since been applied to other fields, including organization development (Isaacs, 1999). A related source of knowledge is various ancestral traditions of peacemaking – also cited by Bohm (1999, p. 16) as an inspiration – which have been revived in the form of circle processes in restorative justice (Pranis, 2005) and as story circles in intercultural competence development (Deardorff, 2020). It is to these fields that we now turn to glean additional insights into the meaning of dialogue before addressing Shuter's (2012) earlier quoted statement that intercultural dialogue as defined in face-to-face literature may be difficult to achieve in virtual communities.

2.3.2. Implementing dialogue in organization development and restorative justice

According to Isaacs (1999), founder of the Dialogue Project at MIT Sloan School of Management, problems within large corporations often stem from an inability to conduct a successful dialogue. Isaacs (1999) proposes dialogue, which he refers to as "shared inquiry, a way of thinking and reflecting together" (p. 9), as an alternative for more conventional approaches to the way meetings are conducted, namely with "an agenda, a clear purpose and predetermined outcome for every step of the process, and someone to 'drive' the process" (p. 331). Table 2 summarizes his understanding of dialogue: it lists the four practices that are key to building the capacity for dialogue, the central questions that are at stake for each practice, and the corresponding principles that inform each of the practices (based on Isaacs, 1999, pp. 419-420). To give an example that already anticipates the intercultural dimension of dialogue: according to Isaacs (1999), the practice of respecting refers to seeing the other as legitimate; as a whole being. "If you respect someone, you do not intrude. At the same time, if you respect someone, you do not withhold yourself or distance yourself from them" (Isaacs, 1999, p. 114). The underlying principle is that of coherence; an understanding of wholeness: "for us to perceive something, it must somehow be in us, or it literally would not connect to anything in us" (Isaacs, 1999, p. 125). Consequently, the central question related to the practice of respecting is *how does this fit?*. What is at stake is the recognition that the otherness and strangeness that you experience when interacting with other people is already in you and part of the whole.

Table 2. Isaacs's (1999) dialogue practices

Core practices	Key questions	Core principles
Listening	How does this feel?	Participation
Respecting	How does this fit?	Coherence
Suspending	How does this work?	Awareness
Voicing	What needs to be said?	Unfoldment

Pranis (2005), who served as a restorative justice planner in the USA, addresses the use of 'talking circles' in the criminal justice system and the wider communities to settle disputes and enable healing. The physical format of the circle is essential because it "symbolizes shared leadership, equality, connection and inclusion. It also promotes focus, accountability, and participation from all" (Pranis, 2005, p. 11). Other structural elements of the circle process are listed in Table 3 (based on Pranis, 2005, pp. 33-37). A talking piece refers to any object "passed from person to person in a group and which grants the holder sole permission to speak" or to offer silence (Pranis, 2005, p. 3). Consequently, as Pranis (2005) points out, two people cannot go back and forth at each other when they disagree. This turns the talking piece into "a powerful equalizer" while it "weaves a connecting thread among the members of the circle" (Pranis, 2005, p. 36). Her description of the circle process clearly echoes the values that the expert practitioners cited with respect to virtual exchange. Aside from the values of connection, inclusion, and participation, Pranis (2005) emphasizes the need to create an environment that is based on "what the participants need to make the space safe to speak in their authentic voices [… and that ensures] respectful speaking and listening and some form of confidentiality" (p. 34).

Given the shared set of values and the strong correspondence of the processes, Pranis's (2005) description provides us with a relevant set of characteristics for exploring to what extent dialogue can be achieved in virtual exchange.

Table 3. Pranis's (2005) structural elements of circle processes

Ceremony	Opening and closing ceremonies mark the time and space of the circle as a space apart.
Guidelines	The commitments or promises that participants make to one another about how they will behave in the circle. The entire circle, not just the facilitator, is responsible for the creation and implementation of the guidelines.
Talking piece	The talking piece slows the pace of the conversation and encourages thoughtful and reflective interactions.
Facilitating	The facilitator's role is to initiate a space that is respectful and safe, and to engage participants in sharing responsibility for the space and their work.

2.4. Intercultural dialogue

2.4.1. The meaning of intercultural dialogue

A recent survey on intercultural dialogue by Unesco (2018) concludes that "to date, there is no universally agreed formal definition of intercultural dialogue or a single one-size-fits-all model of implementation" (p. 16). Nevertheless, various scholars and organizations have provided their own definition, including the Council of Europe (2008):

> "intercultural dialogue is understood as a process that comprises an open and respectful exchange of views between individuals and groups with different ethnic, cultural, religious and linguistic backgrounds and heritage, on the basis of mutual understanding and respect" (p. 17).

However, Van Maele and Mertens (2014) point out that encounters cannot *a priori* be qualified to be intercultural or not by referring to the presence or absence of differences in group memberships. According to Barrett et al. (2013), encounters can be characterized as intercultural when the participants themselves perceive its intercultural dimension and make it salient. In this respect, Borghetti (2017) refers to "how individuals socially position themselves in interactions [...], to their awareness of such positioning, and to their willingness and ability to recognize and negotiate the others' multiple identities as much as their own" (p. 2) as more relevant considerations. Consequently, we could posit that a dialogue can be qualified as intercultural when the cultural diversity within the group is made topical or is experienced as significant by one or more of the participants in the dialogue. Particularly in the case of perceived difference or strangeness, this will create additional challenges – but also chances – for realizing the earlier cited practice of respecting in dialogue. Can the participants in intercultural dialogue see the coherence on which any perceived differences rest, and still engage with the other as a whole being?

2.4.2. Implementing intercultural dialogue in intercultural competence development

The Unesco (2018) survey on intercultural dialogue concludes that there is no one-size-fits-all model of implementation and that instead "the emphasis is placed on the specific context of the country" (p.16). Although Deardorff (2020) acknowledges the situational component, she presents a method for developing intercultural competence that can work across countries, relating the work of Pranis (2005) and others to the universal tradition of storytelling. After testing the method in a variety of contexts around the world, she offers a manual for using story circles as a powerful tool for developing intercultural competence. Her method directs participants to sharing their own experiences of interculturality through the use of prompts like "what is one of the most positive interactions you have had with a person(s) who is different from you, and what made this such a positive experience?" (Deardorff, 2020, p. 35), and through a guided debriefing of their story circle experience.

Intercultural dialogue is named as one of the contexts in which story circles can be put to use. More specifically, story circles can be integrated in dialogue to support participants in empathic listening: "dialogue participants come together first through story circles to practice *listening for understanding* and gaining insights on each other's perspectives before engaging in further dialogue across difference" (Deardorff, 2020, p. 17; italics in original). The central values (openness and respect) and the principal competencies that are honed through story circles bear a strong resemblance to Isaacs' cited practices and principles of dialoguing. Story circles, Deardorff (2020) states, promote the following intercultural competencies: "demonstrating respect for others, practicing listening for understanding, cultivating curiosity about similarities and differences with others, gaining increased cultural self-awareness, developing empathy, and developing relationships with culturally different others" (p. 16; italics deleted). To this she adds further guidelines that remind participants to avoid making assumptions and to refrain from judgmental comments (Deardorff, 2020, p. 53). Table 4 demonstrates the extent to which story circles inscribe themselves in the here articulated view on dialogue. For the first three practices and principles of dialoguing, there is a direct connection between Isaacs's (1999) definition of dialogue and Deardorff's (2020) description of the central competencies in story circles. As far as 'voicing' and 'unfoldment' is concerned, the relation is more implicit. Nevertheless, it is not hard to see that expressing oneself through meaningful life stories would qualify as a fine example of voicing, and that the many distinct stories that we hear from others may well resonate with us because those stories are unfolding "from a common source [... and appear as] the explicate versions of some more implicate order [... that is like a] constant potential waiting to unfold through and around us" (Isaacs, 1999, pp. 166, 168).

In Deardorff's view, story circles are conducted on site with all participants physically present in the room. Virtual story circles are not impossible – as a matter of fact, Unesco has started running virtual story circles and training facilitators (Deardorff, personal communication, September 21, 2020) – but they are not the preferred choice: "[i]t is ideal for participants to be face-to-face when sharing their stories. However, there may be times when this can be done via technology (such as Skype or FaceTime)" (Deardorff, 2020, p. 54). No explanation is given for granting this deficiency position to technology-enabled story circles. In the final section we shall consider to what extent such a position could be justified by examining how dialogue has been implemented in online environments.

Table 4. Comparing characteristics of dialogue (Isaacs, 1999) and story circles (Deardorff, 2020)

Core practices of dialogue	Intercultural competencies through story circles	Core principles of dialogue	Intercultural competencies through story circles
Listening	Practicing listening for understanding	Participation	Developing relationships with culturally different others
Respecting	Demonstrating respect for others	Coherence	Understanding across differences
Suspending	Avoid making assumptions; refrain from judgmental comments	Awareness	Gaining increased cultural self-awareness
Voicing	Expressing oneself through meaningful life stories	Unfoldment	Recognizing individual stories as the explicate version of a common source

3. Virtual intercultural dialogue

Now that we have carefully examined the characteristics of intercultural dialogue, we can return to consider Shuter's (2012) statement that intercultural dialogue, as it has been defined in the face-to-face literature, may be difficult to achieve in virtual communities. Virtual here means 'technology-enabled', "preferably based on regular synchronous or near-synchronous meetings using high social presence media" (Erasmus+ Virtual Exchange, 2019). The discussion below addresses the broader question whether current e-environments promote online dialogue by considering the communicative affordances and constraints of the format and the interface. More specifically, we look at intercultural dialogue as it is enabled in Soliya Connect (Soliya, 2007-2020), which is also the platform that serves as the model in the beginner's course for facilitators on Erasmus+ Virtual Exchange (2019), and discuss how it shapes three of the elements in Pranis's (2005) description of dialogue: the circle, the talking piece, and the facilitator. Together, these elements illustrate how dialogue is reshaped in a virtual environment as it is mediated by the technological context in which it is conducted.

3.1. Virtual talking circle

Dialogues tend to be conducted in a circle because this shape expresses equality and creates connection and inclusion (Pranis, 2005). The idea that the lay-out of the environment can promote or constrain certain communicative behaviors is not new and has also been examined outside the virtual world (see e.g. XML, 2016, on the architecture of parliaments around the world). Virtual dialogues can be conducted in a hybrid onsite-online format or take place in entirely virtual environments. Hybrid virtual meeting systems such as TelePresence can create the illusion that all participants, both participants who are physically present and those joining from a distance, sit together at a single meeting table that stretches from the onsite meeting room into the virtual world (Cisco, 2019). I have not come across this degree of verisimilitude in fully virtual rooms yet although developers have created circular lay-outs there as well. In Soliya, for example, participants are arranged in a circle because this is "held to be more conducive to dialogue" (Helm, 2015, p. 5). It would be rash to conclude from this that a circular seating pattern will avoid power imbalances, though. Circles, whether virtual or face-to-face, may indeed set up a propensity for shared leadership, but there is no guarantee that talking in circles will install or maintain the desired equality just by themselves.

Other imbalances in power distribution may be due to the virtual nature of the dialogue. Some participants, as Helm (2015) points out, may call in from locations with broader bandwidth and higher performance and as a result be more intelligible and more present in the dialogue than their partners in less technologically advanced settings. Power imbalance may also be inscribed in the software. In Soliya, for instance, only the facilitator is able to interrupt other speakers while they hold the floor. Of course, this is not an intrinsic disadvantage of virtual dialogue rooms but users often have no option but to use the interface as it is provided to them. Finally, the mediated nature of virtual dialogue can also affect nonverbal communication. Think for instance of the camera angle that can represent participants as looking up to or looking down on their dialogue partners. And even if they look straight into the camera, participants can still appear to be on top or at the bottom of the circle when their pictures are arranged visually on the screen, creating further perceptions of imbalance. Therefore, the design of the interface will be a crucial factor in determining how conducive the virtual talking circle really is for a genuine dialogue experience.

3.2. Virtual talking piece

The technical restriction of allowing only one participant to speak at a time in some online environments is somewhat reminiscent of the manner in which a talking piece operates in face-to-face dialogue. Sequential turn-taking slows down the pace of the communication and once a participant 'has' the floor, which can be visually affirmed by a lit up frame or an expanded picture, that speaker can mostly keep it without being interrupted. Nevertheless, this right may not be absolute in cases where one or more participants are granted the power to intervene, as indicated in the previous paragraph. Moreover, some platforms, including Soliya, provide a synchronous communication channel through a text chat box where participants can carry on multiple threads of conversation while their colleague holds the talking piece.

Sequential turn-taking in a virtual dialogue can also affect communication from the perspective of the listener. In comparison with face-to-face dialogue, participants will need to make certain adjustments to indicate they are actively listening. Vocal back-channeling, by humming or other sounds, to indicate encouragement or (dis)agreement is also no longer available when the auditory channel rests solely with the speaker. Listeners may have to resort to alternatives (learning forward toward the screen; arranging the camera angle to express 'eye contact'; refraining from fiddling …) to signal they are devoting the speaker their full attention. In addition, nonverbal gestures may be interpreted differently

Chapter 2

depending on the medium. For instance, in online communication nodding will more likely be interpreted as agreement with the points made by the speaker rather than as a gentle encouragement to continue speaking (Erasmus+ Virtual Exchange, 2019).

3.3. Virtual facilitator

Like facilitators in face-to-face intercultural dialogue, online facilitators are foremost process leaders who have to maintain multipartiality as they act to ensure a quality discussion (Soliya, cited in Erasmus+ Virtual Exchange, 2019). Consequently, online facilitators need to bring the familiar facilitator skills set to their task, including skills such as active listening, mirroring, summarizing, asking good questions, and bringing other perspectives into the dialogue. Like all facilitators, they are also expected to create and maintain a safe environment for the dialogue participants in which the desired values of openness, respect, authenticity, and trust can flourish. The virtual nature of the environment, however, adds a technological dimension of security to the aforementioned requirements: what safeguards have been taken by the host to protect the ongoing dialogue and any recordings that may have been made from unwanted hackers?

Next, there is also the matter of the perceived social identity of the host of the exchange. For instance, is the person seen as 'the rich other' reaching out to participants from less economically and technologically developed areas? The perception of neutrality that is expected from the dialogue facilitator may indeed be affected by various aspects of identity (gender; religion; profession; location...), often in an implicit manner. In her analysis of transcripts from Soliya Connect, Helm (2015) shows how the facilitator sometimes discloses information about her identity without offering participants "the chance to align to her transportable identity as may happen in 'normal' conversation in which such prompts would likely open the floor to questions and conversation" (p. 9). One comes across a similar case in the introductory course for dialogue facilitators offered by Erasmus+ Virtual Exchange (2019). The dialogue simulations that serve as illustrations and exercises in the course present a female facilitator who is wearing a hijab. By donning a hijab, the facilitator discloses that she is a Muslim but, in accordance with the principle of neutrality or multipartiality, she does not make this aspect of her identity relevant in the conversation. Nevertheless, given that a central topic of the dialogue concerns attitudes toward and interaction with migrants in Europe, one may wonder to what extent the participants perceive the facilitator as neutral. The issue here is that the format and the interface of the dialogue can be seen to discourage the participants from bringing up this possible conflict whereas, as Helm indicates, this would be more likely to happen in face-to-face environments.

4. Conclusions

From the semantic exploration that we carried out, it can be concluded that the term 'exchange' does not adequately capture the essence of what educators aim for in virtual exchange. Although it comprises a transaction of information, knowledge, opinions, and meaning, the exchange is better understood as an interaction whereby the focus not only rests on the task but also on the relationship. Above all, educators are looking to virtual exchange for the joint creation or spontaneous emergence of something new in a context which upholds values like trust, openness, respect, and authenticity. Virtual exchange even holds a promise of transformation for the participants: what we get back in the exchange is us, ourselves, our interconnected selves. The term 'dialogue', as defined by Bohm (1999) and applied in various domains by Isaacs (1999), Pranis (2005), Deardorff (2020) and others, has been shown to reflect this intended meaning more adequately than 'exchange'. Therefore, it would make sense to specify 'virtual exchange' as 'virtual dialogue' especially in contexts that aim at the interactional and transformative power of the activity. What is more, whenever the intercultural dimension is made salient by participants, this will create additional chances for acknowledging that the strangeness discovered in the other is already part of us, and hence, for a fuller realization of the dialogue principles of participation, coherence, awareness, and unfolding.

The other conclusion concerns the challenge of conducting dialogue in online environments. Specific examples like Soliya demonstrate that some of the structural components of dialogue can indeed be transferred to an online context and applied to foster intercultural understanding. Nevertheless, this transfer is always mediated by the given format and interface, resulting in a number of communicative affordances and constraints, as illustrated in this chapter. Consequently, Shuter's (2012) hesitation to downright accept that definitions of intercultural dialogue that are rooted in face-to-face contexts can be transferred unproblematically to virtual contexts is warranted. What is needed at this point is more empirical research into the actual discourses of online intercultural dialogue by interdisciplinary teams, combining technological, pedagogical, and linguistic expertise. For dialogue remains of pivotal importance and Isaacs' words at the cusp of the 21st century, pondering the dizzying pace of change, ring as true as ever:

> "[f]unctioning with the intensities of our world requires resilience. Dialogue can help by stretching our minds to inquire into point[s] of view we might not naturally accept, and so holding more possibilities and options open" (Isaacs, 1999, p. 334).

With the support of technology, the potential of dialogue can be realized more fully, particularly if we take its core principles, practices, and structural components, as outlined in this chapter, as a starting point for designing virtual intercultural dialogue activities. As illustrated in this chapter, young adults from North America, Europe, the Mediterranean region and the Middle East have had the possibility to engage with each other in such activities through structural initiatives like Soliya and Erasmus+. It is high time that also youngsters from the Asia-Pacific region could join in this virtual intercultural dialogue as they have just as much to give and just as much to learn in making the world flourish in trust, respect, and openness.

5. Acknowledgments

First I would like to thank the organizing committee of the third biennial APVEA conference at Hangzhou Dianzi University in May 2019 for giving me the opportunity to raise some of the ideas expressed in this chapter as a keynote presentation (https://apvea.org/course/view.php?id=13). This chapter has also benefited from the anonymous reviewers' comments on an earlier version of the manuscript. I also express my sincere thanks to the six expert practitioners whose responses have informed much of Section 2 in this text. Finally, I would like to thank the facilitators and co-learners of the online introductory course to dialogue facilitation, offered through Erasmus+ Virtual Exchange, who have helped me in maintaining a beginner's mind, from which I have benefited greatly, including a keen awareness that this text only provides a very tentative attempt at coming to terms with its theme.

References

Avgousti, M. I. (2018). Intercultural communicative competence and online exchanges: a systematic review. *Computer Assisted Language Learning, 31*(8), 819-853. https://doi.org/10.1080/09588221.2018.1455713

Barrett, M., Byram, M., Lázár, I., Mompoint-Gaillard, P., & Philippou, S. (2013). *Developing intercultural competence through education*. Council of Europe.

Bohm, D. (1999). *On dialogue*. Routledge.

Borghetti, C. (2017). Is there really a need for assessing intercultural competence? Some ethical issues. *Journal of Intercultural Communication, 44.* http://mail.immi.se/intercultural/nr44/borghetti.html

Cisco. (2019). *Cisco TelePresence X5000 series*. https://www.cisco.com/c/en/us/products/collaboration-endpoints/ix5000-series/index.html

Council of Europe. (2008). *White paper on intercultural dialogue. Living together as equals in dignity*. https://www.coe.int/t/dg4/intercultural/source/white%20paper_final_revised_en.pdf

Deardorff, D. K. (2020). *Manual for developing intercultural competencies. Story circles*. Unesco Publishing and Routledge. https://doi.org/10.4324/9780429244612-2

Drexler, W. (2010). The networked student model for construction of personal learning environments: balancing teacher control and student autonomy. *Australasian Journal of Educational Technology, 26*(3), 369-385. https://doi.org/10.14742/ajet.1081

Erasmus+ Virtual Exchange. (2019). *Introduction to dialogue facilitation – Spring 19*. https://europa.eu/youth/erasmusvirtual/activity/facilitation-trainings_en

European Union Education Ministers. (2015). *Declaration on promoting citizenship and the common values of freedom, tolerance and non-discrimination through education.* https://ec.europa.eu/assets/eac/education/news/2015/documents/citizenship-education-declaration_en.pdf

Harper, D. (2001-2020). Online etymology dictionary. https://www.etymonline.com/

Helm, F. (2015). Exploring identity and participation in online intercultural exchange [Conference presentation]. *Virtual learning sites as languaging spaces (ViLS-2), Örebro, Sweden.*

Isaacs, W. (1999). *Dialogue and the art of thinking together.* Currency.

Jia, Y. (2019). *Experiencing global intercultural communication.* Foreign Language Teaching and Research Press.

Jones, E. (2013). Internationalization and employability: the role of intercultural experiences in the development of transferable skills. *Public Money & Management, 33*(2), 95-104. https://doi.org/10.1080/09540962.2013.763416

McLuhan, M. (1964). *Understanding media: the extensions of man.* Mentor.

O'Dowd, R. (2020). A transnational model of virtual exchange for global citizenship education. *Language Teaching, 53*(4), 477-490. https://doi.org/10.1017/S0261444819000077

Pine, B. J., & Gilmore, J. H. (1999). *The experience economy.* Harvard Business School Press.

Pranis, K. (2005). *The little book of circle processes. A new/old approach to peacemaking.* Good Books.

Rajagopal, K., Firssova, O., Op de Beeck, I., Van der Stappen, E., Stoyanov, S., Henderikx, P., & Buchem, I. (2020). Learner skills in open virtual mobility. *Research in Learning Technology, 28.* https://doi.org/10.25304/rlt.v28.2254

Shuter, R. (2012). Intercultural new media studies: the next frontier in intercultural communication. *Journal of Intercultural Communication Research, 41*(3), 219-237. https://doi.org/10.1080/17475759.2012.728761

Soliya. (2007-2020). *Soliya Connect program.* https://www.soliya.net/programs/connect-program

Unesco. (2018). *Unesco survey on intercultural dialogue 2017.* Unesco. http://uis.unesco.org/en/news/unesco-survey-intercultural-dialogue

Van Maele J., Baten L., Beaven A., & Rajagopal, K. (2013). e-assessment for learning: gaining insight in language learning with online assessment environments. In B. Zou, M. Xing, C. H. Xiang, Y. Wang & M. Sun (Eds), *Computer-assisted foreign language teaching and learning: technological advances* (pp. 245-261). IGI. https://doi.org/10.4018/978-1-4666-2821-2.ch014

Van Maele, J., & Mertens, K. (2014). Towards an experience-driven approach to teaching intercultural communication. In P. Romanowski (Ed.), *Studia Naukowe, 27, Intercultural issues in the era of globalization* (pp. 122-129). IKSI Scientific Publishing House.

Vertovec, S. (2017). Talking around super-diversity. *Ethnic and Racial Studies, 42*(1), 125-139. https://doi.org/10.1080/01419870.2017.1406128

XML. (2016). *Parliament.* XML. http://parliamentbook.com/

Yorke, M. (2006). *Employability in higher education.* Higher Education Academy.

3. Tackling international controversies in virtual exchange

Masahito Watanabe[1]

Abstract

Since 2000, I have been coordinating a web-based Virtual Exchange (VE) project, *Project Ibunka*. *Ibunka* means different cultures in Japanese. It aims to provide opportunities for authentic interaction among English as a Foreign Language (EFL) and English as a Second Language (ESL) learners all over the world. By the end of our last project, *Project Ibunka 2018*, more than 6,600 students from 22 different countries had participated in this project. The Asia-Pacific countries, such as Japan, China, Taiwan, South Korea, Indonesia, the US, Argentina, and others, have always played an active role in *Project Ibunka*. Though not so often, participants had taken up international controversies, such as territorial disputes, wartime responsibility, compensation for war victims and survivors, and others. Fortunately, the messages posted did not result in fruitless debate among participants. These issues can sometimes be seen to be too sensitive to be taken up in VE. However, the study and discussion of such issues are inevitable if we are to promote mutual understanding especially in the Asia-Pacific region. In my article, I would like to show how VE language teachers and students can take an acceptable, open-minded stance in VE, free from any stereotypes and prejudices. Teachers should set a goal of multicultural understanding and encourage students to gain insights using conflict resolution approaches. They also should push students to reconsider their own values from the standpoint of basic human needs.

---

1. Yokohama University, Yokohama, Japan; wata33@gmail.com; https://orcid.org/0000-0003-0792-7194

How to cite: Watanabe, M. (2020). Tackling international controversies in virtual exchange. In E. Hagley & Y. Wang (Eds), *Virtual exchange in the Asia-Pacific: research and practice* (pp. 61-76). Research-publishing.net. https://doi.org/10.14705/rpnet.2020.47.1146

Chapter 3

Keywords: multiculturalism, conflict resolution, Asia-Pacific region, virtual exchange, intercultural exchange.

1. Introduction

1.1. Episode 1

Japan has had a peace clause in its constitution since the end of World War II. Since then, citizens have formed various grass-root-level peace movements. Among them, those for the elimination of nuclear weapons are most widespread and persistent, since Japan is the only nation ever to experience atomic bombings. When the International Janusz Korczak Conference was held in Japan in 2010, a group of Japanese university students reported their experience of visiting India. They appealed for a nuclear-weapon-free world to the Indian audience there.

The dramatic recitation of an English translation of the poem, *Umashimenkana (Let us be midwives*, in English[2]), was the highlight of the event:

> Let us be midwives
> It was night time in the basement of a building, now in ruins.
> Victims of the atomic bomb crammed into the dark room.
> There wasn't even one single candle.
> The overwhelming smell of fresh blood, the stench of death,
> The nauseating odor of humanity, the moaning…
> And miraculously, out of all of this, came a voice: "the baby is coming"!
> In this hellish place, at this very moment
> A young woman had gone into labor!
> In the dark, without even one single match, what could be done?

---

[2]. http://www.marieauxiliatrice.catholique.fr/Opening-the-door-to-new-life

Suddenly, a raised voice said: "I am a midwife, I will deliver".
It was the voice of a seriously injured woman, who was groaning with pain a minute before.
And so it was that in this hell a new life saw the day,
And so it was, that this midwife covered in blood died before the new day dawned.
I want to bring forth new life,
I want to bring forth new life,
Even if this means losing my own life.

At the end of the session, one of the Indian students in the audience raised his hand and asked, "Was Hiroshima-Nagasaki the right consequence of Pearl Harbor?". The Japanese university students on the stage remained silent. They were not able to reply to him. Why?

1.2. Episode 2

Since 2000, I have been carrying out a VE project every year. It is a web-based online discussion forum where English learners from different cultural backgrounds meet and discuss. In 2010, one of the South Korean students posted a message titled, "Two controversies between Korea and Japan". She referred to the territorial dispute between Korea and Japan, and the compensation for the sex slave survivor from World War II, and concluded, "I hope the controversy will be settled as fast as possible, so the relationship between both peoples will be better than now. I think that we, Korean and Japanese, can be good friends, can't we?".

I posted a message with the title, "Yes! We, Japanese and Korean, can be good friends" as a reply to her. Following me, many Japanese students replied to her with a favorable attitude toward Korea. She made the following reply to the Japanese students' postings: "Although both nations can be the best of partners in the global community, we blame each other. It's really time consuming and worthless. In an attempt to be good neighbors, we should try to understand each other. I really hope that we'll be good neighbors and partners".

Chapter 3

Until the time of writing (2019), the relationship between Korea and Japan has deteriorated more than ever and it still does not show any signs of resolution. How can VE language teachers handle political controversies like this?

1.3. Intercultural Communicative Competence (ICC) discussed in EFL/ESL

Byram (1997) outlined two attitudes we take when we encounter groups with different cultural and linguistic backgrounds: the 'tourist' and the 'sojourner'. The 'tourist' can travel around scenic areas for sightseeing. Although the experience might enrich him/her, it will never change him/her fundamentally. On the other hand, the 'sojourner' moves to a foreign region and leads a life temporarily there. According to Byram (1997), "although tourism has had major economic consequences, it is the sojourner who produces effects on society which challenge its unquestioned and unconscious beliefs, behaviors and meaning, and whose own beliefs, behaviors and meanings are in turn challenged and expected to change" (p. 1). Byram (1997) referred to this internalized knowledge of the sojourner as ICC. Newton (2016, p. 5) suggested the following five strategies for language teachers so they can cultivate learners' ICC:

- situate language in real communicative events/genre/tasks;

- start with self;

- encourage experiential learning and encourage learners to put learning into practice beyond the classroom;

- provide opportunities for learners to compare experiences and reflect on what the experiences felt like, what judgments arise, and for both feelings and thinking, why they feel/think in this way; and

- guide learners to construct understandings: Replace transmission of cultural facts with discovery learning.

Mainly based on Byram (1997), Newton's (2016) suggestions above show how teachers can "prepare students for becoming competent intercultural communicators" (p. 1) in existing EFL courses. The Japanese university students of Episode 1, absorbed in the mission of telling the tragedy of a-bomb victims to people outside Japan, did not study much about how foreigners think of nuclear weapons and react to their appeal. Although they had known the fact that the Japanese had been criticized for ignoring their responsibility as aggressors during World War II by the Asia-Pacific countries, the Indian gentleman's inquiry was completely out of their expectation. In short, they lacked something in their ICC.

Language teachers often shelve international controversies like the ones we saw in Episode 2. Political decisions and cultures are inseparable. The fact that they cannot maintain a healthy atmosphere without shelving political matters also suggests that their students can only be travelers, not sojourners. What should VE language teachers do to bring our learners to the level of sojourners? How can they have learners challenge their own "beliefs, behaviors, and meanings" as Byram (1997, p. 1) said? One of the main purposes of second or foreign language learning is the development of understanding of the cultural diversity that exists in the modern world. However, how can we achieve this goal? Few proposals have been made in VE research to create a coherent roadmap for bridging the political and cultural gaps among the participants although VE has been promoted as an international interaction among students. In this article, I would like to propose that VE language teachers should set a goal of multicultural understanding based on conflict resolution theorizing. It will enrich the current notion of ICC both for students and teachers. Teachers also should push students to reflect on their own values from the standpoint of basic human needs.

2. Multiculturalism

On September 13, 2007, the general assembly of the United Nations (UN) adopted the *Declaration on the Rights of Indigenous Peoples*. Although UN Declarations do not have any legal binding force under international law, "they

Chapter 3

represent the dynamic development of international legal norms and reflect the commitment of states to move in certain directions, abiding by certain principles". The declaration bears significant meaning as the UN acknowledges explicitly that indigenous peoples' are different, specifically that they have ownership rights to their culture, identity, language, labor, health, education, and others. Kymlicka (2007) referred to this global trend toward "the (re-)internationalization of state-minority relations" as "multiculturalism" (p. 1).

We should note Kymlicka (2007) used the word, '(re-)internationalization', not *internationalization*. The prefix '(re-)' implies that there was another internationalization movement and it was not so successful. During the early decades of the twentieth century, European empires that encompassed many ethnocultural communities fell apart resulting in several smaller countries with newly defined borders. Some of the same ethnic communities were divided up into several countries. We found, for example, Germans living in Poland and Polish living in Germany, Hungarians living in Romania and Romanians living in Hungary, and others. They were called 'irredentist minorities'. The states at that time made treaties to protect the rights of minor fellow citizens left outside of their borders. We can define this as *the first* internationalization of state-minority relations.

The issues of irredentist minorities gave some states reasons to wage war, i.e. World War II. The Holocaust in Europe was a form of ethnic cleansing and resulted in a tremendous number of casualties. After WWII, the first internationalization of state-minority relations was replaced with the granting of universal human rights, irrespective of any ethnic backgrounds. Since all citizens have equal human rights, the states considered they did not have to respect specific minority rights anymore. This idea was called assimilation. The UN and most of the post-WWII states seemed to approve it since "there were no references to minority rights in either the Charter of the United Nations, or the Universal Declaration of Human Rights of 1948". (Kymlicka, 2007, p. 30)

Attitudes toward indigenous peoples and minorities started to change in the 1980's. The UN began to revise its assimilation policies into new ones that officially acknowledge specific minority rights, including land ownership, language policy, and customary laws and others. In the 1990's, the emergence of new political issues brought by the end of the Cold War, such as regional conflicts, increased mobility of people, the vast number of refugees, and others, furthered the tendency. Thus, state-minority relations, which had once left the political arena, were *re*-internationalized. Multiculturalism is "understood as a concept that is both guided and constrained by a foundational commitment to principles of individual freedom and equality" (Kymlicka, 2007, p. 7). Thus, we can see multiculturalism as being an outgrowth of post-war universal human rights.

Multiculturalism has a significant impact on ICC and VE. Language teachers often underestimate the diversities among partner students, shelve existing political issues, and pursue collaborative products based on the so-called, big 'C' cultures (European Union, 2017). The concept of multiculturalism may be one solution students can look at to understand and use to resolve current international conflicts within a VE context. If we can elevate VE to a multicultural level, learners may be able to progress more easily from the state of the tourist into that of the sojourner.

Kimmel (1994) proposed five levels of cultural awareness that characterize the subjective culture we have personally: (1) cultural chauvinism, (2) ethnocentrism, (3) tolerance, (4) minimization, and (5) understanding. They are sequentially arranged levels. As the levels rise, socialization and metacognition are augmented gradually.

For ease of explanation, I set up the following four features:

- [± comparison] whether the individual has compared his/her culture with others and is aware of other cultures, or not;

- [± non-C1[3] superiority] whether the individual favors the group he/she belongs to and judges different cultures undesirable, or not;

---

3. C1: First culture, i.e. home country's culture, usually the culture of the country or the area where a person was born and spent a long time.

- [± real-life interaction] whether the individual has experienced much interaction with non-C1 cultures in his/her real-life, or not; and

- [± acknowledgment of non-C1 idiosyncrasies] whether the individual acknowledges the idiosyncrasies of non-C1, or not.

With these features, the following Table 1 shows how the five levels differ.

Table 1. Five levels of cultural awareness

	Comparison	Non-C1 superiority	Real-life interaction	Acknowledgment of non-C1 idiosyncrasies
(1) cultural chauvinism	−	−	−	−
(2) ethnocentrism	+	−	−	−
(3) tolerance	+	−	+	−
(4) minimization	+	+	+	−
(5) understanding	+	+	+	+

At the level of (1) cultural chauvinism, the individual, like a child, learns little about their C1 and non-C1, but has strong confidence in their own C1. At the level of (2) ethnocentrism, they can compare C1 and non-C1 through socialization – "a wider range of symbolic interactions" (Kimmel, 1994, pp. 189-190) – and formal education, but admire nothing other than their own C1. At level (3) tolerance, they have already accumulated some knowledge about their C1 and the non-C1, and experienced real-life interactions with non-C1 people, but still admire their C1 more than others. They often try "to educate, legislate, develop, or coerce" (Kimmel, 1994, pp. 189-190) non-C1 people into adopting the same ways of thinking and behavior as their own. At level (4) minimization, they consider the cultural differences among partners are negligible but underestimate the idiosyncrasies of each culture. Kimmel (1994) defined level (5) understanding as follows:

"[i]ndividuals at this level have discovered (usually through mediated intercultural experiences) that some of their own categories, plans, and rules are cognitively and perceptually arbitrary and that 'appropriate' behavior and feelings and 'realistic' thinking in intercultural situations are not necessarily givens" (pp. 189-190).

This level is entirely compatible with ICC and multiculturalism.

Looking back at the Japanese university students and if they can be positioned at level (2) ethnocentrism, although they seldom show or insist on the superiority of their C1, they have little experience of real-life interaction with non-C1 people. My VE project honors the vast interaction among students with various cultural backgrounds. However, it still cannot provide a rational means to handle international political issues among partners. It can be judged to be in level (4) minimization, and falls short of level (5) understanding.

Multicultural understanding should be set up as a goal of VE, but how can we achieve it? Conflict resolution strategies will give us insights.

3. Conflict resolution

Conflict resolution is the formal or informal process that seeks a peaceful resolution to a dispute among two or more opposing parties. Burton (1972) made the following statement about conflict:

> "[c]onflict, like sex, is an essential creative element in human relationships. It is the means to change, the means by which our social values of welfare, security, justice and opportunities for personal development can be achieved. If suppressed, as is often the case in traditional societies where conflict is settled according to traditionally accepted norms, society becomes static. In highly industrialized communities, rates of technological change are rapid and acceleration, and consequently conflict is widespread and fundamental. There is conflict between the individual and society, between privileged and

underprivileged, between managers and managed, and between those possessing different ideological values. But they are neither to be deprecated nor feared. The existence of a flow of conflict is the only guarantee that the aspiration of society will be attained. Indeed, conflict, like sex, is to be enjoyed" (pp. 137-138).

Here, we should note the following two points: (1) current technological developments mean conflict can affect our life directly from many different angles, and (2) if we can utilize international controversies to attain 'the aspiration of society' (Burton, 1972), they can become the means to multicultural understanding.

Fisher (1994) suggested two "generic principles deemed effective for addressing protracted social conflicts between identity groups. [... They are] the value base of scientific humanism and the approach of planned social change" (p. 48). In what Fisher (1994) calls 'scientific humanism', two notions are significant: 'shared experience' and 'basic human needs'. If statements, responses, comments, criticisms, and others do not accompany any shared experience, they are not prospective. Substantial interaction and cooperative processes among groups involved are essential. It also finds value in basic human needs. The idea originates in Maslow's (1943) hierarchy of needs. The hierarchy takes the shape of a pyramid, and arranges five needs from bottom to top based on the degree of cognitive growth: (1) physiological needs, (2) safety needs, (3) belonging and love needs, (4) esteem needs, and (5) self-actualization needs. The approaches based on basic human needs are of a win-win (or, non-zero-sum) nature. They should pursue mutually beneficial endings, not win-lose (or, zero-sum) ones. Democracy, to improve human welfare through shared experience, and freedom, to ensure individuals' development both physically and spiritually, i.e. basic human needs, often form the base of conflict resolution theorizing.

'Planned social change' is a collaborative process where all parties involved feel it necessary to modify their social structure and agree to do this. When social change is driven simply by market forces or undemocratic political authorities, they are considered unplanned. The planned ones should bring reformation of the fundamental arrangements of living, and reflect shared values, norms, roles, institutions, and others. Although it is collaborative, it requires individual consciousness for change.

> "Change occurs most effectively when individuals are involved in participative processes that apply knowledge to their situation, examine existing values and attitudes, and allow for the emergence of new norms and institutions" (Fisher, 1994, p. 49).

Conflict resolution approaches offer many practical insights for VE language teachers. They should implement the following four: (1) ensuring freedom of expression so that students can express any messages they wish without too much consideration of others, (2) democratizing the learning environment, allowing students to make decisions through discussion, (3) pushing students' win-win type of resolutions that satisfy basic human needs of all the participants, and (4) forming teachers' consensus about conflict resolution in advance.

Based on the four premises above, VE language teachers should promote the opportunities for students to talk frankly and constructively so that they can reach win-win types of resolutions. However, planned social change among students is hard to obtain in educational settings, although it is a part of multicultural understanding and conflict resolution. It requires professional skills of diplomacy and time for consensus-building on both sides.

VE language teachers should encourage students to acknowledge their individual consciousness for the need of change. This will serve as an intermediate step to the goal of the planned social change. However, this is not an easy task. Any time people make an overt criticism of political decisions or the C1 there are chances of conflict developing. Teachers need another educational strategy to facilitate students' reviewing of their own values. I would like to suggest nurturing students' naive sentiments for basic human needs.

Chapter 3

4. Nurturing naive sentiments for basic human needs

History textbooks often have a long list of past wars and devote most of the pages to the detailed description of them. We tend to consider humans having genetic predispositions to violence and war. However, we can also find many scholastic works that try to deny this and give evidence of peaceable cultures and societies. According to these works, behind some of the major institutional changes, such as slavery abolition, empowerment of women, elimination of racism, and others, ordinary citizens' naive sentiments often assumed a crucial role. For example, Swanson (2013) made the following description about the naive sentiments in the slavery abolition movement of the nineteenth century:

> "[t]his was a movement that made ending the slave trade and slavery a moral cause, a cause to be sacrificed for on behalf of distant, unknown people very different from oneself. It was a movement of public pressure. It did not use violence and it did not use voting. Most people had no right to vote. Instead it used so-called naive sentiments and the active ignoring of the supposed mandates of our supposed human nature" (p. 21).

The naive sentiments of ordinary people, i.e. the belief that we should end slavery because slaves are so poor and in misery, were the driving force of the ending of slavery. Further, the beliefs were instinctively understandable and had the potential to appeal globally despite cultural differences.

Swanson (2013) and other peace study scholars elevate the idea of slavery abolition to war abolition. They consider war itself can be abolished as slavery was. Swanson (2013) denied the possibility of a *just war*. He even denied the two types of wars authorized by the UN Charter: defensive wars and UN-authorized wars. Since these two types of wars threaten our basic human needs, they cannot be exceptions.

> "We must not oppose one war on the grounds that it isn't being run well or isn't as proper as some other war. We must not focus entirely on the

harm wars do to the aggressors. We must acknowledge the victims. We must see one-sided slaughters for what they are and grow appropriately outraged. A 'good war' must sound to all of us, like it sounds to me, as no more possible than a benevolent rape or philanthropic slavery or virtuous child abuse" (Swanson, 2013, pp. 156-157).

Even a few military superpowers cannot guarantee their citizens' perfect physical security by themselves. The bankruptcy of one private company in NY caused a chain of economic crises around the globe. Environmental issues such as global warming, deforestation, desertification, extreme weather, and others, extend across borders. We need cooperation, not competition among us. From these ideas comes the notion of common security, "[n]o one is safe until all are safe" (Shifferd, Swanson, & Hiller, 2018, p. 6). It also reflects our naive sentiments for basic human needs.

The idea of basic human needs has a global appeal. VE language teachers should give sufficient learning materials and information from the past and the present that can nurture students' naive sentiments for acknowledging basic human needs. When students confront international controversies in VE, their naive sentiments will give them opportunities to challenge their fixed beliefs and behaviors. This might give them some courage to take a step toward planned social change in the long run.

5. Conclusion

In this chapter, the need for enriching the concept of ICC is shown for students and VE language teachers. Multiculturalism that leads to an understanding among people is the key to this endeavor. We should acknowledge the idiosyncrasies of minorities, not minimize them. Since political resolutions of each state are closely related to the culture therein, it is inevitable to see clashes on political matters. We should not shelve political issues from our students' online discussions but rather offer recourse to conflict resolution theorizing if we see clashes, and have students seek solutions among themselves democratically. Although their final

Chapter 3

solutions might not reflect each participant's state policies, we should encourage them to arrive at what sincerely reflects their naive sentiments considering basic human needs. Naive sentiments have the potential to give way to planned social change in our students.

Since students from different cultural backgrounds can meet in VE projects, they offer good opportunities to see cultural diversity. However, VE language teachers should also organize a learning environment where students can notice that some values, specifically, basic human needs, are global, and, based on this understanding, offer opportunities for them to reconsider their own values. These values have the potential to go beyond cultural differences. To this end, teachers cannot shelve international controversies, where different value systems clash.

In my VE project, *Project Ibunka*, there are three main discussion themes, i.e. (1) school life, (2) cultures, and (3) social issues – world peace. This sequence facilitates students to proceed from big 'C' to small 'c' cultures gradually. During the project, I provide examples of successful international collaboration that might help our students tackle controversies and picture a peaceable world. They are given for the purpose of nurturing students' naive sentiment. In fact, the amount of input is still not sufficient for multicultural understanding. VE language teachers need to collaboratively accumulate and organize both the information and their expertise for this.

I would like to conclude my chapter by offering the following reply to the Indian inquirer in Episode 1 above, *is Hiroshima-Nagasaki the right consequence of Pearl Harbor?*

> "We, of course, do not admire the fact that the Japanese Navy once attacked Pearl Harbor which resulted in the death of a lot of American citizens. The victims were sure to be thinking why did they have to die due to the sudden military attack of Japan".

> "You can say, 'Hiroshima-Nagasaki was the right consequence of Pearl Harbor'. It might be correct as a description of historical facts.

However, none of the victims of Hiroshima-Nagasaki would have died, considering they should not have attacked Pearl Harbor. They died thinking why did they have to die due to the unusual bombing. The victims of Pearl Harbor and those of Hiroshima-Nagasaki are the same in this respect".

"We, Japanese, (should) refuse to resort to any type of violence or war to solve problems. Children and adults alike, men and women alike, irrespective of the difference in race, culture, religion, thought, and others, all of the people on the globe have the right to live in safety and enjoy life, that is, basic human rights. We, Japanese, regret that we had pursued our own happiness while neglecting the human rights of the people other than us, and even developed hatred toward non-Japanese".

"When unreasonable hatred toward some people remains deeply in your mind, it might cause another catastrophe comparable with Hiroshima-Nagasaki or the Holocaust of World War II. You cannot isolate yourself from these historical tragedies".

"We cannot win our happiness from others. One hostility produces another. No one can win. We should cooperate with others to bring happiness for all. No one is safe until all are safe. Can you love people who share little with you? Can you love people who live in a foreign country and whose religion, language, lifestyle, and values are different from yours? You can love them. We were born to love each other despite differences. We can believe in our morality. We are all good by nature".

References

Burton, J. W. (1972). *World society.* Cambridge University Press.
Byram, M. (1997). *Teaching and assessing intercultural communicative competence.* Multilingual Matters.

European Union. (2017). *"Big C" culture, "little c" culture*. Erasmus+ KA2 Project Co-funded by the European. https://erasmusmyway.wordpress.com/2017/05/19/big-c-culture-little-c-culture/

Fisher, R. J. (1994). Generic principles for resolving intergroup conflict. *Journal of Social Issues, 50*(1), 47-66. https://doi.org/10.1111/j.1540-4560.1994.tb02397.x

Kimmel, P. R. (1994). Cultural perspectives on international negotiations. *Journal of Social Issues, 50*(1), 179-196.

Kymlicka, W. (2007). *Multicultural odysseys: navigating the new international politics of diversity.* Oxford University Press.

Maslow, A. H. (1943). A theory of human motivation. *Psychological Review, 50*(4), 370-396.

Newton, J. M. (2016). Cultivating intercultural competence in tertiary EFL programs. *Crossing Borders in Language Teaching and Business Communication: Proceedings of the 11th ELT Conference at AE CYUT*, (pp. 1-22).

Shifferd, K., Swanson, D., & Hiller, P. (2018). *A global security system: an alternative to war (2018-2019 edition)*. World BEYOND War.

Swanson, D. (2013). *War no more: the case for abolition.* David Swanson

4. ICC cultivation in a multiform course mode

Ran Liu[1] and Yi'an Wang[2]

Abstract

With the present situation of economic globalization, simple inter-flows of information within and between countries have become standard to meet the development needs of college and university students, who now require and demand intercultural communication to improve their understanding of the globalized world. In recent years, online platforms have dramatically changed the traditional face-to-face communication methods and provide a learning environment without time and place restrictions. With the construction of international online platforms, real intercultural communication conditions have been provided for students to improve their Intercultural Communication Competence (ICC) and English skills where they were not available before. This study outlines an online teaching method and design of a new multiform course mode that consists of two online platforms. Eleven random classes of 330 university students were observed in this study. All of them were enrolled in a four-month course of intercultural communication in the spring semester of 2017 at a science and technology university in China. Students were divided into two groups, Group A had five classes of students who participated in the new course mode and Group B was the other group which had six classes under the traditional classroom teaching mode. This study aims to find if the special course mode would help develop ICC among college students who stay in a domestic context, through an analysis of the variation of

1. Freelance researcher, Hangzhou, China; romantic364130@sina.cn; https://orcid.org/0000-0003-2894-0259

2. Hangzhou Dianzi University, Hangzhou, China; wangyian2003@hotmail.com

How to cite: Liu, R., & Wang, Y. (2020). ICC cultivation in a multiform course mode. In E. Hagley & Y. Wang (Eds), *Virtual exchange in the Asia-Pacific: research and practice* (pp. 77-102). Research-publishing.net. https://doi.org/10.14705/rpnet.2020.47.1147

© 2020 Ran Liu and Yi'an Wang (CC BY)

Chapter 4

the two groups' ICC before and after the course. This research adopts a mixed methods approach that includes questionnaires, online platform observations, and students' reflective journals to test students' cultural intelligence before and after they have had the intercultural communication course. The findings provide a basis and reference for future ICC cultivation, especially regarding the construction of online ICC cultivating platforms.

Keywords: college students, intercultural communication competence, online learning platform, cultural intelligence.

1. Introduction

1.1. Cultivation of ICC

Traditionally in college English courses in China, the most important thing for students was to pass different tests and get certificates. Cultivation of ICC was not taken seriously. Students could only learn from books and teachers, that is, without being in a real intercultural environment. Such English language learning would lead to cultural mistakes when they really interacted with people from another culture. Therefore, the mode needed to be changed urgently and many Chinese scholars have begun to try.

As new teaching methods in language courses emerged, application of network technologies became widespread. E-teaching is now a major trend and has become increasingly popular. Colleges and universities have already built some online learning platforms to change students' traditional learning methods and help teachers gain access to more teaching resources. As a part of language learning, ICC cultivation is the same. Network teaching platforms provide teachers and students with a virtual communication means where teachers are able to attain information and feedback efficiently. Students have no limitations of time or space when studying in online courses. They can choose when and what to learn. Additionally, teachers can make full use of the network teaching platform, utilizing multimedia learning resources on the Internet and creating different courseware for learners. Younos (2012) considers the main goal of online teaching platforms as being to create social interactions to motivate students. Kuo, Walker, Schroder, and Belland (2014) indicate that in online programs, "interaction is a critical indicator of student satisfaction" (p. 36). The main aim of an ICC platform should therefore be to provide students with a real intercultural communication space to improve their ICC.

In China, Internet teaching platforms are still a new emerging teaching media. Many online platforms have been constructed by the government to reform the education system. This research is based on a multiform course mode consisting of two online platforms, one is the *Zhejiang Institutions of Higher Learning Online Open Course Sharing Platform* which contains various online courses. The other is an online intercultural exchange platform sponsored by the ministry of education in Japan, named the *International Virtual Exchange (IVE) project*. The two platforms are inseparably interconnected in the course mode of this research.

1.2. Main models of ICC

In cultivating students' ICC, studies on the constituent elements of ICC occupy an important position. For example, Deardorff (2006) has proposed the *Process Orientation* model to measure an individual's ICC. This model is divided into four dimensions, *Attitudes, Knowledge and Comprehension, Internal Outcome*, and *External Outcome*. The first thing to consider is *Attitudes*. Concretely, it contains three aspects, *Respect, Openness and Curiosity*, and *Discovery*. The embrace of these attitudes is critical for good intercultural communication. Once these attitudes have been acquired, an intercultural process can occur.

In 2003, Earley and Ang formed the CQ (cultural intelligence) theory with four dimensions, metacognitive, cognitive, motivational, and behavioral based on Sternberg and Detterman's (1986) framework. In that framework, Sternberg and Detterman (1986) collected varied opinions of CQ to complement the CQ theory on individual level: (1) metacognitive intelligence is how individuals acquire information and obtain knowledge subconsciously; (2) cognitive intelligence is how knowledge structured individually; (3) the intelligence that motivates individuals to focus and learn is regarded as motivational intelligence; and (4) behavioral intelligence underlined individuals' capabilities to behave.

This study takes Earley and Ang's (2003) CQ Scale (CQS) as the measurement, who state that the above four dimensions are effective and functional under various cultural backgrounds and aims to do a comprehensive study of students' ICC learning processes and to determine if the new course mode helps them improve ICC.

2. Research methodology

2.1. Research questions

The fundamental objective of this research is to examine the effects of the online learning platform on students' ICC improvement using the CQS to examine any change. Hence this study is going to answer the following main questions:

- Is there any change in students' ICC if they participate in the new multiform course mode?

- Depending on the findings above, what are the characteristics of the changes?

- If there were any changes, what suggestions could be extracted to build future intercultural network learning platforms in China?

2.2. Research design

The study is based on students' participation in a multiform course mode. The mode is a combination of classroom teaching and two online learning platforms which allowed students to interact with others both domestically and internationally. It also included an interview task that was carried out from the course beginning to end. The two online platforms are the *Zhejiang Institutions of Higher Learning Online Open Course Sharing Platform* (*Zhejiang Sharing Platform*) and the *IVE project*.

For the quantitative research, the CQ survey instrument was used and given to both groups of 330 students before they started the intercultural communication course. As for the quantitative research, observation of how Group A of 150 students acted in the two platforms was needed. An analysis of each of their reflective reports on the course was carried out.

2.3. The different platforms

2.3.1. Zhejiang Sharing platform

Zhejiang Sharing Platform is an online platform launched by the government of Zhejiang Province, China. The platform consists of courses from a number of colleges and universities. For Group A students, in this platform they can access content from an *intercultural communication course* that adds to the classroom content. The advantage of this online course is the clear guidance for students: they can see the course outline, know the exact content of each unit and finish tasks and homework using their personal computer. There are a large number of books, audio, and video resources offered on this platform and students can also watch short video courses of their teacher.

2.3.2. The IVE project

To assist with the interview task, another online exchange platform, the *IVE project* was considered suitable for the new course mode. The *IVE project* was created by Eric Hagley and his team. It was created with assistance from a Japanese government Kaken grant. In the spring semester of 2017, students from Japan, China, and Columbia, in addition to a lesser number of students from the United Arab Emirates and Thailand, took part in the platform. It is like an open forum where students can socialize with each other under the supervision of their teachers. The main aim of putting Group A students in this platform was to help them find a person from a different culture but with similar interests so they can build a relationship with each other and Group A students can launch their interview task better.

There were five sections in the platform that provided students a place to discuss the topics 'self-introduction', 'about my hometown', 'events in our lives', 'future plans', and one open forum. During the period of this research, the Chinese students were interacting with students from the other countries. Most of the students were just beginners of cultural learning, so the above simple topics could arouse their interest, making their integration into the platform easy and quick.

2.4. The intercultural interview

An important part of the study was the interview task that was assigned to Group A students to guide them toward building connections with the foreign students through the *IVE project*. It is a special interview task of this multiform course mode. At the beginning of the course, the task was assigned to Group A students (students who participated in the new mode) which acted as a guideline in their ICC learning. Each of them was asked to interview a person from a different culture (nation, country, social background). It was a long-term task that required students to submit their schedule and rate of progress at different learning phases during the whole semester.

The interview was divided into four parts: *My Culture Story, Interview Proposal, Record of Culture Exchange,* and *Final Report*. Figure 1 below is the clear steps of the interview. *My Culture Story* was the first step, which asked students to outline their basic cultural background including their basic information (name, gender, age, hometown, etc.) and many other aspects about their life. It is worth noting that the *intercultural communication course* is an optional course that students can choose based on their interests. Since the majority of the students are interested in cultural knowledge, the culture stories they wrote often had substantial content and expressed their basic understanding of culture.

Figure 1. Interview steps

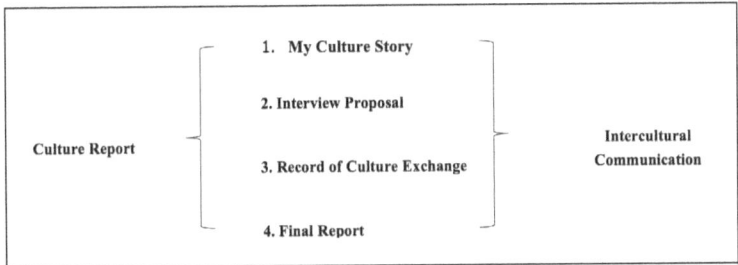

Creation of the interview proposal was the second step of the interview task. In this part, students give a brief introduction about the interview they intend to do and the basic information of the interviewee. The basic format of the proposal is as follows (Table 1).

Table 1. The interview proposal

The interview proposal	
1) Information of the Interviewer:	(name, gender, age, religious belief, hometown, etc., language)
2) Information of the Interviewee:	
3) The way you found your partner:	(how you choose them from the platforms)
4) The reason you chose that partner:	(why are you interested in them, is it relevant to your interview theme? etc.)
5) Interview method:	(virtual exchange platform discussion, other chatting tools)
6) The theme of your interview:	(the main topic you designed to discuss)

Step 3 was the interview journal. In this part, students give some details about their current interviewee. On the platform they can freely discuss any topic they are interested in and can also expand on it using additional video chat or texts through other tools based on their needs, thus deepening communication. Both sides are able to express their thoughts sincerely over the period of communication. The students have some basic thoughts prepared for the interview and also participate in intercultural communication. In this step, teachers do not interfere in student communication unless students need some extra help to ensure they have an experience of intercultural communication.

Step 4 is the final report on the interview. In this part, students sum up the whole interview and give a conclusion about the topic they chose for discussion. They write about their experiences on the platform with screenshots and describe their individual feelings (such as culture shock, cultural exchanges, misunderstandings, and what they think were the most interesting cultural interactions). After hopefully acquiring some cultural knowledge and participating in the platform for one semester, they would have a variety of related ideas about cultural differences and possessing intercultural sensitivity which would help in doing the post-research.

Together, these four sections make up the whole interview task of the multiform course mode and it also serves as a necessary part to make students focus on the learning of cultural knowledge. The final cultural report they hand in at the end of the semester which contains the four sections also serves as the reflective journal of this study.

2.5. Research subjects

To show a clear comparison of ICC changes and/or a systematic learning of culture, this study observed two groups of students. Group A had 150 students in five classes that took part in this online learning platform and Group B had 180 students in six classes that did not participate in the project but rather learned in a traditional classroom.

Group A was taught by two teachers and Group B was taught by one teacher. All three teachers were from the same course group, in the same science and technology university in China. Before teachers started the *intercultural communication course* teaching, they had set teaching plans and had made the teaching program together. All of them are experienced teachers. There were not many differences in the classroom teaching aspects of the two groups. This study considers the variable as the new multiform course mode.

All students were non-English majors, sophomores, and junior students (Table 2). Both groups were selected randomly. The participants they communicated with on the platform were same-age students from Japan and Columbia who also participated in one of the platforms, the *IVE project*.

Table 2. Two groups of students

Students	Grade		Number	Gender		Major
	Sophomore	Junior		Male	Female	
Joined the project	128	22	150	60.7%	39.3%	Non-English Majors
Didn't join the project	171	19	180	66.7%	33.3%	

2.6. Research instrument and procedures

As mentioned above, this survey study is a combination of both quantitative and qualitative research approaches which uses a questionnaire and reflective journals to discover if the networked teaching and learning platform has an effect on the ICC of college students and the characteristics of any changes. Therefore, questionnaires and students' reflective journals are served as the instruments of this study. In addition, the students' interactions on the platform were also observed for qualitative reference.

2.6.1. Questionnaire

This study adopted Earley and Ang's (2003) CQS. They produced the self-testing scale to gauge changes brought about due to globalization as this needed to be examined. They discovered people's behavior and working performance were different under different cultural conditions, which could not be explained by *Emotional Intelligence* (Salovey & Mayer, 1990). CQ can be deemed as an individual's capability of information collection and processing in a different cultural background and take effective actions to adapt to the new environment. The CQS was produced to measure this.

As mentioned above, metacognitive CQ, cognitive CQ, motivational CQ, and behavioral CQ, the four dimensions of CQs, work together to affect the

Chapter 4

individual's level of CQ. In the CQS, there are 20 items corresponding to the four dimensions mentioned above. The questionnaire uses a Likert scale score, from one to seven, one indicating 'strongly disagree' and seven indicating 'strongly agree'. The subjects who take the survey report on themselves according to their actual situation. The original questionnaire of CQS can be found in Ang and Van Dyne (2008, p. 389).

As this research aimed to study the effectiveness of a multiform course mode on ICC where cultural interactions between students occurred through the Internet, the final questionnaire of CQS given to students had some minor modifications to suit the online nature of the study. It maintained the four dimensions but had a total of 21 items.

All 330 students were non-English majors. To ensure they could thoroughly understand the questionnaire and to keep the accuracy of the data, the questionnaire given to students was in English and Chinese. To prevent students falling into formulaic replies, the items were randomly disorganized. Table 3 is the English version of the questionnaire, and the bilingual version students received is in the supplementary materials.

To make it more salient and logical, Table 4 shows the final form of the CQS for this study and the corresponding numbers for items in the four dimensions.

Table 3. Modified CQS

CQ Factor	Corresponding Number	Questionnaire Items
Metacognitive CQ	MC1/Q6	I am conscious of the cultural knowledge I use when interacting with people with different cultural backgrounds.
	MC2 / Q11	I adjust my cultural knowledge as I interact with people from a culture that is unfamiliar to me.
	MC3 / Q15	I am conscious of the cultural knowledge I apply to cross-cultural interactions.
	MC4 / Q9	I check the accuracy of my cultural knowledge as I interact with people from different cultures.

Cognitive CQ	COG1 / Q24	I know the education system of other cultures.
	COG2 / Q8	I know the rules (e.g. vocabulary, grammar, how to use language politely and appropriately) of other languages.
	COG3 / Q16	I know the cultural values and religious beliefs of other cultures.
	COG4 / Q10	I know the norms of dealing with interpersonal relationships (e.g. friendship, kinship) in different cultures.
	COG5 / Q17	I know the arts (e.g. music, painting, movies) of other cultures.
	COG6 / Q13	I know the rules for expressing nonverbal behaviors (e.g. smile, gesture) in other cultures.
Motivational CQ	MOT1 / Q14	I enjoy interacting with people from different cultures.
	MOT2 / Q4	I am confident that I can socialize with local people in a culture that is unfamiliar to me.
	MOT3 / Q 18	I am sure I can deal with the stresses of adjusting to a culture that is new to me.
	MOT4 / Q20	I am sure I can deal with miscommunications and problems in intercultural interactions arising from cultural differences.
Behavioral CQ	BEH1/ Q 19	I change my verbal behavior (e.g. accent, tone) when a cross-cultural interaction requires it.
	BEH2 / Q 22	I use pause and silence differently to suit different cross-cultural situations.
	BEH3 / Q21	I change my nonverbal behavior (e.g. facial expression, smile) when an intercultural situation requires it.
	BEH4/ Q7	I vary the rate of my speaking when a cross-cultural situation requires it.
	BEH5 / Q 23	I change my communication styles (e.g. direct vs. indirect) when an intercultural interaction requires it.
	BEH6 / Q12	I try to rephrase or explain when problems arise from intercultural communication.
	BEH7 / Q6	I use pictures, photos, and emoji to express myself when an intercultural situation requires it.

Table 4. Correspondence classification of four dimensions

Metacognitive CQ	Q6, Q11, Q15, Q9
Cognitive CQ	Q24, Q8, Q16, Q10, Q17, Q13
Motivational CQ	Q4, Q14, Q8, Q20
Behavioral CQ	Q19, Q22, Q21, Q7, Q23, Q12, Q6

2.6.2. Reflective journals

As already stated above, both groups of students were assigned with a cultural report task, which functioned as a reflective journal of the subjects. In the report, students recorded the process of intercultural communication and gave comments about themselves and how their thoughts have changed after the virtual exchange communication with people from different cultural backgrounds. The journals which reflect students' inner viewpoints were completed at the end of the course. Therefore, their journals were fresh and valid.

2.7. Data analytical approaches

Quantitative and qualitative statistics were collected to support the research with the process of data collection lasting from March to July, and through the spring semester of 2017 of the sample science and technology university.

2.7.1. Quantitative data collection

The CQS used for the research was given as a pre- and post-study. The pre-study wanted to ascertain if different groups' CQ was obvious in different levels. The same CQS questionnaire was used as the post-study which measured any changes. The post-survey was given to students in the last class of the course. Considerations of privacy and data authenticity of the self-test were taken into consideration. This survey was administered as an online questionnaire which students could do using their cell phone too. The pre- and post-study were both taken in the classroom. The pre- and post-study of Group A (150 students who participated in the online platform) had 139 and 144 valid questionnaires recovered. As for Group B, there were 166 and 132 valid questionnaires recovered from the pre- and post-surveys.

2.7.2. Qualitative data collection

For students who participated in the new multiform course mode, the final culture reports they wrote served as qualitative data in this research. There were four sections to the journal, *My Culture Story, Interview Proposal, Record of Culture Exchanging*, and *Final Report*. The journal, being one task of the course, was taken seriously by students. A total of 149 journals were collected both in electronic form and printed form.

2.8. Data analysis

In this study, qualitative and quantitative research was conducted using different methods simultaneously with the adaptation of the four dimensions of the CQS. Both results are used in the discussion of the research.

2.8.1. Quantitative data analysis

Results from the surveys were exported and IBM SPSS 23.0 used as the analytic tool to compute the exact numerical value of mean, standard deviation, and Standard Error of Mean (SEM) of both groups' pre- and post-tests. As for independent samples, this study used Levene's test for equality of variances and the t-test for equality of means to examine the data dependency and differences between pre- and post-data.

2.8.2. Qualitative data analysis

As mentioned above, there are four dimensions on the CQS. Through analyzing any changes in CQ of the students who participated in the online learning platform, results on how the four dimensions of CQS are also shown in their reflective journals and summarize the characteristics of the changes. Further, some suggestions for the future construction of networked teaching and learning platforms is offered as well.

3. Results and discussions

Using the data collected and analysis results outlined above, this section now turns to the following aspects: (1) a contrast of the pre- and post-study outcome of the two groups; (2) the characteristics of changes in Group A students; and (3) for college students in China, what constitutes an ideal online intercultural communication learning and teaching platform.

3.1. Changes between the groups

As stated above, this research included both pre- and post-studies to test the level of students' CQ before and after they participated in the intercultural communication course. Table 6-1 (in supplementary materials) shows the results of both students before they started the intercultural communication course.

Tables 6.1 and 6.2 (in supplementary materials) are the statistics of the pre-study of the two groups of students. From the column of 'Mean', the average score of each item is similar between the two groups. The column 'SIG (2-tailed)' showing results from the *t-test for equality of means*, shows the exact difference. If the *p*-value is less than 0.05, it illustrates that there are significant differences between the two groups' data, otherwise there are not. It is thus clear that p-values in the tables are greater than or equal to 0.05 (only Q11 equals 0.05, other items are greater than 0.05), which means there are no significant differences between the two groups. Before they started the *intercultural communication course*, the students of the two groups had nearly the same level of CQ.

The post-survey was conducted after both groups of students had finished their one-semester *intercultural communication course*. Group A students had also participated in the *IVE project* and interacted with foreign students through this online learning platform, while Group B students had not. The following data shows the results of the post-study. Tables 6-3 and 6-4 (in supplementary materials) note the statistics from the post-study for the two groups of students. In Table 6-3, the column 'Mean' shows great differences between the average scores. It is visible that Group A students who joined the *IVE project* have relatively higher average scores. The exact differences can be examined using the *t*-test for equality of means in Table 6-4, with column 'SIG (2-tailed)' giving the *p*-values ($p<0.05$). If the *p*-value is smaller than 0.05, it illustrates that there are great differences between the two groups' data, otherwise there are not. From

Table 6-4 (in supplementary materials), nearly all *p*-values of the items are less than 0.05 except Q24 which means, compared with the non-participating Group B, Group A had significant improvement.

3.2. Characteristics of the improvement

To make the comparison clearer, Table 5 below lists the average scores broken down into the four dimensions of both the pre- and post-tests of the two groups.

Table 5. Improvement of Group A students

	Total (pre)	Total (post)
Group B	94.51	94.26
Group A	95.34	102.81
	Cognitive (pre)	Cognitive (post)
Group B	25.67	25.83
Group A	25.38	28.39
	Behavioral (pre)	Behavioral (post)
Group B	32.30	31.75
Group A	32.81	34.57
	Metacognitive (pre)	Metacognitive (post)
Group B	18.07	18.09
Group A	18.55	19.32
	Motivational (pre)	Motivational (post)
Group B	17.42	17.70
Group A	17.46	19.66

Table 5 above shows an improvement in Group A students who participated in the online platform, and for Group B students, their total score basically had no change and there were few improvements in the cognitive, motivational, or behavioral CQ dimensions.

As displayed in Table 6-4 (in supplementary materials), the statistics of the post-study showed the improvement of Group A students. In the following items: Q4, Q8, Q10, Q12, Q17, Q18, and Q23 ($p<0.05$) are approximately equal to zero, thus these six items could be considered as the items with the greatest degree of improvement. The *p*-values of Q13, Q14, Q19, Q20, Q22 were no higher than 0.02, which means the development in these items was relatively obvious. Since the following section is going to analyze the improvement of the four dimensions of CQS, Table 6 outlines the classifications of the above items and the corresponding numbers of the four dimensions of CQS.

Table 6. Improved items

	Most improved items		Relatively improved items	
Cognitive CQ	COG2	Q8	COG6	Q13
	COG4	Q10		
	COG5	Q17		
Motivational CQ	MOT2	Q4	MOT1	Q14
	MOT3	Q18	MOT4	Q20
Behavioral CQ	BEH6	Q12	BEH1	Q19
	BEH5	Q23	BEH2	Q22

The following sections analyze Group A students' improvement in ICC showing both the improved items and their cultural reports (reflective journals). As stated above, Group A and Group B students were all assigned the task of writing a *cultural report*. With regard to their cultural reports, as connections between Group A students and foreign students had been developed through the IVE project, they were able to finish the task carefully with details of interactions with their foreign partner. However Group B students were perfunctory with regard to their cultural report. For Group B students, they did not have a serious cultural interview with people from other cultures.

Since this study focuses on the improvements in students who participated in the online platform, the following section looks at details from Group A students' reports.

3.3. Improvement in metacognitive CQ

Metacognitive CQ refers to "an individual's cultural consciousness through cross-cultural interactions" (Ang & Van Dyne, 2008, p. 5). Flavell (1979) and Nelson (1996) consider metacognitive CQ as a high individual capability to explore higher-level strategies in fresh cultural environments by deepening information recognition.

Those with higher levels of metacognitive ability CQ can more clearly know what knowledge to use when interacting with foreigners and it also helps them revise their communication strategies. It is a mental process that incorporates cultural knowledge, understanding, and acquirement thereof.

For both Groups A and B students who participated in the intercultural communication courses, the cultural knowledge they acquired has no doubt improved through learning from their teacher and books. But for students who took part in the online platform, the improvement is through actual practices. Therefore, as illustrated by the statistics above, compared with the non-participating Group B, Group A's level of CQ improved more in this area than in the other three dimensions.

3.4. Improvement in cognitive CQ

Cognitive CQ is the knowledge that is acquired from learning and practicing in different cultural backgrounds, it can be cultural norms, conventions, etc. (Ang & Van Dyne, 2008, p. 5). In simple terms, Cognitive CQ is the basic cultural knowledge that affects people's ideas and behaviors. As Ang and Van Dyne (2008) note, "cultural knowledge includes knowledge of oneself as embedded in the cultural context of the environment" (p. 5). For students, when they are in a 'real' environment, this ability can be improved more easily. The IVE project is such a platform. The most improved items of cognitive CQ are as follows (see Table 7).

Both Groups A and B students are non-English majors. For Group A students, on the online platform all students from the different countries used English as the lingua franca to communicate with each other. Many of them mentioned it was their first time to use English to communicate with a foreigner. To keep the communication going fluently, they needed to learn more rules of English.

Table 7. Improved items on cognitive CQ

Cognitive CQ	Q8	I know the rules (e.g., vocabulary, grammar, how to use language politely and appropriately) of other languages.	Most improved items
	Q10	I know the norms of dealing with interpersonal relationships (e.g., friendship, kinship) in different cultures.	
	Q17	I know the arts (e.g., music, painting, movies) of other cultures.	
	Q13	I know the rules for expressing nonverbal behaviors (e.g., smile, gesture) in other cultures.	Relatively improved item

Here are some words from their reflective journals (numbers are used to protect individual's anonymity):

> "This course not only helped me improve my English, but also made me use English to communicate with a foreigner for the first time which has great significance to me. Communicating with a real English user is quite different from the usual exams and various English exercises" (150632290).

> "This interview was my first cross-culture communication with a foreigner. I firstly found that to communicate with a foreigner is so interesting and wonderful" (15141511).

As for the improvement noted due to changes in response to Q10, after real interaction with foreign students, most students in Group A learned more basic norms of dealing with interpersonal relationships than they had known. The students they communicated with were the best samples for them to learn those norms.

> "Japanese show great respect for seniority. The junior must use honorifics when speaking to the elders no matter in their families, schools or companies. But in China, we do not pay special attention to such typical honorifics" (15063314).

> "I think it is general in China and Japan to not talk too much about privacy things at the beginning of communication" (15081612).

Art was a common topic and nearly everyone talked about the music and movies of their own culture. There were a lot of students from Japan, so many Group A students started their communication talking about Japanese manga and anime.

> "I have learned that in Japan, there is an art form called *Haiku* which is similar to ancient Chinese poetry" (15031325).

> "I saw the official trailer of the Tokyo Olympic Games. At that time, I didn't know why so many comic and animation elements were put in it. But in fact, all aspects of Japan's social life and mental state are displayed in their anime. Different kinds of animation are created for all ages. Animation culture can be one of the symbols of Japan and it's an important point for us to know about Japan" (14051318).

Though not fluent in English, both sides of students communicated in a relaxed and happy manner.

> "There were several times that we did not understand each other in words, but with a smile, the embarrassment seems to have been resolved. Even the most intelligent person can not learn all the languages of the world. However, this does not mean that we have lost opportunities for communication. We still have body gestures" (15031325).

> "When we facetime with each other, there were many times that she folded her hands in front and said 'a li ga to u' (thank you) which made me feel she is so polite. But Yoko told me it is common in Japan" (15141511).

3.5. Improvement on motivational CQ

Motivational CQ is the intelligence that drives individuals to focus and learn under cultural interactions (Ang & Van Dyne, 2008, p. 5). Deci and Ryan (1985) consider students with high motivational CQ are those who have intrinsic interests and are active in cross-cultural situations (Table 8). Bandura (2002) also thinks such active students are also confident in intercultural communication.

Table 8. Improved items on motivational CQ

Motivational CQ	Q4	I am confident that I can socialize with local people in a culture that is unfamiliar to me.	Most improved items
	Q18	I am sure I can deal with the stresses of adjusting to a culture that is new to me.	
	Q14	I enjoy interacting with people from different cultures.	Relatively improved items
	Q20	I am sure I can deal with miscommunications and problems in intercultural interactions arising from cultural differences.	

For Q4 and Q18, the average scores of Group A students was 4.39 and 4.47 respectively, but after the course, the score had reached 5.01 and 4.99. Group B students' scores of the two items improved from 4.30 and 4.40 to 4.43 and 4.52 respectively. From the statistics and journals of Group A students, this study shows that for Group A students, there is an obvious improvement in motivational CQ as shown by their answers to Q4 and Q18. This was derived from their real interactions with foreign students. Through the intercultural communication practice, they gained experiences about how to socialize with people from different cultural backgrounds, adjust to their habits, and learn from the new culture. As many of them made friends with the foreign students, it gave them the courage and confidence to have good communication with people from different cultures. In the process, they faced many communication problems but solved them well.

> "Sometimes I could not understand what he wanted to express, and my English was not fluent. But the biggest harvest for me is I have learned the efficient way to communicate. I would pay attention to details to avoid cultural misunderstandings. Interacting with foreigners has

changed me and my communication style which will be a great help in the future" (15063231).

"There were many language and cultural barriers in the conversation between Akiko and I, but we were communicating with our hearts. An affable will can easily conquer cultural difficulties" (15031325).

"Not until I participated in the platform did I learn that there are great differences due to 'cultural difference'. But luckily I also had the chance to learn how to deal with them through my own experiences" (15141537).

3.6. Improvement in behavioral CQ

The behavioral dimension refers to the level of how an individual adopts new verbal and nonverbal behaviors in a cross-cultural situation (see Table 9). "Behavioral CQ is a critical component of CQ, because verbal and nonverbal behaviors are the most salient features of social interactions" (Ang & Van Dyne, 2008, p. 7). As Hall (1959) underlined, nonverbal behaviors are even serious because they pass on meaning subtly as a 'silent language'.

Table 9. Improved items on behavioral CQ

Behavioral CQ	Q12	I try to rephrase or explain when problems arise from intercultural communication.	Most improved items
	Q23	I change my communication styles (e.g. direct vs. indirect).	
	Q19	I change my verbal behavior (e.g., accent, tone) when a cross-cultural interaction requires it.	Relatively improved items
	Q22	I use pause and silence differently to suit different cross-cultural situations.	

The above four items are very precise behaviors when communicating across cultures. For Group A students, through their intercultural communication, Q12, Q23, Q19, and Q22 are related to all the items mentioned in Table 6 and

Table 7 above. To maintain smooth communication, students have tried their best to understand their foreign friends and be understood. In this research, it was speculated that most students would merely communicate as necessary to complete the task. However, from the results, it is palpable that most of them have made friends and gained a lot from the communication and also indicates they have expressed themselves commendably.

> "In our continuous communication, from typing to voice messages, we have improved the efficiency of communication. It not only improved our oral English, but also the ability to understand people from a different culture" (15141516).

> "Because we are facing people from other nations and cultures, and they are different to us in ways of living, thinking and acting, cultural clashes are unavoidable. But we should try to change our fixed way of talking and thinking, to adapt to the new culture and understand others in order to communicate effectively" (15071105).

> "The most important thing is not to use one's own communication mode and take so many things for granted. Both sides should try to understand each other through changing communication styles" (15031236).

4. Suggestions for future online ICC platform construction in China

As the statistics show, Group A students' showed improvements in aspects of cognitive CQ, motivational CQ, and behavioral CQ. This research attempted to find out if those improvements were due to students' participation in the online learning platform and whether it helped students improve their ICC. The online platform provides communication chances for students from different cultures and their improvement in the three dimensions is due to the real practice they were able to have therein. Therefore, in the future construction of network platforms to cultivate students' ICC, this study suggests teachers improve and perfect the aspect of metacognitive CQ. In such online learning websites, sections of special cultural knowledge could be added with the starting point of stimulating students' participation. For instance, there could be different ICC tests and knowledge competitions which encourage students to learn more cultural knowledge.

Furthermore, in addition to the content of the online learning platform, the form of it could also have some improvement. Summing up from students' feedback, the construction of the online exchange platform's system could be improved in the following aspects: (1) instead of the IVE project's post and reply asynchronous mode, students prefer real time communication through the platform – for the online exchange platform, the convenience of communication should be of vital importance; and (2) for students from different cultural backgrounds, long-term communication could help them find more cultural phenomena and understand a different culture deeper. Maintaining students' follow-up communication is also an area to be considered in the construction of future online ICC cultivating platforms.

As a final addition, from the reflections in students' cultural reports, the multiform course mode also helps in the promotion of English communication ability. In the future construction of network learning platforms, sections such as "English corner" can be added for students to communicate orally in English.

5. Summary and implications

It is clearly visible from the statistics and students' pleasure reflected in their journals that the multiform ICC course mode is worth popularizing to cultivate students' ICC in China.

From the results of this study, we can see that students who have real interaction with people from another culture are more interested in intercultural communication. To cultivate students' ICC, real practice with people from another cultural background can arouse students' learning interest and make course teaching more efficient. Many of the Group A students mentioned in their journals that the online platform made them communicate with foreigners for the first time. It is common for college students in China that only a few of them have the opportunity to communicate with people from other cultures. Therefore, it is particularly significant to establish more online platforms to create an intercultural context for them.

The formulation of a multiform course mode is an innovative method of education. From the extracts of students' journals above, it is obvious they have had a good learning experience using this multiform mode. Many researches have tried promoting ICC cultivation domestically and this multiform course mode integrates some of these previous studies in this field. From the research findings and students' feedback, this mode is worth making standard in educational settings where ICC should be included such as foreign language classes and other culture based classes.

6. Limitations of the present study and implications for future study

Through the current research, the effectiveness of online learning platforms on developing students' ICC has been shown and this mode of education is worthy of being advocated. However there are limitations in this research. As the teaching mode incorporates an online learning platform which is not popularized at the moment, the study is limited to the 330 non-English majors of a science and technology university. Thus this research is based on the statistics of the involved Chinese students only, but with no study of the ICC changes in the foreign students that they communicated with. For future studies, research could be carried out with students from different countries.

The focus of this study was on whether the online platform had helped students cultivate their ICC. Future studies could also examine students' communication processes and feedback reports to analyze many other questions such as how ethnography might be embodied in cross-cultural communication.

Lastly, for a more comprehensive understanding of the changes brought about by this multimode method, multiple effective procedures could be carried out rather than single measures. This research adopted a mixed methods approach that included questionnaires, online platform observations and students' reflective journals. For future studies, researchers could also use many other research techniques such as face-to-face interviews to make the research more detailed.

7. Supplementary materials

https://research-publishing.box.com/s/xiospc4byknu1j5gi04fpw7f2742adhm

References

Ang, S., & Van Dyne, L. (2008). (Eds). *Handbook of cultural intelligence: theory, measurement, and applications*. M. E. Sharpe.

Bandura, A. (2002). Social cognitive theory in cultural context. *Applied Psychology: An International Review, 51*, 269-290.

Deardorff, D. K. (2006). Identification and assessment of intercultural competence as a student outcome of internationalization. *Journal of Studies in International Education, 10*(3), 241-266. https://doi.org/10.1177/1028315306287002

Deci, E. L., & Ryan, R. M. (1985). *Intrinsic motivation and self-determination in human behavior*. Plenum.

Earley, P. C., & Ang, S. (2003). *Cultural intelligence: individual interactions across cultures*. Stanford University Press.

Flavell, J. H. (1979). Meta-cognition and cognitive monitoring: a new area of cognitive inquiry. *American Psychologist, 34*, 906-911. https://doi.org/10.1037/0003-066x.34.10.906

Hall, E. T. (1959). *The silent language*. Doubleday

Kuo, Y., Walker, A., Schroder, K., & Belland, B. (2014). Interaction, internet self-efficacy, and self-regulated learning as predictors of student satisfaction in online education courses. *The Internet and Higher Education, 20*, 35-50. https://doi.org/10.1016/j.iheduc.2013.10.001

Nelson, T. O. (1996). Consciousness and metacognition. *American Psychologist, 51*(2), 102-116. https://doi.org/10.1037/0003-066X.51.2.102

Chapter 4

Salovey, P., & Mayer, J. D. (1990). Emotional intelligence. *Imagination Cognition & Personality, 9*(6), 217-236.

Sternberg, R. J., & Detterman, D. K. (1986). *What is intelligence? Contemporary viewpoints on its nature and definition*. Ablex.

Younos, A. (2012). Online education for developing contexts. *XRDS: Crossroads, The ACM Magazine for Students, 19*(2), 27-29. https://doi.org/10.1145/2382856.2382868

Section 2.

Virtual exchange in the language and intercultural studies classroom

5. Collaborative tasks in telecollaboration: their challenges and potentials

Hisae Matsui[1]

Abstract

This chapter reports the challenges that both the students and the teachers experienced in a telecollaborative project between a Japanese university and an American university. In this semester-long project, the students in groups of three to five from both universities worked collectively mainly asynchronously and in occasional synchronous sessions. The project was originally designed in 2017 with the expectation of incorporating 'collaborative tasks' (O'Dowd & Ware, 2009), then redesigned in 2018. To examine how the students in both years perceived their collaborations and effectiveness, the results from online surveys from both years were compared. Furthermore, two groups from 2018, which experienced difficulties, were examined to reveal the causes of the problems. These results indicate that rather complicated tasks raised more logistical challenges than linguistic challenges. It became clear that the students experienced various challenges, which include scheduling synchronous sessions, unaligned visions on the final products, and lacking consideration for non-native speakers in synchronous sessions. These challenges in 'collaborative tasks' suggest that the success of a project is heavily dependent on the simplicity of the project design, sharing the same understanding at the beginning of the project, as well as the linguistic consideration to their group members.

Keywords: project design, collaborative tasks, team learning behavior, team effectiveness.

---

1. Princeton University, Princeton, New Jersey, United States; hmatsui@princeton.edu; https://orcid.org/0000-0002-8211-3433

How to cite: Matsui, H. (2020). Collaborative tasks in telecollaboration: their challenges and potentials. In E. Hagley & Y. Wang (Eds), *Virtual exchange in the Asia-Pacific: research and practice* (pp. 105-124). Research-publishing.net. https://doi.org/10.14705/rpnet.2020.47.1148

Chapter 5

1. Background

Telecollaboration has been adopted to various disciplines for online intercultural exchange, interaction and collaboration (Unicollaboration, 2014). The focus of the prominent telecollaborative projects, such as Cultura, Soliya, and eTandem, has been on the development of linguistic and intercultural competences (Helm, 2015). As a result, the collaboration aspect of telecollaboration is often overshadowed by these elements.

Collaboration is primarily conceptualized as a process of shared meaning construction in computer-supported collaborative learning. As pointed out by Ilic (2013), "[t]he meaning-making is not assumed to be an expression of mental representations of the individual participants but is an interactional achievement (Stahl, Koschmann, & Suthers, 2006)" (p. 33). Van den Bossche and his colleagues, who described collaboration as building mutually-shared cognition, identified Team Learning Behavior (TLB) in effective groups, namely 'construction' (describing a problem), 'co-construction' (building a shared conception), and 'constructive conflict' (negotiating different interpretations) (Van den Bossche et al., 2011). Among these elements, they pointed out that "[c]onstructive conflict was found to be a significant behavior in the process of building [a] shared mental model" (Van den Bossche et al., 2011, p. 295).

Furthermore, TLBs are considered to give rise to mutually-shared cognition, and it leads to higher perceived team effectiveness (Van den Bossche et al., 2011). Team effectiveness, which can be defined as a team's capacity to achieve its goals and objectives (National Research Council, 2015), has three dimensions: "the degree to which the team's output meets the standard of quality [...], the degree to which the process of carrying out the work enhances the capability of members to work together in the future [...], and the degree to which the teamwork contributes to the professional growth of the team members" (Van den Bossche et al., 2011, p. 296). Although these studies focused on face-to-face collaboration, these elements also seem crucial in telecollaboration, especially in telecollaboration that requires building mutually-shared cognition.

In terms of collaboration in telecollaboration, the types of activities and tasks have significant influences on the nature of collaboration. O'Dowd and Ware (2009) classified various telecollaborative activities into 12 categories and then identified three types of communicative activities in telecollaboration: information exchange tasks, comparison analysis tasks, and collaborative tasks.

The first type, information exchange tasks, is designed for sharing personal and cultural information and opinions (e.g. Lee, 2006; Vinagre, 2005). While this type of task mainly focuses on providing a partner with personal information, comparison analysis tasks, the second type, go beyond that as they require comparisons or critical analysis of cultural products from both sides (e.g. Furstenberg, Lewet, English, & Maillet, 2001). The third type, collaborative tasks, requires working together to produce a joint product or conclusion (e.g. Belz, 2007; Zaehner, Fauverge, & Wong, 2000). Although this type of task usually involves a great deal of coordination and planning, they are also expected to bring about substantial amounts of negotiation of meaning both on linguistic and cultural levels as the students are trying to reach agreement on their final product (O'Dowd & Ware, 2009, p. 178). Even among tasks categorized under 'collaborative tasks', the nature of collaboration varies. While some tasks require students to complete their written works, such as translations, in their target language with help from their partners who are native speakers of the target language (Ware & O'Dowd, 2008; Ware & Perez-Canada, 2007), the other tasks involve decision-makings in collaboration such as creating joint presentations (Zaehner et al., 2000).

Considering their characteristics, collaborative tasks, especially those of the tasks, which require decision-making processes, seem to be suitable for building mutually-shared cognition and increasing team effectiveness as a result; however, there is no previous study which dealt with TLBs and team effectiveness in collaborative tasks. Therefore, in this study, two projects, which were similar in design, were analyzed to reveal how the students collaborate and consider their effectiveness in terms of the nature of collaboration, that is, 'construction', 'co-construction', and 'constructive conflict' (Van den Bossche et al., 2011).

2. Case study

2.1. Participants

The students from an English class in a Japanese university and the students from a Japanese class in an American university participated in this study. The students were grouped into groups of four to six students which had one to four students from each university per group.

In 2017, the number of students in a Japanese university outnumbered the number of students in an American university while it turned out to be the opposite in 2018. These numbers are dependent on the enrollment number each year, which is beyond the researcher's control (Table 1).

Table 1. Participants of each school in each year

Year	Students in a Japanese university	Students in an American university
2017	27	12
2018	11	20

2.2. Project description

In both years, the goal of the project was creating two short video clips, and each clip should include clips from both universities as Figure 1 below indicates.

Figure 1. Model for the final video

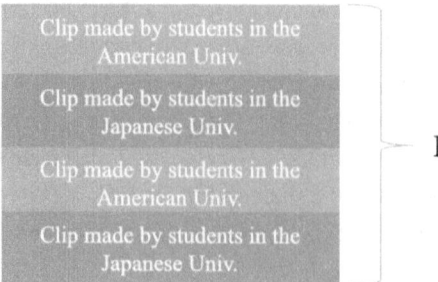

In both years, the video production process took the following steps: (1) outline, (2) storyboard, (3) scripts, and (4) video clips (Figure 2).

Figure 2. Stages for video production

Outline	Storyboard	Scripts	Video clips
Discuss what should be included in the video clip (Google Docs)	Draw storyboards for the clips	Write scripts for each clip (Google Docs)	Shoot video clips, edit them, and make them into one clip

For the project in 2017, the students made two separate video clips: one in Japanese and the other one in English. These two clips had different themes and different storylines. The one in Japanese was a promotion video for studying abroad for a Japanese audience while the one in English was a promotion video for studying Japanese for an American audience.

Although all the students were expected to dedicate their efforts to both clips, the Japanese students were assigned to lead discussions for the final English video and then edit the clips to complete the final video, while the American students were assigned to lead discussions for a final video in Japanese and edit the clips to complete a final Japanese video. Therefore, the Japanese students took the initiative in making a final video in English and the American students took the initiative in making a final video in Japanese.

The students in the project in 2018 also made two clips; however, they had one theme and one storyline. The theme of the video was promoting studying foreign languages. The students had to discuss and agree on one storyline and storyboard for the story. Subsequently, the Japanese students were assigned to take the initiative to write scripts and edit clips to complete the final video in English. In contrast, the American students were assigned to take the initiative to write scripts and edit clips to complete the Japanese final video. The comparison of the process of video production is shown in Figure 3.

Figure 3. Stages for video production in 2017 and 2018

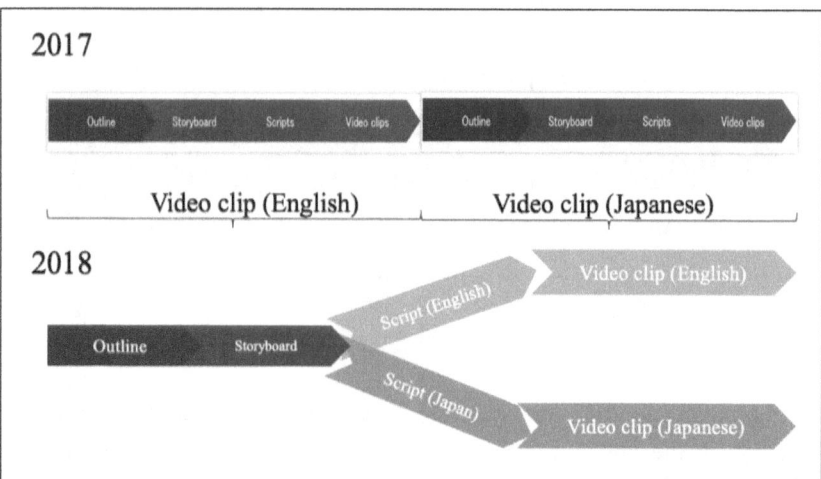

As Figure 3 indicates, the students in the 2017 project had a short discussion period for each step. Each step was led by the assigned group (Japanese or American), which was in charge of the clip (English or Japanese). On the other hand, the students in the 2018 project had a more extended discussion period for each step. Meanwhile, they had to have clear mutually-shared cognition for the outline and storyboard since they would write scripts based on them.

The students in both universities had discussions with the students from the other university using the online discussion board Slack and video conferences on Skype (2017) and Zoom (2018) over 11 weeks in both years. After about two weeks of a 'getting to know each other' stage in asynchronous and synchronous means, the students moved into the planning stage. The students initially exchanged their opinions on online discussion boards; thereafter, they concluded their discussion in video conferences.

In 2017, the students from a Japanese university were able to have synchronous sessions with their group members from an American university during their class time; therefore, the scheduling for Skype sessions never became a problem.

However, in 2018, it was impossible to have synchronous sessions during their class time because the class times were either too early or too late for their partner schools. Therefore, they had to decide synchronous session times on top of the discussion for the content.

In both years, the students exchanged their opinions both in English and Japanese as the projects were parts of the world language curricula. In 2017, all exchanges for a final video in English were conducted in English, and all exchanges for a final video in Japanese were conducted in Japanese. In 2018, all exchanges for the outline stage were conducted in English, all exchanges for the storyboard stage were conducted in Japanese, and discussions on the English script were carried out in English while discussions on the Japanese script were done in Japanese. The language choice (English or Japanese) for a synchronous session for the script stage was left to the students.

2.3. Data collection and analysis

The analysis of the students' perception of collaboration was conducted in the following stages. First, the results from the survey on the students' perceptions of TLBs and team effectiveness in both years were analyzed and compared to see if there were any tendencies in each year. Next, the results in 2018 were more closely analyzed by groups to examine the similarities and differences among groups. Lastly, two problematic groups were selected based on the analysis in the previous stage and both survey results and actual interactions were analyzed to reveal the causes of the problems.

2.3.1. Instruments

In order to investigate students' perceptions of the project and collaboration, an online survey was developed. The survey had both structured and unstructured items. The structured items were expected to measure two elements of the students' perceptions; TLBs and team effectiveness. The questionnaire was adapted from the instruments that Van den Bossche and his colleagues (2011) developed, and had five-point Likert scales, which allowed the students to express how much they agree or disagree with a particular statement. The sample items for each aspect in the questionnaire are shown in Table 2.

Table 2. Sample items for the aspects (adapted from Van den Bossche et al., 2011, p. 298)

Category	Aspect (shortened version)	Sample item
TLBs	Construction (construction)	"If something is unclear, we ask each other questions"
	Co-construction (co-construction)	"Information from team members is complemented with information from other team members"
	Constructive conflict (conflict)	"Opinions and ideas of team members are verified by asking each other critical questions"
Team effectiveness	Team performance (satisfaction)	"I am satisfied with the performance of our team"
	Team viability (future)	"I would want to work with this team in the future"
	Team learning (learning)	"As a team, we have learned a lot"

The unstructured items included questions for overall impressions and suggestions for future projects. The questionnaire was translated into Japanese for the students in a Japanese university to eliminate the language barrier.

2.3.2. Data collection procedure

Two types of data were collected for this study: data from the online survey and actual interactions among students on Slack and Zoom in 2018. The online survey, which was mentioned above, was distributed to the students of both universities. Participation in the survey was completely voluntary, and the responses were collected anonymously.

The actual interactions were also collected upon each student's consent. At the beginning of the courses, the researcher distributed the consent forms in class to the students. After receiving the responses from the potential participants, the project groups were formed. Only the interactions both on Slack and Zoom, which all group members had agreed to, were recorded. Only the participants' voices on Zoom were recorded through the audio recording software, Audacity, and no visual information was saved for this study.

After the interactions were recorded, the recordings were transcribed for analysis. All of the participants' names and group names were coded through the process of transcribing so that no identities of the students were saved. The names which appear on the discussion board will also be coded in the same manner as described above.

3. Results

3.1. Comparing 2017 and 2018

To see the tendencies of students' perceptions in both years, the mean scores for each aspect of TLBs were displayed separately for each university and each year in Figure 4. The graph indicates that the scores for 'construction' in both universities and the score for 'co-construction' in a Japanese university decreased in 2018 while the score for 'co-construction' in an American university and the scores for 'conflict' in both universities increased in 2018.

In a similar manner, the mean scores for aspects of team effectiveness are shown in Figure 5. The graph indicates that all aspects except for the score for 'satisfaction' of Japanese students decreased in 2018.

The result of the overall impression of the success in the project, which is shown in Table 3, reflects these results. In 2017, all the students were satisfied overall with the process and outcome of the project; however, in 2018, a small number of students from both universities expressed their dissatisfaction.

Although the majority of the students in 2018 were satisfied overall, it is worthwhile looking into the details of students' perceptions in 2018; therefore, in the next section, the data from 2018 will be analyzed group by group.

Figure 4. Aspects of TLB (2017 vs. 2018)

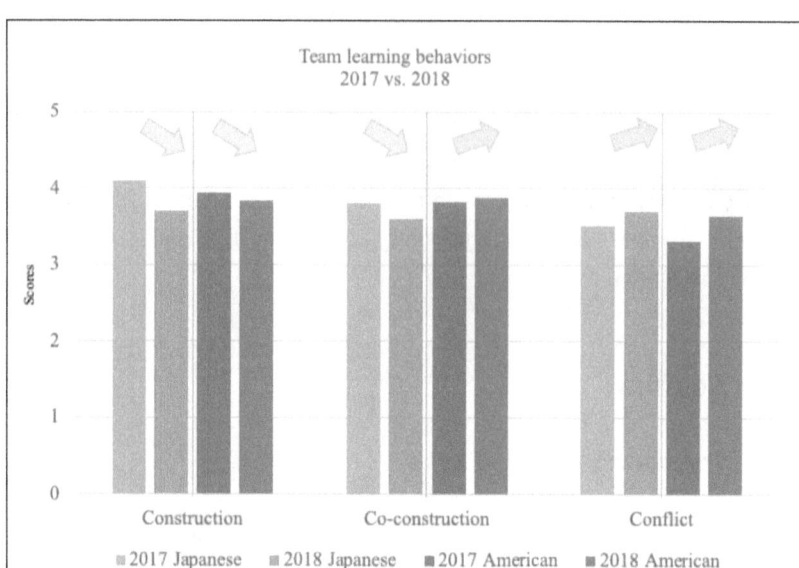

Figure 5. Aspects of team effectiveness (2017 vs. 2018)

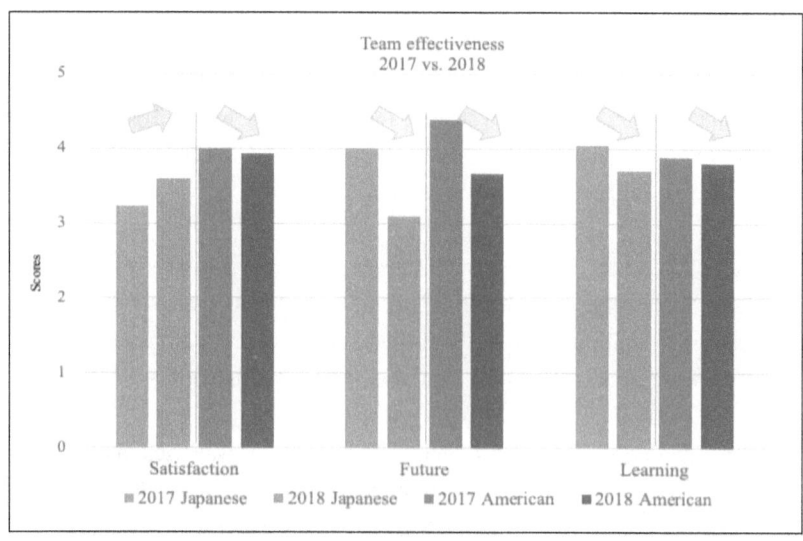

Table 3. Percentage of the students who thought the project was successful

Year	Japanese side	American side
2017	100%	100%
2018	95%	91%

3.2. Comparing groups in 2018

In order to investigate further on the details of problematic groups, the mean scores of each aspect in TLBs and team effectiveness from 2018 were analyzed group by group.

The mean scores of the TLBs from each group are presented in Figure 6, and the mean scores of the team effectiveness from each group are presented in Figure 7. Both graphs indicate that Group C had the least successful collaboration overall.

As Figure 6 shows, all the aspects of TLBs are the lowest among groups, and 'conflict' has the lowest score among three aspects: 3.38 in 'construction', 3.00 in 'co-construction', and 2.75 in 'conflict'. These scores indicate that although the group members shared their ideas and asked each other questions, they had difficulty with negotiating different interpretations and building a shared conception.

Figure 7 shows similar tendencies. Group C has the lowest scores in all three aspects; 2.75 in 'satisfaction', 1.75 in 'future', and 2.5 in 'learning', which was by far the lowest among the groups. Considering the fact that the mean score for 'future' is significantly low, the group members were not satisfied. These results clearly indicate that Group C had difficulty carrying out the project.

Furthermore, the results from the question *Do you think this project was successful?* were examined further to identify which groups of students did not think the project was successful. The results indicate that one student from a Japanese university and one student from an American university did not think so as Table 4 shows. These students are from Group C and Group F.

Figure 6. Aspects of TLBs by a group from 2018

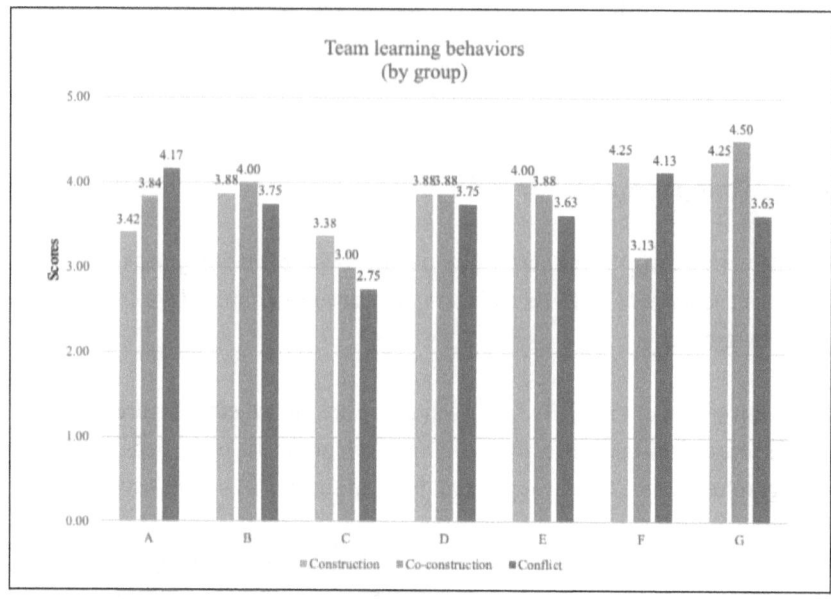

Figure 7. Aspects of team effectiveness by a group from 2018

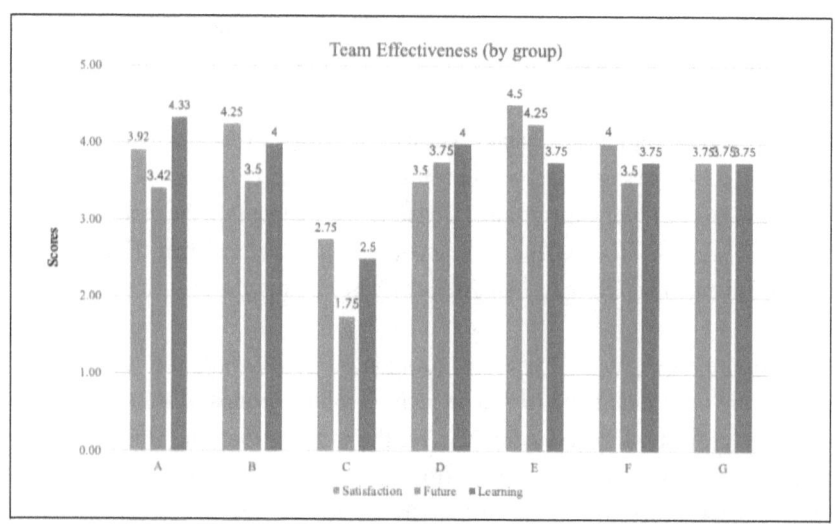

Table 4. Number of the students who thought the project was successful in 2018

Yes/No	Japanese side	American side
Yes	10	19
No	1	1

The mean scores of both TLBs and team effectiveness in Group F were not significantly low compared with other groups; however, there would be value in looking at their interactions. Therefore, in the next section, the actual interactions and narrative comments on the survey of Group C and Group F will be analyzed to reveal possible causes of the problems that the group members of these groups encountered.

3.3. An in-depth look of Group C and Group F of 2018

3.3.1. Group C

To analyze how they interacted with each other on Slack, words in the post from each group member were counted in three stages of video production: (1) discussion for an outline, (2) discussion for storyboard, and (3) discussion for video clip productions. All exchanges were conducted in English in Stage 1, in Japanese in Stage 2, and also in Japanese in Stage 3. Furthermore, the words on Slack in Group A were also counted in the same manner since Group A has higher mean scores for TLBs with an ideal ratio of three aspects, 4.17 in 'conflict' as the highest, followed by 3.84 in 'co-construction', and 3.42 in 'construction'.

Since the interactions among group members of Group C on Slack showed their struggles with scheduling synchronous sessions, the words were categorized further into two groups: one for scheduling and the other for other purposes, including discussion for the contents of the video.

These results are shown in Figure 8. Although the members of Group A also spent some time for scheduling, the members of Group C spent more time than the members of Group A. It is also noteworthy that the students from a Japanese

Chapter 5

university posted less as they progressed. Especially in Stage 3, they posted close to nothing.

Figure 8. Word count for Group C and Group A

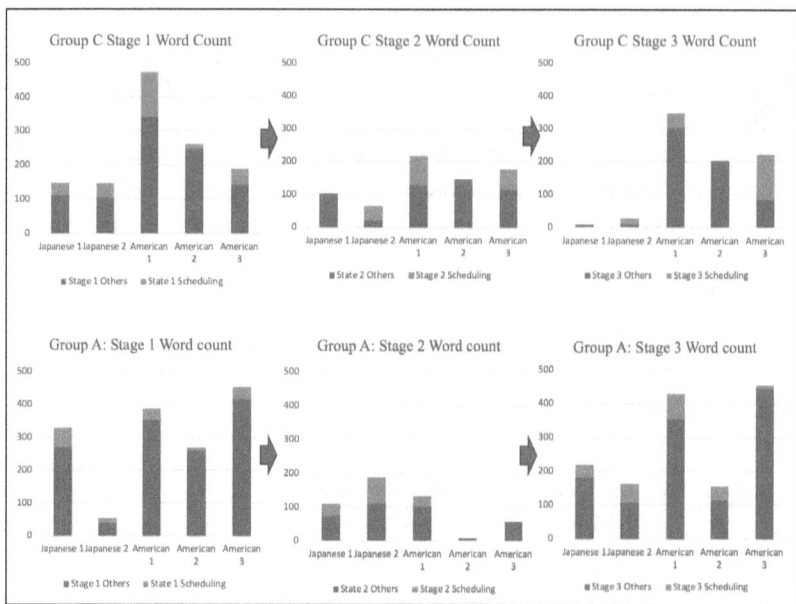

In Zoom sessions, it was often observed that certain students from an American university dominated the conversation in both Japanese and English sessions, and a student from a Japanese university often spoke fast and used his/her dialect in this group. These tendencies made it hard for non-native speakers to understand and speak out.

The responses to the narrative part of the survey revealed the reasons behind the phenomenon. Student B answered that he/she participated more actively in Zoom in his/her native language even though he/she participated actively both in English and in Japanese in Slack. He/she reflected on the sessions and mentioned: "it was hard to join the heated discussion among the students from xx university because (target language) is my second language". The same student also responded 'no' to the question *Do you think this project was successful?*, and commented, "it was not very fruitful. I'm not sure what I learned through this activity". To the question *What do you want to change to improve the project?* he/she answered, "make the purpose clear. There were often times that I got lost with what I was learning during the activities". Summarizing the above, Student B could not join the synchronous discussion and was at a loss with the purpose of the activity. As a result, he/she had the impression that he/she did not learn much from the project.

Student C said he/she participated more actively in his/her native language in Slack as well as in Zoom. He/she reflected on the exchange and mentioned: "I felt less comfortable and unable to express some of the more complicated ideas and suggestions that I had in (my target language), but in (my native language), I was fine". He/She also commented about the collaboration: "collaboration with (the partner university's) students does not seem worthwhile and adds extra work and stress without much, if any, benefits". To the question *If you have another opportunity to work with students (from other countries), what would you like to do?*, he/she answered, "if I had to work with students (from other countries) again, I would like to work with them while we are all on the same academic schedule and time zone (or at least +/- two hours)". These comments indicate that he/she could not participate in the synchronous sessions as much as he/she wanted. Moreover, he/she put value on being able to schedule the sessions. Due to these issues, he/she could not find this project valuable.

Student D claimed that he/she participated actively both in English and in Japanese in Slack but did not participate as actively in English nor in Japanese in Zoom:

> "Speaking with people over Zoom was just a little difficult because the conversation was often dominated by the same people, and I had a hard time getting a word in, though I didn't have a lot to say anyway".

Even though he/she did not have many opinions that he/she wished to express, he/she experienced a hard time joining the conversation both in Japanese and

English sessions because the conversation was often dominated by the same people, which was also observed in Zoom sessions.

3.3.2. Group F

This group did not have the lowest scores, like Group C. The mean scores of aspects of TLBs were not low. As Figure 6 indicates, the mean score of 'construction' was the highest (4.25) among groups and that of 'conflict' was the second-highest (4.19) among groups. The mean scores of aspects of team effectiveness were not very low as well. The mean score of 'satisfaction' was the thirst highest (4.00) yet that of 'future' was the third from the bottom and that of 'learning' was the second from the bottom.

In order to shed light on the problems, the contents of both Slack and Zoom sessions were analyzed. The analysis shows that they did not reach mutual understanding several times. During Zoom sessions, the teacher had to intervene in the discussion to clarify the points, which did not happen often in the other groups. In Stage 2, one part of the storyboard was not completed by one of the group members. Furthermore, one of the final videos did not have clips from the other university, and the other final videos did not make it on time. There were clearly misunderstandings among group members.

In the narrative part of the survey, Student A responded 'no' to the question *Do you think this project was successful?* and mentioned, "we came together out of haste and made a lot of poor last-minute decisions. Communication and language skills were not practiced very well" for his/her reasons.

Student B responded 'yes' to the question *Do you think this project was successful?*; however, his/her comment shows his/her discontent toward the group members from the other university. He/she mentioned,

> "I think (xx) university (Student B's university) student(s) is/are obviously more capable and dedicated to completing the project. The student(s) in (yy) university (the other university) took it not seriously

enough. When I watched the final version of our video, I wanted to delete the (the other university's) part(s)".

These comments show the problems that they encountered were caused by misunderstanding, miscommunication (possibly partially from lack of language skills), and uneven expectations from each side.

4. Limitation

Since the two projects in this study took place over two years with different groups of students, and also not being in a laboratory setting, it suffers from low external validity; therefore, results cannot be generalized to a population of interest yet. It is, therefore, necessary to conduct further studies to generalize an outcome of this study.

Furthermore, it is possible that other factors, such as their genders, ages, cultural backgrounds, personalities, and intercultural competences, also affected how they collaborated. In this study, however, only the factors mentioned in the narrative part of the survey were taken into consideration during the analysis. Further studies are necessary to examine other possible factors.

5. Pedagogical principles

Collaborative tasks indeed could facilitate collaboration as it is necessary to have a shared concept to create final products. However, if a project requires clearer shared concepts among telecollaborative groups, it could be very challenging. For the project in 2017, since each side took the initiative to make the assigned final clip, students from the other side often followed what the students from the university who took charge suggested. For the project in 2018, on the other hand, the students from both sides had to come together to share a clear understanding of the final products because there was only one outline and one storyboard for the final video clips as Figure 3 shows. It was extremely challenging for some groups due to a lack of communication, language skills, and consideration of language use for their non-native group members. Moreover, logistic problems, such as scheduling conflicts, made communication more difficult. These problems may not be seen in face-to-face collaboration as Van den Bossche and his colleagues observed (Van den Bossche et al., 2011).

Having said that, collaboration with international peers has been and will be unmistakably crucial in the workforce in an increasingly globalized world. Experiences that the students are able to have through telecollaborative projects could be very beneficial for their future careers.

6. Conclusion

To make a telecollaborative project meaningful, instructors should consider various factors. First, it is vital to decide the type of collaboration while considering students' language levels. For example, a collaboration that involves decision-making requires an understanding of shared concepts. If the project requires a very clear idea about the final product, the students from both sides should be able to have a shared mental model, which could be very challenging for students with lower language skills. If the students have limited language skills, it may be a good idea to limit collaboration to ones which do not involve decision-making, 'information exchange tasks', or 'sharing cultural information' in teams (O'Dowd & Ware, 2009) and keep collaboration local for tasks which require shared mental models.

It is also extremely important to consider the types of tasks and means of communication if there are potential logistical issues such as scheduling. This is especially true if the countries are geographically apart, and the time difference is hard to work with. Having a 14-hour difference, finding times for synchronous sessions was extremely challenging for some groups in 2018. Their valuable exchange time could be consumed by mere scheduling. Although synchronous communication has its advantages, having only asynchronous might be a better choice if a potential problem exists.

Furthermore, making the students realize how they should communicate with non-native speakers is also important. Domination of the conversation, speed of the utterance, as well as usage of unfamiliar terms and dialect for non-native speakers, are important elements to consider during synchronous sessions. With consideration of these various elements mentioned above, telecollaborative projects could be successful, and meaningful learning experiences take place for our students.

References

Belz, J. A. (2007). The development of intercultural communicative competence in telecollaborative partnerships. In R. O'Dowd (Ed.), *Online intercultural exchange, an introduction for foreign language teachers* (pp. 127-166). Multilingual Matters. https://doi.org/10.21832/9781847690104-009

Furstenberg, G., Lewet, S., English, K., & Maillet, K. (2001). Giving a virtual voice to the silent language of culture: the Cultura project. *Language Learning & Technology, 5*(1), 55-102.

Hackman, J. R. (1989). (Ed.). *Groups that work (and those that don't). Creating conditions for effective teamwork.* Jossey-Bass.

Helm, F. (2015). The practices and challenges of telecollaboration in higher education in Europe. *Language Learning and Technology, 19*(2), 197-217.

Ilic, P. (2013). *The impact of mobile phones on collaborative learning activities.* Doctoral dissertation. University of Exeter.

Lee, L. (2006). A study of native and non-native speakers feedback and responses in Spanish-American networked collaborative interaction. In J. Belz & S. Thorne (Eds), *Internet-mediated intercultural foreign language education* (pp. 147-176). Heinle & Heinle.

National Research Council. (2015). *Enhancing the effectiveness of team science.* The National Academies Press.

O'Dowd, R., & Ware, P. (2009). Critical issues in telecollaborative task design. *Computer Assisted Language Learning, 22*(2), 173-188. https://doi.org/10.1080/09588220902778369

Stahl, G., Koschmann, T., & Suthers, D. (2006). Computer-supported collaborative learning: an historical perspective. In R. K. Sawyer (Ed.), *Cambridge handbook of the learning sciences* (pp. 409-426). Cambridge University Press.

Chapter 5

Unicollaboration. (2014). *Position paper: virtual exchange in the european higher education area.* http://www.unicollaboration.org/wp-content/uploads/2016/06/Position-paper_1.pdf

Van den Bossche, P., Gijselaers, W., Segers, M., Woltjer, G., & Kirschner, P. (2011). Team learning: building shared mental models. *Instructional Science, 39*, 283-301. https://doi.org/10.1007/s11251-010-9128-3

Vinagre, M. (2005). Fostering language learning via email: an English-Spanish exchange. *Computer Assisted Language Learning, 18*(5), 369-388. https://doi.org/10.1080/09588220500442749

Ware, P. D., & O'Dowd, R. (2008). Peer feedback on language form in tellecollaboration. *Language Learning & Technology, 12*(1), 43-63.

Ware, P. D., & Pérez-Cañado, M. L. (2007). Grammar and feedback: turning to language form in telecollaboration. In R. O'Dowd (Ed.), *Online intercultural exchange: an introduction for foreign language teacher*s (pp. 107-126). Multilingual Matters. https://doi.org/10.21832/9781847690104-008

Zaehner, C., Fauverge, A., & Wong, J. (2000). Task-based language learning via audiovisual networks: the LEVERAGE project. In M. Warschauer & R. Kern (Eds), Network-based language teaching: concepts and practice (pp. 186-203). Cambridge University Press. https://doi.org/10.1017/cbo9781139524735.011

6. The practical realities of virtual exchange

Sandra Healy[1] and Olivia Kennedy[2]

Abstract

This chapter examines practical issues regarding Virtual Exchanges (VEs) for educational purposes in the university context and covers language use, cultural differences, time management, teacher collaboration, technology-related issues, assessment, and context specific factors. It charts the establishment of three academic collaborations between a university in Kyoto, Japan, and institutions in Asia, Africa, and Europe. The first collaboration follows a new hybrid model created at the Japanese university described here. In the Teaching Online Together (TOT) model, teachers in the Philippines interact with students in a tutorial style system to improve the students' English presentation skills via video conferencing. The second project, with a university in Kenya, is modelled on the intercultural telecollaboration or Cultura-type exchange approach (O'Dowd, 2018). Students from the respective institutions work together asynchronously to complete tasks related to the development of intercultural understanding and sensitivity. The third collaboration, with a university in Belgium, follows a shared syllabus approach (O'Dowd, 2018) in which teachers create course materials for students who then work together both synchronously and asynchronously to achieve their goals.

Keywords: virtual exchange, telecollaboration, teaching online together, TOT, developing intercultural sensitivity, online collaboration.

1. Kyoto Institute of Technology, Kyoto, Japan; sandyhealy26@googlemail.com; https://orcid.org/0000-0003-4387-259X

2. Nagahama Institute of Bioscience and Technology, Shiga, Japan; o_kennedy@nagahama-i-bio.ac.jp; https://orcid.org/0000-0003-0144-2516

How to cite: Healy, S., & Kennedy, O. (2020). The practical realities of virtual exchange. In E. Hagley & Y. Wang (Eds), *Virtual exchange in the Asia-Pacific: research and practice* (pp. 125-144). Research-publishing.net. https://doi.org/10.14705/rpnet.2020.47.1149

Chapter 6

1. Introduction

VE, or 'telecollaboration' as it is also known in the sphere of foreign language learning, describes the online interactions of learners, or groups of learners, in different contexts who collaborate as part of their education. Teachers from all over the globe, in different teaching environments and with different educational goals, have engaged in very diverse approaches to VE and this has led to the development of an enormous variety of projects. Because of this diversity, no model has dominated, which in turn has given educators the freedom to creatively address the different needs of their learners (O'Dowd, 2017). This chapter will describe the establishment of three individual VEs taking place between the university in Japan where the two authors of this chapter teach, and institutions in three other countries. It will explore the process of setting up these telecollaborations and some issues to be aware of when embarking on such projects.

2. Background

Various VE models have been developed and are divided into three approaches by O'Dowd (2018): subject-specific, shared syllabus, and service-provider. The first approach can be further divided into exchanges that are grounded in foreign language learning and those that are from business studies. The eTandem model is one of the oldest examples of this first approach to VE. In this model, students from different linguistic backgrounds are partnered together in order to learn one another's language. Developed from a long history of learners pairing up formally and informally in the years before such mediating technology existed, the first documented computer-mediated exchange occurred between Ruhr-Universität Bochum and the University of Rhode Island (Brammerts, 1996). Because the focus of eTandem learning is often the development of language skills, much of the research in this area is in the field of second language acquisition and explores linguistic development (O'Rourke, 2007).

Another model that falls under the subject-specific approach is the Cultura model which was first used in an exchange between a French language class at Massachusetts Institute of Technology (MIT) and an English class at the National Higher French Institute of Aeronautics and Space (SUPAERO) in Toulouse, France (Furstenberg, 1998). It was later further developed at MIT by Furstenberg, Levet, English, and Maillet (2001) and used in English. As the name suggests, Cultura model exchanges focus on the intercultural aspects of VE. Projects using this model often require students to compare and contrast different areas of culture from the students' respective countries. The dual goals of the Cultura model are to improve both intercultural competence and students' linguistic ability.

In recent years, shared syllabus approaches, in which teachers from different educational institutions collaborate to provide their students with opportunities to work on shared content, have become common. These types of exchanges enable students to learn about their subject area from differing cultural perspectives while also developing their intercultural communication skills and language skills (Starke-Meyerring & Wilson, 2008). One of the most well-known models of the shared syllabus approach is Collaborative Online International Learning (COIL) which was developed at the State University of New York (SUNY) network of universities (Rubin, 2016). Classes of students studying similar subjects are connected and work together on materials that instructors from both universities have developed. The emphasis on content and the different cultural interpretations that people from different countries bring to the collaboration are the difference between this and other approaches.

The third approach described by O'Dowd (2018) is the service-provider approach which refers to projects created by organizations rather than individual teachers. One of the first examples was the New York/Moscow Schools Telecommunications Project which was set up in 1988 to connect young people from the United States and the Union of Soviet Socialist Republics (USSR) during the Cold War to discuss socio-political issues (Helm, 2018). The goals of this initiative are still relevant today and can be seen in the Erasmus+VE project, launched in 2018, which endeavors to connect young people in Europe with those in the Southern Mediterranean. iEARN (iearn.org) and Soliya (soliya.net), which connects students from the US and Europe and the Arab and/or Muslim worlds to help them develop friendships and deepen their understanding of one another are other well-known examples of the service-provider approach.

3. Case study

3.1. Participants

The authors of this chapter both teach English as a foreign language at a national university in Kyoto, Japan, where the students are studying either science and technology or architecture and design. The majority of the students continue onto graduate programs, and from there either move into academia, or take up research positions in companies, both domestic and international. As such, the need for strong communicative abilities, both in terms of language skills and intercultural awareness, is recognized to be of importance by both the students themselves, and the university administration. All domestic students have previously studied English as a foreign language for six years, in junior and senior high school, and their resulting English ability is assessed early in their first semester on campus. At the start of the programs described here, they had an average Test of English for International Communication (TOEIC) score of 570.

3.2. Project description

The three VE initiatives described here are currently being undertaken in the English department. They are mainly classroom-based, with all of the synchronous work and a large percentage of the asynchronous work occurring during class-time. Students are required to prepare outside of this time so as to be ready for interchanges with their distant learning partners.

The students at the Japanese institution use a class set of iPad tablets for synchronous work that have been preloaded with the Skype application and their own devices, mainly laptop computers, for asynchronous work. The collaborators in Belgium, the Philippines, and Kenya use a combination of computers and mobile devices. Technological issues have been rare, and mainly relate to unstable Wi-Fi. Careful contingency planning for when such problems occur means that any repercussions can be minimized.

3.2.1. TOT

The first exchange underway at the university is a collaboration with an online English conversation school based in the Philippines and is the longest running exchange we are involved in. It does not follow any of the traditional models and was developed for our specific context in a Japanese university. We named this new model TOT. TOT combines elements of traditional tutorial style learning with the service-provider approach. In this approach, learners do not connect with other learners. Instead, small groups of students in one country, Japan, are connected with teachers in another country, the Philippines. Instructors in our university collaborate with instructors in the other institution, teaching online together. The advantages that this approach has provided to both our university and to the institution in the Philippines will be discussed in more detail below.

The exchange benefits from the fact that many English language schools based in the Philippines now provide online conversation lessons to people in Japan. The number of Japanese learners choosing such virtual conversation classes has increased rapidly recently (Tajima, 2018) because of their convenience, flexibility, and affordability. The VE described in this section is based on a relationship with such a school called QQEnglish (qqeng.com), and we have been working together for more than five years. The exchange is classroom-based and focuses on improving the presentation skills of the Japanese undergraduate students. It mirrors a traditional tutorial classroom where students work in small groups with teachers. The students engage in four VE sessions using Skype during the autumn semester and work in small groups with a Filipino teacher. All are assigned roles and take turns presenting, timing, recording, and evaluating one another as well as taking part in group discussions with the online teacher. These four online sessions are an integral part of the curriculum, with much of the remaining 12 weekly lessons devoted to preparing and practicing for them.

Chapter 6

3.2.2. Cultura-type exchange

The second collaboration is an exchange with university students in Kenya. This small exchange is based on the Cultura model. Master's level students in Kyoto engage with undergraduate students in Kenya both synchronously and asynchronously and exchange information on issues related to culture in order for students on both sides of the exchange to develop intercultural competence. The course consists of three tasks. The first of these is the exploration of 'Cicada' by Shaun Tan (2018), an Australian writer and illustrator. This picture book is aimed at older readers and is written in simple English. It was chosen due to the low linguistic load that it provides, while providing a good starting place to discuss both human rights and human relations. Because the main character is a cicada rather than a human, the text is racially and culturally neutral, and allows students to explore the themes of racism, discrimination, acceptance, self-worth, and the place of work in our lives. The second task the students are asked to do also focuses on literature, but this time students choose a story to share that they feel is representative of their own country. They discuss why they chose it and the different meanings that could be ascribed to it with their VE partners. The final task is to create a digital story in a medium of their choice. Themes in these student-produced stories connect to the concepts introduced in the course such as collective/individualistic societies, high/low context cultures, monochronic/polychronic attitudes toward time, and verbal/nonverbal language. By telling their own stories, students reach a further, deeper level of understanding of these concepts and how they function in different cultures.

3.2.3. Shared syllabus approach

The third VE project is our most recent undertaking and is a shared syllabus collaboration with a university in Belgium. The language teachers from both these universities met at a computer assisted language learning conference in Europe and started working together on the VE project. Initially, we hoped to include content teachers in a central role, however this proved difficult and so the exchange has instead been established between language teachers who have students from the same discipline, in this case architecture. The process of negotiating and setting up the exchange took place over a two year period and included visits from both institutions to their partner institution.

3.3. Issues in VE

Creating VEs is an exciting opportunity for both teachers and students to connect with peers around the world and the potential benefits are numerous. A large body of research documents the development of linguistic skills (Guth & Marini-Maio, 2010; Polisca, 2011), intercultural communication skills (Belz & Müller-Hartmann, 2003; Hoffstaedter & Kohn, 2015), critical thinking skills (Von Der Emde, Schneider, & Kötter, 2001), digital literacy skills (Helm, 2014) and multiliteracies (Guth & Helm, 2011). Multiliteracies is a concept that expands traditional views of language learning and literacy to recognize and encompass the variety of linguistic and cultural differences that have become part of our world due to globalization and increased diversification (Guth & Helm, 2011). However, the process of setting up exchanges also involves a variety of issues that need to be addressed, and forethought in these areas can increase both efficacy and efficiency. Issues covered in this section include language use, cultural differences, time management, teacher collaboration, technology-related issues, assessment, and context-specific factors.

3.4. Issues to be aware of surrounding the use of English as a Lingua Franca (ELF)

It is important that all participants who take part in VE understand its aims and parameters before meeting their online learning partners. An important consideration to make clear to learners is the language of the proposed exchange. When the exchange will follow the eTandem model, for example, the two languages being practiced will be the focus, and participants will work together specifically on language. In other models, however, it has become increasingly common for VEs to use ELF.

In ELF contexts, an adherence to Native English Speaker (NES) standards is not required as long as interlocutors understand one another. This is very different from the experiences of most Japanese learners of English. In the Japanese national education system, students between the ages of 13 and 18 study a program of English largely based on NES norms, and which emphasizes the superiority of linguistic accuracy over fluency. Many Japanese students and their teachers therefore lack the ability to communicate effectively with international students (D'Angelo, 2018). Japanese students report having low motivation to learn languages and an overall lack of confidence in their linguistic capabilities and these low levels of self-esteem may be related to an over-reliance on NES norms (Yujobo, 2019). It is important, therefore, for students to be guided toward an image of themselves as language users acting on a global stage to replace their present self-image as failed language learners. Using VE can help build students' self-esteem and help them to understand the changing role of ELF as a valid and valuable tool in the globalized world. Once learners are immersed in the VE, many find the use of ELF means that they feel less anxious than they would communicating with a native speaker of the language. Guarda (2013) found similar results.

This change toward the use and acknowledgment of ELF reflects the effects of globalization and worldwide changes in the usage of and attitudes toward English. The nexus of English has moved from the centrality of native speakers to encompass wider communities, and ELF can be "defined functionally by its use in intercultural communication rather than formally by its reference to native-speaker norms" (Hülmbauer, Böhringer, & Seidlhofer, 2008, p. 27). A consequence of this is a sense of ownership of the language by different communities, which is reflected in the way English has become 'multiplex' (Sergeant, 2012), meaning that English no longer has one center, for example the United Kingdom, that shapes the language and its usage, but rather has many different centers located in different communities around the world. As such, the usage of ELF moves toward addressing issues of cultural imperialism. In the past, some efforts at internationalization have been seen as neo-colonialist because the competencies of one group or culture have been valued more highly than those of another (Stier, 2006). By using ELF, the contributions of all participants can be more easily recognized as having equal value.

3.5. Issues surrounding language proficiency

ELF is the language used to teach, coordinate, and develop the exchanges and is also the language the learners use in the three VEs described here. In the Philippines, English is an official language and so the online teachers based there have high levels of linguistic proficiency. Some of the coordinators are Japanese, but this does not pose a problem as all the coordinators have extensive knowledge of both English and Japanese. The exchange with the university in Kenya follows a similar pattern as English is also an official language, and is used as the language of instruction in the education system from grade four onwards (Mose, 2018). The official languages in Belgium are Dutch, French, and German, but because all the coordinators and teachers have very high levels of English proficiency there are no issues related to language difficulties at an organizational or teaching level.

Differing communication styles have occasionally brought misunderstandings. One example of this is the way that Japanese speakers often include brief periods of silence in spoken discourse which may be unfamiliar to speakers of other languages. Some research describes the Japanese as using "implicit and non-direct forms of communication" like silence (McDaniel, Samovar, & Porter, 2003, p. 255) which may be uncomfortable for people used to different communicative styles. As a result of this dissonance, the participants sometimes responded using high involvement strategies to fill the silence and in turn the Japanese interlocutors found this upsetting. By identifying these issues, by offering reassurance and guidance, and through the use of multimodal communication, these communication difficulties can be somewhat ameliorated.

Perceived differences in linguistic proficiency are important for the students. Many of the Japanese students reported feeling nervous and anxious before the exchange that they were to take part in began, believing the level of their English to be insufficient for the activities proposed. They soon discovered their fears were unfounded, however, and many expressed relief and happiness at being able to be understood by their interlocutors. In order for this to occur it is of vital

Chapter 6

importance that teachers create tasks that the students from both of the countries in the exchange can achieve successfully.

3.6. Cultural issues to be aware of when establishing a VE

VE can be a way for students who are unable to take part in study abroad programs because of financial or personal reasons to experience communication with people from other countries. For many of the students at the university described in this chapter, it is the first time they have interacted at length autonomously, or semi-autonomously, with a person from another country. A large number report that the experience was important to them for this reason. Some examples of comments from students, included here verbatim, include: "This was a precious experience"; "This was the first time to talk to a foreign person. I had fun"; and "I am fun speaking English, before I hate[d] it"; "Why didn't we do this in the first semester too?".

This lack of experience with intercultural exchange means that students are often ill-prepared to confront the realities of working with people from other cultures. Japan is often viewed as a largely homogenous society with a unique culture and separate from the rest of the world (Liddicoat, 2007, 2013). This perspective results in a certain lack of knowledge about the cultural backgrounds of people from other countries, and also in an almost fatalistic belief that people from separate countries cannot understand one another. Without the knowledge that people from different cultural backgrounds view the world very differently, learners taking part in VE can potentially form damaging opinions of their distant learning partners that must be addressed if an exchange is to be beneficial to learners. One way to do this is by providing guidance, including careful introductions combined with ongoing self-reflection and feedback throughout the process. For example, in the exchange with the Filipino teachers, the Japanese students are introduced to cultural relativism through studying the basic principles of Hofstede's (1980) cultural dimensions and examining the ideas of cultural essentialism and are asked to reflect on their own understandings of the interactions they take part in in ongoing learning journals. One telling example of cultural dissonance was revealed when the Japanese students were asked to find three examples of interaction between people from the two nations in preparation for their first interaction with the Filipino instructors. The goal was to create positive connections for the students between the two countries. Many students were shocked, however, to learn that Japan had invaded the Philippines during the Second World War and their research led them to explore events such as the Bataan Death March. They had not previously considered that people in the Philippines may hold anything other than positive feelings toward Japan. Supporting students as they learn about such disturbing information is important and activities need to be designed to acknowledge both past difficulties and cooperation between nations. Additionally, it cannot be assumed that increased intercultural competence will develop automatically. Boehm, Aniola-Jedrzejek, and Kurthen (2010) have warned that instructors, institutions, and researchers have been overly optimistic as to how much intercultural awareness is achieved through VE without specific intercultural guidance.

3.7. Issues surrounding time

Time is an important factor in all VEs. Firstly, depending on the countries that the exchange is taking place between, there may be a significant time difference. This needs to be taken into account when considering whether the exchange will be synchronous, asynchronous, or a combination of the two. Our exchange with the Philippines is synchronous because there is only one-hour time difference between the two countries. Between Kenya and Japan, however, there is a six-hour difference, and between Belgium and Japan, seven. This means that synchronous sessions have to be held in the morning in Kenya and Belgium and in the late afternoon in Japan which has caused scheduling conflicts for teachers, students, and all of the universities involved. As such, in these two exchanges, much of the communication between partners is asynchronous, with partners on each side communicating and responding at a convenient time as they prepare in the lead up to synchronous sessions which take place on Skype, BigBlueButton, a web conferencing system designed for online learning, or Zoom.

In addition, universities in different countries follow different academic schedules. When class is in session in one country, students in another are deep in summer internships or on holiday break. While the Belgian academic year begins in September, Japanese students begin in April, meaning that while the students on one side of the exchange are settled into university life, the students on the other are only just starting out as university students. They are therefore not ready for the challenges that VE can bring. Examination periods also fall at very different times, and the intense periods of preparation that precede them are not suitable for VE. The fact that participants are busy at different times of the year causes many logistical challenges.

Finally, and perhaps most importantly, setting up and running VEs is extremely time-consuming for all involved. This burden on the teachers involved has until recently been largely unrecognized by institutions with little or no extra preparation time allocated. Many teachers, passionate about the potential benefits of VE, presently spend this time as a labor of love (Helm, 2015).

3.8. Issues to be aware of in teacher collaboration

Collaboration between teachers is at the heart of VE, and in order for projects to be successful, good relationships are essential. To build such relationships takes time, effort, patience, and determination from all involved, but without them, projects soon collapse. The dynamics between the staff involved in the three projects described here are all different, but all are based in a mutual respect and the understanding that all members want the best for the students in their care.

Of the three exchanges described here, the Philippine exchange is progressing the most smoothly largely because QQEnglish is a private company and therefore works differently to a traditional educational institution. Because roles are clearly defined, there is little need for negotiation. While the teachers in Japan control the project in terms of overall design, content of lessons, methods of instruction, activities to be undertaken, and types of assessment to be carried out, the staff in the Philippines are consulted as to their recommendations. Materials developed in Japan are shared with the teachers in the Philippines, and their suggestions for improvements implemented. Korthagen's (1985) five phase ALACT method of professional reflection is constantly in progress. The acronym

ALACT describes a cyclical approach which moves through five stages, firstly action, secondly reflecting on the action, thirdly developing an awareness of the important aspects of the action, fourthly developing alternative actions and finally trialing the new action, at which point the cycle begins again. Feedback from the Filipino teachers has been invaluable in improving the exchange, and each iteration of the course improves upon the one before it.

This relationship has resulted in a number of benefits for both partners. First, it has led to other kinds of collaboration in different educational contexts (not covered in this chapter) that are beneficial to both organizations. The Philippine teachers have benefited from opportunities to teach groups of emerging adults, rather than the individual adults who form their usual client base. As such, they have learned how to teach presentation skills to small groups and cope with a very different classroom dynamic involving a much more active approach to class management. Additionally, several teachers have come from the Philippines to observe face-to-face classes in Japan. This non-virtual interaction has dramatically improved the relationships between everyone involved in the organization of the exchange.

The collaboration with the university in Belgium has taken more time to establish. There are several issues that have contributed to this. First, the number of stakeholders is much larger, which provides great flexibility, but also complicates the decision-making process. Next, it is difficult to coordinate everyone's schedules, taking into account different working hours, academic cultures, time constraints, and time zones.

The Kenyan exchange exemplified one of the most basic problems of VEs: finding suitable partners. In this case, we relied on existing personal relationships to make a connection with a teacher who wanted to improve the intercultural communication skills of the students at their university.

In all of the VE projects, the teachers at all the institutions spent a long time negotiating with exchange partners as to the content, length, and timing of both synchronous and asynchronous activities, all designed toward the achievement

Chapter 6

of the disparate goals of the students and their institutions. Largely, all of the participants were open-minded and flexible, and keen to learn as much as they could during the process. The time needed for planning, consultation, and negotiation was thereby vital in order for the exchanges to move ahead smoothly.

3.9. Issues surrounding technology

While some teachers are not confident in their technological skills and hesitate to foray into uncharted waters using them in their teaching, the recent advances in intuitive technology mean that VE is often now possible without specific technological support. Allowing both teachers and learners to use technology they feel comfortable with is important. Because both instructors and learners use smartphones as part of regular daily life, and the tools for VE use a similar operating system, there are few difficulties in set up or operation. This is the case at the university where these three projects are based, and our collaborators in the Philippines, Belgium, and Kenya are similarly situated.

The exception to this, for all contexts, is problems maintaining a fast, stable wireless connection. VE can place a heavy burden on the sometimes fragile network, and time-lags, choppiness, and sudden cut-offs are not uncommon. Flexibility in planning is important: Activities should be prepared in advance that can be accomplished asynchronously should the connection drop out, and teachers on both sides of the exchange should be familiar with one another's roles. On one occasion during a session with the Philippines, the connection was completely lost and a teacher on the ground in Japan was asked to come into the classroom and teach face-to-face as a substitute. Students should also be forewarned that changes to the planned schedule may be necessary to prevent disappointment.

3.10. Issues concerning assessment

As VE has developed and moved toward the incorporation of intercultural competence as well as linguistic competence, methods of assessment have needed to be re-evaluated, and new methods found to reflect these new learning goals, particularly as measuring intercultural competence has proved to be difficult. One method of measuring VE interaction that has been trialed measures student participation levels, and counts either how many times participants send emails or post messages, or how much time they have spent using the software (O'Dowd, 2013). Unfortunately, however, simply leaving the software open on their desktop is often counted as active study time, leading to high scores for little or no activity. High levels of participation, whether measured by time online or number of interchanges, have not been found to correlate with learning of the target material (O'Dowd, 2013). As such, it was decided rather that rubrics, portfolios, and reflections would be used to assess student progress across the three VE projects. Rubrics were chosen as they are easily understood and managed by both students and teachers. Table 1 (supplementary materials, Appendix A) contains which shows an example of part of a rubric used in the Filipino exchange which documents visible examples of students' anxiety as perceived by the Filipino teachers and assesses their presentation skills. Table 2 (supplementary materials, Appendix B) is an adaptation of the rubric from the international cross-cultural experiential learning evaluation toolkit from SUNY (2015) for use in classes focusing on intercultural communication. Portfolios are another popular method, which although still do not necessarily address the potentially unwieldy issue of intercultural competence directly, provide a method of assessment that is more holistic. The final method we use is reflective journaling as it provides a space in which it is easier to address issues of intercultural competence as well as other factors concerning the exchanges.

In the Philippine exchange, all assessment of the activities done synchronously is carried by the Filipino teachers using a rubric. The use of a rubric forces these instructors to focus specifically on the presentation skills that are the target of the course. Nonverbal aspects of communication such as eye contact, posture and facial expressions, verbal skills such as pacing and volume, and content and organization are all able to be evaluated in this way. Specific English linguistic ability is not assessed because students are not streamed by ability into class groups, and, while all students are expected to make linguistic progress, this progress is not assessed for their course grade. The students are also graded by their teachers in Japan on the practice and preparation activities that they undertake in class. Finally, students are asked at several points during the semester to write reflections on their learning experiences, and these are also used to assess the achievement of learning goals.

In the Kenyan exchange, student achievement on the Japanese side of the exchange is measured with a portfolio approach. Students keep the various artifacts they create during the various activities, and choose how to present and organize them. An introspective journal forms a large part of this portfolio, where they reflect on their experiences and what they have learned from the exchange.

A difficult challenge that many teachers involved in VEs face is in deciding how courses created jointly can be officially accredited. Students on both sides of exchanges require assessment and course credits for the work they do. In Japan, there has been a slow acceptance of credits for online education and this will need to be addressed in the future.

3.11. Context-specific issues

Each VE is unique to its context and the scale of the exchange is important. The Kenyan exchange is small and due to this it is easy to be flexible with both content, types of interaction, and time. The organization of the Filipino exchange takes place between individual teachers in Japan and a privately run Japanese company and thus is relatively straightforward and manageable. The exchange with the university in Belgium is larger than either of the other exchanges and also has more institutional constraints on both sides. The structure of university systems can present barriers to collaboration due to traditional ways of working and curriculum constraints. Trying to match classes from the respective institutions within the present curriculum has proved to be difficult and at present we are trying to put compatible courses in place for the future.

4. Conclusion

VEs are versatile, flexible, and inclusive, and provide incredible learning experiences for both students and teachers. They allow students who might otherwise never interact with people from other backgrounds to engage in what may prove to be eye-opening and life-changing opportunities and as such are a wonderful addition to most educational programs. However, building VEs is an ongoing process and further research is needed on how to create more sustainable models. Additionally, more training and support is necessary for teachers both at an individual and institutional level, and rather than individuals repeating the same processes in isolation, we need to focus on developing generic models that can be easily used in various contexts.

5. Acknowledgments

This work was supported by JSPS Kakenhi grant number 19K00820.

6. Supplementary materials

https://research-publishing.box.com/s/j4jwtm354ywoh18w2dmkdz0rmyppak3n

References

Belz, J., & Müller-Hartmann, A. (2003). Teachers as intercultural learners: negotiating German-American telecollaboration along the institutional fault line. *Modern Language Journal, 87*(1), 71-89. https://doi.org/10.1111/1540-4781.00179

Boehm, D., Aniola-Jedrzejek, L., & Kurthen, H. (2010). Do international online collaborative learning projects impact ethnocentrism? *E-Learning and Digital Media, 7*(2), 133-146. https://doi.org/10.2304/elea.2010.7.2.133

Brammerts, H. (1996). Tandem language learning via the internet and the international e-mail tandem network. In D. Little & H. Brammerts (Eds), *A guide to language learning in tandem via the internet* (pp. 9-22). Trinity College Dublin.

D'Angelo, J. (2018). The status of ELF in Japan. In J. Jenkins, W. Baker & M. Dewey (Eds), *The Routledge handbook of English as a lingua franca* (pp. 165-175). Routledge. https://doi.org/10.4324/9781315717173-14

Furstenberg, G. (1998). Nouveaux outils, nouvelle pédagogie. *Revue internationale d'éducation de Sèvres, 18*, 87-91. https://doi.org/10.4000/ries.2922

Furstenberg, G., Levet, S., English, K., & Maillet, K. (2001). Giving a virtual voice to the silent language of culture: The Cultura project. *Language learning & technology, 5*(1), 55-102.

Guarda, M. (2013). *Negotiating a transcultural place in an English as a lingua franca telecollaboration exchange*. Unpublished PhD thesis. http://paduaresearch.cab.unipd.it/5337/1/guarda_marta_tesi.pdf

Guth, S., & Helm, F. (2011). Developing multiliteracies in ELT through telecollaboration. *ELT Journal. 66*(1), 42-52. https://doi.org/10.1093/elt/ccr027

Guth, S., & Marini-Maio, N. (2010). Close encounters of a new kind: the use of Skype and wiki in telecollaboration. In S. Guth & F. Helm (Eds), *Telecollaboration 2.0. languages, literacies and intercultural learning in the 21st century*. Peter Lang.

Helm, F. (2014). Developing digital literacies through virtual exchange. *Elearning Papers, 38*, 1-10.

Helm, F. (2015). The practices and challenges of telecollaboration in higher education in Europe. *Language Learning & Technology, 19*(2), 197-217.

Helm, F. (2018). *Emerging identities in virtual exchange*. Research-publishing.net. https://doi.org/10.14705/rpnet.2018.25.9782490057191

Hoffstaedter, P., & Kohn, K. (2015). Research on results on telecollaboration: General part. *TILA Research Results on Telecollaboration*. http://www.tilaproject.eu/moodle/pluginfile.php/2694/mod_page/content/15/TILA%20Research%20Results%20on%20Telecollaboration.pdf

Hofstede, G. (1980). Motivation, leadership, and organization: do American theories apply abroad? *Organizational Dynamics, 9*(1), 42-63. https://doi.org/10.1016/0090-2616(80)90013-3

Hülmbauer, C., Böhringer, H., & Seidlhofer, B. (2008). Introducing English as a lingua franca (ELF): Precursor and partner in intercultural communication. *Synergies Europe 3*, 25-36.

Korthagen, F. A. J. (1985). Reflective teaching and preservice teacher education in the Netherlands. *Journal of Teacher Education, 36*(5), 11-15. https://doi.org/10.1177/002248718503600502

Liddicoat, A. J. (2007). Internationalising Japan: Nihonjinron and the intercultural in Japanese language-in-education policy. *Journal of Multicultural Discourses, 2*(1), 32-46. https://doi.org/10.2167/md043.0

Liddicoat, A. J. (2013). *Language-in-education policies: the discursive construction of intercultural relations*. Multilingual Matters. https://doi.org/10.21832/9781847699152

McDaniel, E. R., Samovar, L. A., & Porter, R. E. (2003). Japanese nonverbal communication: a reflection of cultural themes. In L. Samover & R. Porter (Eds), *Intercultural communication: a reader* (pp. 253-261). Thomson Wadsworth.

Mose, P. (2018). Language-in-education policy in Kenya: intention, interpretation, implementation. *Nordic Journal of African Studies, 26*(3), 215-30.

O'Dowd, R. (2013). Telecollaboration 2.0. In S. Guth & F. Helm (Eds), *Telecollaboration 2.0. languages, literacies and intercultural learning in the 21st century*. Peter Lang.

O'Dowd, R. (2017). Virtual exchange and internationalising the classroom. *TLC Journal-Training Language & Culture, 4*(1), 8-24. https://doi.org/10.29366/2017tlc.1.4.1

O'Dowd, R. (2018). From telecollaboration to virtual exchange: state-of-the-art and the role of UNICollaboration in moving forward. *Journal of Virtual Exchange, 1*,1-23. https://doi.org/10.14705/rpnet.2018.jve.1

O'Rourke, B. (2007). Models of telecollaboration (1): eTandem. In R. O'Dowd (Ed.), *Online intercultural exchange. An introduction for foreign language teachers* (pp. 41-61). Multilingual Matters. https://doi.org/10.21832/9781847690104-005

Polisca, P. (2011). Language learning and the raising of cultural awareness through Internet telephony: a case study. *The Language Learning Journal, 39*(3), 329-343. https://doi.org/10.1080/09571736.2010.538072

Rubin, J. (2016). The collaborative online international learning network. In R. O'Dowd & T. Lewis (Eds), *Online intercultural exchange: policy, pedagogy, practice* (pp. 263-272). Routledge. https://doi.org/10.4324/9781315678931

Sergeant, P. (2012). English and linguistic globalisation. In P. Sergeant & J. Swan (Eds), *English in the world: history, diversity, change* (pp. 178-187). Routledge.

SUNY. (2015). *International cross-cultural experiential learning evaluation toolkit from SUNY*. http://www.crossculturetoolkit.org/

Starke-Meyerring, D., & Wilson, M. (2008). Learning environments for a globally networked world: emerging visions. In D. Starke-Meyerring & M. Wilson (Eds), *Designing globally networked learning environments: Visionary partnerships, policies, and pedagogies* (pp.1-17). Sense Publishers. https://doi.org/10.1163/9789087904753_002

Stier, J. (2006). Internationalisation, intercultural communication and intercultural competence. *Journal of Intercultural Communication*, 11, 1-12.

Tajima, M. (2018). *Engagements with English in Japan: ideological constitutions of the language and its speakers*. Doctoral dissertation. University of Technology Sydney

Tan, S. (2018). *Cicada*. Hodder Children's Books.

Von Der Emde, S., Schneider, J., & Kötter, M. (2001). Technically speaking: transforming language learning through virtual learning environments (MOOs). *Modern Language Journal. 85*(2), 210-225. https://doi.org/10.1111/0026-7902.00105

Yujobo, Y. J. (2019). Reconceptualizing 'Global Jinzai' from a (B)ELF Perspective. *The Center for English as a Lingua Franca Journal, 5*, 11-22.

7 The affordances of wikis for virtual exchange

Thomas Kaufmann[1]

Abstract

This chapter will describe the ways wikis can benefit students, teachers, and administrators as well as provide examples of ways they can be used in the language and culture classroom for Virtual Exchange (VE). It will specifically examine how the tool was used for a collaborative research paper and explore how students can think critically to decide how to draft, edit, and revise the paper into a unified voice. Throughout the process, writers are thinking metacognitively about their writing and that of their counterparts. Furthermore, using written or verbal comments and visual markup within the wiki itself, recursive feedback loops between teachers and students are created in real-time but also recorded for later reflection. Finally, the tool also allows for a multitude of data points to be collected and analyzed for fair and valid assessment that is data driven. Teachers and administrators can see exactly who wrote what, when, and how long it took them. Therefore, the quantity and quality of the contributions can be assessed. Wikis are a powerful tool that can be harnessed in the language classroom for intercultural VE in a myriad of ways with an assortment of benefits.

Keywords: virtual exchange, wikis, metacognitive, recursive feedback, data-driven assessment.

---

1. The University of Illinois Champaign-Urbana, Illinois, United States; thomask5@illinois.edu; https://orcid.org/0000-0002-3706-0459

How to cite: Kaufmann, T. (2020). The affordances of wikis for virtual exchange. In E. Hagley & Y. Wang (Eds), *Virtual exchange in the Asia-Pacific: research and practice* (pp. 145-163). Research-publishing.net. https://doi.org/10.14705/rpnet.2020.47.1150

Chapter 7

1. Introduction

1.1. Wikis

A wiki, as mentioned elsewhere (Kaufmann, 2018), is a living document that exists online. The term 'wiki' is derived from the Hawaiian phrase, wiki-wiki, which means quick. A wiki is a collaborative web site whose content can be viewed and modified by visitors to the site. This allows users to easily create and edit the web pages, or wikis, collaboratively (Chao, 2007). Users who have permission can view and modify it in real-time. Each team member of the project can store, collate, and restructure ideas together (Howland, Jonassen, & Marra, 2013). The most well-known example of one is Wikipedia. Most Learning Management Sites (LMSs) now have wiki tools which are very useful for a variety of collaborative projects. Popular word processing software applications like Google Docs, Microsoft Word Online, and QQ Docs have a 'track changes' feature or 'revision history' that can emulate the features of a wiki. Dropbox Paper, Crocodocs, PBwiki, Wetpaint, and ZohoWriter are additional websites that focus solely on wiki creation and collaboration.

Wikis support writing instruction (Lamb, 2004) and have many benefits that assist teachers and students working on improving the writing process: reflection, reviewing, publication and watching the process unfold (Fountain, 2005). Such a process encourages higher levels of thinking that are aligned with Bloom's (1956) taxonomy. Some of the first to use wikis in education were Chao (2007), Evans (2006), and Schaffert et al. (2006). Parker and Chao (2007) explained that wikis are tools for group authoring. Previously, group members would have to collaborate on a document by emailing files to each other while they made revisions on their respective computers, then they would attempt to coordinate the edits into a single combined voice. A wiki exists on the internet rather than individual computers and allows the group members to work from a single, central wiki page. Wikis allow for a self-contained document where multiple users can collaborate within the same digital space. Through the use of wikis, educators can give their students the benefits detailed by Fountain (2005) and gain insight into the metacognitive strategies used by their students.

Another beneficial metacognitive strategy is recursive feedback, "[t]he feedback can be recursive in the sense that it prompts a response that prompts further feedback. Feedback on feedback ('That was helpful/not helpful') can also produce a quick response. Such feedback is immediately actionable in specific ways" (Cope & Kalantzis, 2016, p. 7). This can allow for more personalized learning and can help the reader as well as the writer.

The teacher's comments can form a continued dialog between them and the student as a means of formative grading. In terms of assessing collaboration, McNely et al. (2012) have studied the learning analytics of collaborative writing in similar online writing environments and how it can be used as a form of intervention for non-collaborating learners. Their learning environment and research findings were similar in many ways. They found, "much of our participants' workflow practices in co-located collaborations are ephemeral and thus do not render metrics that can be easily captured and measured" (McNely et al., 2012, p. 2). Through the use of wikis in non-co-located environments, teachers and researchers can capture and measure the very interactions that were previously ephemeral.

Using the track changes or revision history features new things can be examined. The edit histories contain a robust amount of unstructured, incidental data (Cope & Kalantzis, 2016). The information garnered from this feature can transform the assessment process to one that is more ubiquitous, recursive, fair, and valid to students. Wikis are ubiquitous forms of assessment in the sense that the instructor or teaching assistant can log in and provide feedback at any time and from anywhere during the writing process. Furthermore, if the students are logged in at the same time, they can even see the comments taking place in real-time. This feature has the potential to transform assessment from something very linear (e.g. grading a final, polished paper) into something more recursive and process-oriented – e.g. grading quantity and quality of involvement in the process (Cope & Kalantzis, 2016).

Through the usage of wikis, metacognitive strategies are essential to the entire process of producing a work as students need to think about the work of their peers and how their contributions can be combined to create a more cohesive final product.

> "The arbiters of quality are readers and other writers, and all can engage in dialogue about the veracity or otherwise of the content in the edit, and edit history areas, a public metacommentary on the page. The roles of writers and readers are blurred. Textual validation is an open, explicit, public and inclusive process. This represents a profound shift in the social relations of writing and reading" (Kalantzis & Cope, 2011, p. 45).

They also posit,

> "in fact, many web spaces have these kinds of metadialogue or dialogue about dialogue, for instance, in blog comments, video reviews or wiki edit histories for instance. We need to be able to read not just the text, but the subtexts. New media writing environments work as reciprocal ecologies of knowledge validation. They are full of metadialogues about perspective and interest" (Kalantzis & Cope, 2011, p. 69).

1.2. Wikis as pedagogical tools

As explained above, wikis can be used to monitor and properly assess student contributions on collaborative research papers. This allows students to work on their paper with their peers anywhere they have an internet connection. Wikis are particularly useful where group members are contributing from a variety of times of day, time zones, and from geographically dispersed locations. Through this tool, students can be in different geographic regions and still collaborate on assignments and projects.

The tool also allows the instructor to make revisions and comments in real-time that students can see instantly. This way the students do not need to wait until after they turn in an assignment to see the instructor's feedback. This process generates a recursive feedback loop that fosters metacognitive thinking (McNely et al., 2012). Furthermore, this eliminates the excessive use of paper and printing costs, making it more eco-friendly.

A common pitfall of collaborative writing assignments is where one student does all the work but there is no way for the instructor to truly determine and prove if this was the case or not. Wikis overcome this problem due to their comprehensive revision history which displays all of the edits to the document for the instructor. This granularity of data is useful to verify student contributions and provide sufficient evidence to grade each student in a fair and reliable manner. With this tool everything that is entered into the wiki, from infinitesimal, incidental data to macroscopic changes, is recorded, viewable, and can be quantified into a variety of metrics.

There are drawbacks to wikis and the biggest one is the learning curve. It takes some time for students to familiarize themselves with the software and they often forget to log in and make changes under their own names. This can be scaffolded with in-class activities like chain stories, live peer review sessions, or explicit writing instruction. Any activity that allows students guided practice to interact with the software and for the teacher to show their administrator view to the class will be extremely useful.

Learning communities are essential to any good VE (Wihlborg, Friberg, Rose, & Eastham, 2018) and Gilbert, Chen, and Sabol (2008) have outlined a straightforward approach to using wikis to build learning communities (ColumbiaLearn, 2008).

Thus, there are a variety of ways to implement a wiki into different contexts and for different purposes. Later in this chapter, some ideas for potential uses for using wikis in VE contexts will be examined, but the next section focuses on a particular context. It will attempt to depict a more detailed example of how a wiki can be used. It was for a 12-week introduction to research writing course in a Sino-American partnership program in a small city in China. While the course was conducted primarily onsite and co-located, the use of a wiki and videoconferencing software could allow it to be taught with the instructor in

Chapter 7

America and the students in China. It should also be noted that often the students were in different regions of China when they wrote and collaborated on their research paper. The students were tasked to write an ethnography on linguistic landscape analysis or ethnographic linguistic landscape analysis pedagogy (Kaufmann, 2019).

2. Method and study details

2.1. Course design

In a 12-week introduction to research writing course, sophomore English majors in a Sino-American degree program were instructed on the fundamentals of research. They were asked to choose a research site, conduct ethnographic research on the visibility and saliency of languages (English) in the world around them (Landry & Bourhis, 1997) and write a research paper on their findings.

The course progressed with instruction on a given component of a research paper followed by guided practice in class. Next, the students were tasked to draft given components of the paper and submit it for grading. They were instructed not to use any other word processing software other than the wiki. The instructor checked in on their work periodically throughout the week to offer guidance and support through comments and revisions creating recursive feedback. In 2020, due to the impact of COVID-19, this same course will be conducted while the instructor is in the US and the students are quarantined in their homes throughout China.

Every three weeks, teacher-student feedback sessions were held to discuss salient features of the papers and offer guidance with revisions. In the first phase, much of the discussion centered on explaining how to use the wiki and the importance of doing so. It should be noted that this might prove to be more difficult in a virtual environment but would not be impossible. Showing the instructor and student view in real-time during a scaffolded activity has proved to be an effective means of navigating students through the system. The biggest issues of the conferences during Phase 2 related to finding a unified voice and collaborating effectively which the wiki aided in through things like recursive feedback loops. Finally, Phase 3 workshops centered on organizing the papers and using the software for formatting and style issues.

2.2. Activities

There are a variety of activities that can be done to scaffold the learning and assist in helping the students become successful. These revolve around modeling the task from the computer and projector for the students and having them attempt it within their own wikis. As their skills improve, they can also peer review other groups' wikis and think critically about the changes they are making and also the changes that have been made to their own papers.

Furthermore, some students have a tough time transitioning into how to write collaboratively and what to look for when proofreading. Some managed to divide the work up well while others required extensive tutorials. Oftentimes in collaborative writing, the document will contain distinct paragraphs on the same topic but in different voices. The revision history makes this even more apparent when each paragraph is attributed to a unique student. Showing students this revision history allows them to see the lack of cohesiveness, and it can help them understand what is expected in terms of active collaboration and contribution.

2.2.1. Live demos

Students were asked to view some sample abstracts and color code them, (e.g. make the thesis statement blue, research questions red). This was also done on the wiki platform in real-time to introduce students to the platform and scaffold the learning process. In addition to teaching about the components of an abstract a live demonstration of the wiki was also possible. The instructor can monitor all of the students' progress, handle technology issues, and assist with the features of the abstract by using the software to color code it. This type of visual markup activity was used by Cope and Kalantzis (2016) to diagram the text. Outlining structures was also used by Olmanson et al. (2015) to show the pedagogical benefits of students supporting one another in the writing process. In order to stimulate motivation further, this activity was made into a game and the first groups to finish the task correctly were awarded participation points for the day. Once the relevant features were understood and analyzed through a class discussion, the students were equipped to draft their own abstracts.

2.2.2. Peer review

It is beneficial to have students review other groups' papers for the benefits of a peer review (metacognitive) and to understand what revising looks like in a wiki. Permission to view and edit can be granted or revoked to specific users within the software in order to facilitate the peer review process. Students can be instructed to proofread or look for key features within a given text. They can be instructed to highlight all the in-text citations, elements of modern language association style, or look for transition markers. It is also very beneficial for students to observe the use of active and passive voice and first-person pronouns throughout the paper as these are common pitfalls made when writing research papers. This is another type of activity that can be done with or without a wiki to improve students' understanding of the software and to help them write better research papers.

2.2.3. Comments

Face-to-face discussions are very valuable to provide feedback to students, but web conferences offer similar benefits. Another feature of wikis is where the instructor can highlight certain portions of text and comment on them. This could potentially facilitate an asynchronous discussion of sorts with the student commenting on the comments or making the prescribed revisions and seeking clarification. The comments are generally visible on the right-hand side of the manuscript and they can even be made via voice recording in some software. The instructor can also access the wiki and proofread or modify certain portions within the document directly and the students can review the changes that were made. It is like having a mentor or collaborator assisting with the writing process from the very moment you log in. Students are given a notification that a change has been made and can view the feedback as soon as they access the wiki. This type of functionality can expedite the review process by providing feedback in real-time.

2.3. Assessment

Understanding how wikis are used to assess based on the name of the student and their contribution was a difficult concept for students to grasp at first. There is certainly a learning curve in using the software as students sometimes mention that they wrote the paper on their friends computer while they were signed in, or they wrote it while they were co-located (if they are in a VE environment, this will not be an issue). Some even provided data of where they supplied the ideas in the L1 (Mandarin) in another app while teammates translated for them into the wiki. These are potential threats to validity in that students may in fact be contributing, but there is no data to support it in the wiki. This is a common pitfall of the platform but stern grading aids the students in ascertaining expectations for the class and their conduct within it.

Sometimes, students start by writing their own paragraph in a word processing software like Microsoft Word and paste it into the wiki. This would be rather obvious in traditional print due to redundancies in the writing, but wikis make it abundantly clear who wrote what and when. If the students copy entire paragraphs into the wiki in a matter of seconds, the teacher can see that they are not using the tool properly. Again, live demos and 'wiki-scaffolds' (Higginbotham, May-Landy, & Beeby, in ColumbiaLearn, 2008) are essential to eradicating this behavior. This summarizes one way a wiki could be used in a particular context, in this case a dual degree program, but there are many others.

2.4. Ways to incorporate wikis into VE

How can wikis be implemented into other VE contexts? They can be used for small assignments or even large projects depending on the needs of the class, but they are all tasks. Nunan (1989) defines a task as "a piece of classroom work which involves learners in comprehending, manipulating, producing or interacting in the target language while their attention is principally focused on meaning rather than form" (p. 10). The emphasis is not on linguistic structures of language but holistic meaning. It should also be noted that when using web 2.0 tools such as wikis, anything that simply replicates pen and paper for keyboards and monitors is not harnessing the power of the platform effectively. Digital literacy tasks should be immersive and engaging[2]. While one could simply use a wiki as a means of creating a simple website, it is not effectively harnessing everything that the tool affords. As described above, the benefits of the tool lie in the recursive feedback loops that are created and the ability to track and trace the quantity and quality of participation and collaboration. While several studies have used wikis (Forsythe, 2014; Mitchell, 2016) in VE environments, they have not used them to their fullest potential. The following tasks are collaborative and participatory, engaging a broader audience, where a group of students negotiate meaning and decide on a final text to be used by a group of learners that can interact with the ideas.

In joint venture programs like the one previously mentioned between a university in the US and China, wikis could also be used for a type of pen pal exchange activity. Students could simply introduce themselves like (Forsythe, 2014) did. Groups of students from one country could also collaborate on a page related to some unique aspect of their culture like how different holidays are celebrated or a popular news article. If the university hosts any service learning projects or study abroad experiences, the participants could create a page that culminates on the experience with pictures, text, and even video. Students could get together and discuss critical incidents like plagiarism. They could do this with something as simple as sharing a Turnitin report and discussing why it had been flagged for plagiarism or more nuanced where students could help each other to draft a properly cited essay and explain the importance of doing so. Finally, if some students have matriculated to the host institution they could reflect on their experiences and tell future students what to expect. This could not only entice more students to go abroad but allow traveling students to maintain a connection to their home culture and stay abreast of happenings there. These are just some

---

2. https://www.iste.org/standards

of the ways that a dynamic page could be developed and maintained by groups of authors and readers around the world in a partnership program.

There are many more reasons and benefits for a wiki. If an instructor of a course is traveling for a conference or for some reason unable to physically attend class, they could upload a lecture video and assign their students a writing task. The metadata of the wiki will show exactly who is contributing, when they are contributing, and how much. Any type of collaborative academic paper could also harness the affordances of a wiki and transparent assessment. Additionally, students could use a wiki to take notes from a class and share them with others who are watching the lecture videos asynchronously.

Wikis can also be used in classroom activities like brainstorming or exit tickets. In this case, a wiki could take the place of a forum or chat tool. The teacher could post a few warm up questions to the wiki and let the students 'talk with their fingers' in real-time and show their background knowledge. This could give students who are reticent to speak a chance to share their thoughts in another medium. The page can be viewed in real-time and it can also serve as a springboard into a deeper discussion or lecture. Exit tickets can also be done with wikis where the teacher asks students a simple question at the end of class and they reflect on the day's instruction. This can be used to either supplement the chat tool in a videoconference session and/or allow students to contribute asynchronously. Instead of one student speaking and the others listening, they can engage in an act of participatory culture (Jenkins, 2006).

Hagley's (2016) international VE project and similar platforms could use wikis for more complex tasks than forum posts. With a wiki they could engage in discussing and agreeing on a polished final product, e.g. a travel brochure or food recipe. Students could work together on designing their ideal house and explain the cultural elements within it. In groups, they could devise a travel itinerary for their exchange partners. The teachers in the project could use it as a platform to collaborate on a single rubric for assessment criteria or discuss progress among their students. They could even create an entire curriculum together from different locations in the world. In terms of assessment, a wiki would allow the instructor to see the minutiae of data that corresponds to keystrokes into creating shared documents. In a small-scale exchange, two teachers could simply use a wiki as the platform for the entire VE environment.

University writing centers could utilize wikis in a way to discuss works in progress when the participants are not co-located. If students are participating in a study abroad program or connecting with other schools in the target language to work on a text, through annotations and revisions made to the wiki by writing center tutors, students can understand the explicit areas of their paper that need improvement. Ideally, this would be coupled with video chat synchronously to really explain the comments, but it need not be. Wikis allow for audio feedback and the writing center staff can record their voice to explain complex aspects of feedback.

Massive Open Online Courses (MOOCs) could also benefit from using wikis. Research has shown that social learning communities and participation in forums is effective at curbing attrition rates (Crossley et al., 2015). MOOCs could be designed to incorporate wikis for student assignments to demonstrate mastery of course material. Chi, Zhang, and Kulich's (2016) intercultural communications MOOC could have the students do the assignments in a wiki as opposed to a forum. Or, in groups, they could synthesize a final draft of several of the assignments. Furthermore, the mentors and groups could use a wiki to organize all of the discussions instead of WeChat (Chi et al., 2016).

A hyperdoc is a standalone lesson where students are given a set of instructions and are asked to complete them within the document. It is like a digital worksheet, but much more engaging and inquiry-based learning driven. They could be given a link to a page and asked to summarize or reflect on its contents. The students could be asked to complete an outline or table or simply find the answer to a question. Hyperdocs are used in flipped classroom and blended learning modalities where students take charge of their learning and seek out the answers on their own (Highfill, Hilton, & Landis, 2016), but they could also be employed in a VE setting. The teacher could lecture on salient features of the hyperdoc that students struggle to demonstrate mastery in.

Wikis could even be used as a forum for debate. They could supply research to support their opinions and attempt to persuade the moderators of their ability to create compelling arguments. A wiki could allow for teams of students to work together on a draft of arguments and refine each other's statements.

Online learning environments like VIPKid and 51Talk for native speakers of English (often in western countries) could also be used to interact with students in non-English speaking contexts like China. These platforms have been a successful means of spoken VE but seem to lack a real written component. Using a wiki, a student or a group of students could work on a writing assignment and get feedback from a team of teachers around the globe (Ko, 2019).

3. Pedagogical and workplace principles

One of the benefits of using a wiki for collaborative writing involves fair and valid assessment for every student based on their individual contributions to the paper. Students can benefit from individualized feedback in real-time from their instructors and peers. They are also able to collaborate with peers and form a unified voice in the living documents. Furthermore, students can communicate with people all around the globe and exchange ideas in a myriad of ways.

Teachers can use the tool to organize materials and assignments in one place and assess contributions in a fair and valid manner. Teachers can see exactly who wrote what and when in a collaborative environment. They can see the process of learning taking shape and unfold through the revision history of the wiki. Furthermore, this technology can be harnessed to create new pedagogical methods that were not possible with pen and paper.

The tool benefits administrators in allowing them to have a transparent view of what types of things the students are learning and producing. They can assess adherence to curriculum and standards and make more informed decisions based on the data from the wiki. Different schools and colleges can communicate with one another from anywhere on the planet and exchange in a virtual environment.

There are challenges to the validity of this assessment method. Times when students do not make changes to the wiki while logged in under their own username, e.g. using a friend's computer, can be problematic. The changes made could erroneously be attributed to the person who was signed into the wiki and not the one physically behind the keyboard making the contribution is another area the teacher needs to be cognizant of.

The amount of data that can be harvested from a wiki allows assessment in new ways and offers other pedagogical possibilities. Cope and Kalantzis (2016) state,

> "[c]omputer-mediated environments can support immediate machine feedback by means of natural language processing, [computer adaptive testing], and procedure-based games, for instance. They can also offer extensive peer and teacher feedback by streamlining the complex social processes of machine-mediated, argument-defined human feedback" (p. 7).

Wagner (2008) posits there are seven skills necessary for students to learn in order to be successful in the workplace: (1) critical thinking and problem solving, (2) collaboration across networks and leading by influence, (3) agility and adaptability, (4) initiative and entrepreneurism, (5) effective oral and written communication, (6) accessing and analyzing information, and (7) curiosity and imagination. Writing collaboratively in a wiki allows students to develop many of these skills that are viewed as desirable by employers across the globe. Parker (cited in Wagner, 2008, n.p.) adds,

> "[o]ur business is changing, and so the skills our engineers need change rapidly, as well. We can teach them the technical stuff. But for employees to solve problems or to learn new things, they have to know what questions to ask. And we can't teach them how to ask good

questions – how to think. The ability to ask the right questions is the single most important skill".

We are seeing an emphasis on soft skills and using wikis can certainly help develop collaborative problem-solving skills in VE contexts through questions and answers with teachers and classmates.

The very process of writing a research paper is a very critically thought out one. It encompasses history, methodology, and a deeper understanding of complex issues. Collaborating on a research process metacognitively strengthens the students' understanding of these skills. Workplaces of the future will involve or already involve collaborating with others from all over the globe on various facets of unique projects. Annmarie Neal (cited in Wagner, 2008, n.p.) mentioned,

> "[w]hat do I really need to understand about this; what is the history; what are other people thinking about this; how does that all come together; what frames and models can we use to understand this from a variety of different angles and then come up with something different?".

Using wikis for intercultural learning can lead students to a deeper understanding of the world and allow them to formulate answers to these types of questions. This will make their lives more culturally rich, their learning experience more fruitful, and ultimately, make them better employees in workplaces of the future. Again, through using a wiki, students will gain the very soft skills employers are looking for in terms of having metadialogs with superiors and coworkers. These are only the first two skills mentioned but many more of the essential seven are harnessed through this activity, e.g. accessing and analyzing information.

4. Conclusions

This chapter introduced wikis and how they can be used for collaborative writing. It also looked at reflections from students' papers. It showed how using wikis in collaborative writing projects has helped students find their own unified voice as academic writers, develop metacognitive strategies, and generate opportunities for recursive feedback. This same tool can be used to allow students to work on writing tasks asynchronously when they are not co-located. Furthermore, wikis allow the teacher the opportunity to see exactly what has been written, when, and by whom, and this can be beneficial in a variety of VE contexts. This tool can help teachers assess individual contributions to group writing projects fairly and accurately. Additionally, the time it takes for students to receive feedback on their work is lessened dramatically.

Specifically relating to VE, there are several affordances. Firstly, digital tasks of any kind are beneficial to student's technology skills[3]. In the context of discussing plagiarism, a wiki can stimulate robust, enriching conversation surrounding deeper understanding of the concept and higher order thinking skills. Without tools like wikis, VE would be very difficult if not impossible. Wikis provide a shared space for students to formulate ideas and hash them out collectively. In VE, it is not always possible to have everyone speak at the same time, even during a synchronous session. This results in a muddle of voices and ultimately just noise. Having a discussion in a wiki allows everyone's voice to be heard without overloading the participant's listening abilities. Real-time collaboration can serve to give everyone a chance to 'speak' and be 'heard' that can also be utilized asynchronously to reflect on what was said and built upon previous statements. Forums are great at facilitating conversations in virtual environments but certain tasks lend themselves to more unified products. In a sense, forums are static while wikis are dynamic. Writing centers can also benefit from using wikis to be immersed within the document during the revision process. Wikis can actually be used in lieu of certain features of an LMS. Learning guides complete with links to content and directions for assignments can be created and shared. If a student has a question about a certain aspect of the learning guide they can ask it right inside the wiki and the instructor can provide an answer for all students to view. Finally, wikis provide a means for feedback and revision in writing instruction to take place in asynchronous VE environments.

---

3. https://www.iste.org/standards

References

Bloom, B. S. (1956). Taxonomy of educational objectives: the classification of educational goals. In M. D. Engelhart, E. J. Furst, W. H. Hill & D. R. Krathwohl (Eds), *Taxonomy of educational objectives: the classification of educational goals; Handbook I: Cognitive domain*. David McKay.

Chao, J. (2007). Student project collaboration using Wikis. *In 20th conference on software engineering education & training (CSEET'07)* (pp. 255-261). IEEE. https://doi.org/10.1109/cseet.2007.49

Chi, R. B., Zhang, H. L., & Kulich, S. J. (2016). Transforming traditional courses into MOOCs: a case analysis of the intercultural communication courses. *Computer-assisted Foreign Language Education, 6*, 29-34.

ColumbiaLearn. (2008, November 3). *Promoting collaborative learning using wikis*. https://www.youtube.com/watch?v=ul9YM7QZZis

Cope, B., & Kalantzis, M. (2016). Big data comes to school: implications for learning, assessment, and research. *AERA Open*. https://doi.org/10.1177/2332858416641907

Crossley, S., McNamara, D. S., Baker, R., Wang, Y., Paquette, L., Barnes, T., & Bergner, Y. (2015). Language to completion: success in an educational data mining massive open online class. In *Proceedings of the 8th International Conference on Educational Data Mining* (pp. 388-391).

Evans, P. (2006, January). The wiki factor. *BizEd*. https://bized.aacsb.edu/articles/2006/january/the-wiki-factor

Forsythe, E. (2014). Online intercultural collaborations using wikis: an analysis of students' comments and factors affecting project success. *JALT CALL Journal, 10*(3), 255-271. https://doi.org/10.29140/jaltcall.v10n3.179

Fountain, R. (2005). Wiki pedagogy. *Dossiers technopédagogiques*, 319-325.

Gilbert, D., Chen, H., & Sabol, J. (2008). Building learning communities with wikis. In R. Cummings & M. Barton (Eds), *Wiki writing: collaborative learning in the college classroom* (pp. 71-89). University of Michigan Press. https://doi.org/10.2307/j.ctv65sx6q.8

Hagley, E. (2016). Making virtual exchange/telecollaboration mainstream – large scale exchanges. In S. Jager, M. Kurek & B. O'Rourke (Eds), *New directions in telecollaborative research and practice: selected papers from the second conference on telecollaboration higher education* (pp. 225-230). Research-publishing.net. https://doi.org/10.14705/rpnet.2016.telecollab2016.511

Highfill, L., Hilton, K., & Landis, S. (2016). *The HyperDoc handbook: digital lesson design using Google apps*. EdTechTeam Press.

Howland, J. L., Jonassen, D. H., & Marra, R. M. (2013). *Meaningful learning with technology*. Pearson New International Edition.

Jenkins, H. (2006). *Confronting the challenges of participatory culture: media education for the 21st century*. The MIT Press.

Kalantzis, M., & Cope, B. (2011). The work of writing in the age of its digital reproducibility. *Yearbook of the National Society for the Study of Education, 110*(1), 40-87.

Kaufmann, T. (2018). *e-Learning ecologies MOOC* [comment]. CGScholar..https://cgscholar.com/community/community_profiles/e-learning-ecologies-mooc/community_updates/35085

Kaufmann, T. (2019). Ethnographic linguistic landscape analysis pedagogy. *Asian EFL Journal, 25*(5.1), 83-101.

Ko, S. (2019). *VIPKID: revolutionizing language teaching and learning*. SAGE Publications. https://doi.org/10.4135/9781526490308

Lamb, B. (2004). Wide open spaces: wikis, ready or not. *EDUCAUSE Review, 39*(5).

Landry, R., & Bourhis, R. Y. (1997). Linguistic landscape and ethnolinguistic vitality: an empirical study. *Journal of language and social psychology, 16*(1), 23-49. https://doi.org/10.1177/0261927x970161002

McNely, B. J., Gestwicki, P., Hill, J. H., Parli-Horne, P., & Johnson, E. (2012, April/May). Learning analytics for collaborative writing: a prototype and case study. *Paper presented at the 2nd International Conference on Learning Analytics and Knowledge, Vancouver, BC*. https://doi.org/10.1145/2330601.2330654

Mitchell, C. (2016). Web 2.0 use to foster learners' intercultural sensitivity: an exploratory study. In P. Rucks & A.E. Fantini (Eds), *Dimension* (pp. 147-168). SCOLT Publications.

Nunan, D. (1989). *Designing tasks for the communicative classroom*. Cambridge University Press.

Olmanson, J., Kennett, K., McCarthey, S., Searsmith, D., Cope, B., & Kalantzis, M. (2015). Visualizing revision: leveraging student-generated between-draft diagramming data in support of academic writing development. *Technology, Knowledge and Learning, 21*(1), 99-123. https://doi.org/10.1007/s10758-015-9265-5

Parker, K., & Chao, J. (2007). Wiki as a teaching tool. *Interdisciplinary Journal of e-learning and Learning Objects, 3*(1), 57-72.

Schaffert, S., Bischof, D., Buerger, T., Gruber, A., Hilzensauer, W., & Schaffert, S. (2006). Learning with semantic wikis. *Proceedings of the First Workshop on Semantic Wikis – From Wiki To Semantics, SemWiki2006* (pp. 109-123).

Wagner, T. (2008). *The global achievement gap: why even our best schools don't teach the new survival skills our children need, and what we can do about it.* Basic Books. https://newlearningonline.com/literacies/chapter-2/wagner-on-new-workplace-capacities

Wihlborg, M., Friberg, E. E., Rose, K. M., & Eastham, L. (2018). Facilitating learning through an international virtual collaborative practice: a case study. *Nurse education today, 61,* 3-8. https://doi.org/10.1016/j.nedt.2017.10.007

8. The role virtual exchange could play in helping prepare students for real-life study abroad

Andrew Ryan[1]

Abstract

More and more Japanese students are studying abroad and the Japanese government has set a target of 180,000 students to study abroad each year by 2020 and is providing financial assistance to students to help achieve this goal. However, is financial assistance enough? Surveys conducted with students from a national education-focused university in northern Japan, before and after their study abroad experience, show that they feel underprepared before they leave to go overseas and regret not fulfilling the opportunities they had while abroad. The key areas identified where they needed assistance were with their English language ability, confidence building, and intercultural awareness. This paper suggests that doing a Virtual Exchange (VE) before they travel could help students in all of these areas. It could provide much needed language support, motivation to explore other cultures and share their own, and deliver the confidence to enable them to become more outgoing and make the most of the opportunities presented by studying overseas. Additionally, there is a case to be argued, that VE could help reduce the impact of culture shock. Overall, it is very likely that the use of VE prior to departure could improve students' study abroad experience. The author also understands that more research is needed on this and proposes a further study comparing students who have studied abroad without

---

1. Hokkaido University of Education, Sapporo, Japan; andyryanjapanwork@gmail.com; https://orcid.org/0000-0002-4972-921X

How to cite: Ryan, A. (2020). The role virtual exchange could play in helping prepare students for real-life study abroad. In E. Hagley & Y. Wang (Eds), *Virtual exchange in the Asia-Pacific: research and practice* (pp. 165-177). Research-publishing.net. https://doi.org/10.14705/rpnet.2020.47.1151

Chapter 8

conducting VE in advance to those who have, to try and assess its impact on the study abroad experience.

Keywords: study abroad, virtual exchange, student exchange, intercultural communication, language learning, ESL.

1. Introduction

The number of Japanese students who study abroad is increasing. Some students join long-term exchange programs, many more short-term intensive language courses, others take part in cultural exchanges or research trips. This increase has been driven by the Japanese government who, in 2013, set a target of doubling the number of university students who went abroad from 60,000 to 120,000, and high school students from 30,000 to 60,000 by the year 2020 (Lee, 2018).

To achieve this goal, the Ministry of Education, Culture, Sports, Science, and Technology introduced the 'Tobitate' scheme, which uses a combination of public and private money to provide 10,000 scholarships for university and high school students to study abroad (MEXT, 2015). According to the Japan Student Services Organization, the number of students studying abroad steadily rose from 36,302 in 2009 to 105,301 in 2017 (JASSO, 2019). With more and more students deciding to study abroad, it is important that they are given the preparation to allow them to make the most out of their overseas experience, both in terms of formal education, but also, what can be learned simply by living in a different culture. Clearly, students will be given advice and help by their teachers in their home institution but what role could VE play in helping them succeed while abroad?

To assess this question properly it is important to understand the feelings of the student. Firstly, their concerns and fears about studying abroad. If these can be eased then they might have a more productive and enjoyable time at their host institution. Secondly, the regrets returnee students feel need to be investigated. If these are assessed and acted on then future students may not make the same mistakes as their predecessors.

2. Method and study details

To discover students' anxieties before they go overseas and their regrets after they have returned, two surveys were conducted. The first (Survey 1) regarding students' concerns about study abroad involved 25 undergraduate students from a national education-focused university in northern Japan; all were traveling abroad to study (Table 1).

Twenty-one of these students were studying English education while the other four studied humanities (2), school nursing (1) and technology (1). All the students were between 19 to 21 years old and consisted of 15 female students and ten male students. The vast majority were mainly studying English while overseas with the opportunity to take some other undergraduate courses. However, the students who went to Norway, Korea, and Taiwan had the opportunity to study other languages. Two students did not study at all, they went to America to complete teaching internships working in elementary and middle schools.

Table 1. Number of students and their destination and duration of their planned study abroad

Country	Duration	No. of Students	Country	Duration	No. of Students
USA	10 months	5	Norway	12 months	1
	6 months	2		4 months	2
	4 months	1	Canada	4 months	1
	10 weeks	1	New Zealand	10 weeks	1
UK	12 months	2	Korea	3 months	1
	6 months	4	Taiwan	4 months	1
Australia	11 months	2			
	8 months	1			

Chapter 8

The second survey (Survey 2) was conducted with students who had returned from their overseas experience (Table 2). This time 21 undergraduate students from the university previously mentioned were questioned.

Table 2. Students and their destination and duration of their study abroad

Country	Duration	No. of Students	Country	Duration	No. of Students
USA	10 months	2	Norway	12 months	1
	6 months	2		4 months	2
	4 months	1	Canada	4 months	1
	10 weeks	1	New Zealand	10 weeks	1
UK	12 months	1	Korea	3 months	1
	6 months	4	Taiwan	4 month	1
Australia	11 months	2			
	8 months	1			

In the survey prior to departure, the students were asked to assess the following statements (Table 3) and if they strongly agreed, agreed, disagreed, or strongly disagreed with each statement.

Table 3. Statements contained in Survey 1

1	I am anxious about making friends.
2	I am anxious about communicating with my host family or roommates.
3	I am anxious about finding food that I like.
4	I am anxious about finding health care if I get sick.
5	I am anxious about being homesick.
6	I am anxious about not understanding the culture of my host country sufficiently.
7	I am anxious about having enough money.
8	I am anxious about communicating with my classmates.
9	I am anxious I will not be able to speak in class.
10	I am anxious about the level of my second language reading skills.
11	I am anxious about the level of my second language listening skills.
12	I am anxious about the level of my second language writing skills.

In the survey after the students had returned, they were asked to assess the following statements and, again, if they strongly agreed, agreed, disagreed, or strongly disagreed with each one (Table 4).

Table 4. Statements contained in Survey 2

1	I regret not being more outgoing.
2	I regret not communicating more with my host family or roommates.
3	I regret not being more adventurous with food.
4	I regret not learning more about the culture of my host country.
5	I regret not traveling enough in my host country.
6	I regret not taking more photographs or documenting my experiences.
7	I regret spending too much time with other Japanese people.
8	I regret spending too much time thinking about my home country.
9	I regret not communicating more with my classmates.
10	I regret not speaking more in class.
11	I regret not studying harder in class.
12	I regret not doing more home study.
13	I regret not joining a club or society.

3. Results and discussion

3.1. Survey results

The following two tables, Table 5 and Table 6, show the results of the surveys both before the students left Japan and when they returned.

Table 5. Results of Survey 1

	Strongly Agree		Agree		Disagree		Strongly Disagree	
	No.	%	No.	%	No.	%	No.	%
I am anxious about making friends.	9	36	11	44	5	20	0	0
I am anxious about communicating with my host family or roommates.	10	40	13	52	2	8	0	0
I am anxious about finding food that I like.	6	24	11	44	6	24	2	8
I am anxious about finding health care if I get sick.	7	28	16	64	2	8	0	0
I am anxious about being homesick.	6	24	12	48	6	24	1	4

Chapter 8

I am anxious about not understanding the culture of my host country sufficiently.	4	16	12	48	6	24	3	12
I am anxious about having enough money.	3	12	12	48	9	36	1	4
I am anxious about communicating with my classmates.	11	44	12	48	2	8	0	0
I am anxious I will not be able to speak in class.	11	44	12	48	2	8	0	0
I am anxious about the level of my second language reading skills.	7	28	16	64	2	8	0	0
I am anxious about the level of my second language listening skills.	8	32	16	64	1	4	0	0
I am anxious about the level of my second language writing skills.	7	28	16	64	2	8	0	0

Table 6.   Results of Survey 2

	Strongly Agree		Agree		Disagree		Strongly Disagree	
	No.	%	No.	%	No.	%	No.	%
I regret not being more outgoing.	10	47.6	8	38	3	14.3	0	0
I regret not communicating more with my host family or roommates.	9	42.8	9	42.8	3	14.3	0	0
I regret not being more adventurous with food.	2	9.5	8	38	8	38	3	14.3
I regret not learning more about the culture of my host country.	4	19	9	42.8	7	33.3	1	4.8
I regret not traveling enough in my host country.	5	23.8	13	61.9	3	14.3	0	0
I regret not taking more photographs or documenting my experiences.	1	4.8	9	42.8	10	47.6	0	0
I regret spending too much time with other Japanese people.	4	19	12	57.1	5	23.8	0	0
I regret spending too much time thinking about my home country.	2	9.5	10	47.6	8	38	1	4.8
I regret not communicating more with my classmates.	4	19	16	76.2	1	4.8	0	0
I regret not speaking more in class.	5	23.8	15	71.4	1	4.8	0	0

I regret not studying harder in class.	0	0	9	42.8	11	52.4	1	4.8
I regret not doing more home study.	0	0	5	23.8	15	71.4	1	4.8
I regret not joining a club or society.	0	0	11	52.4	10	47.6	0	0

The main point to be taken from Survey 1 is the students' concerns, worries, and fears. When traveling abroad, especially for the first time, for many students everything is new and frightening so the majority of students agreed with all the statements. However, when drawing together the two surveys and linking the fears and regrets then it can be seen that the concerns the students felt before going overseas may have actually become a reality (Table 7).

Table 7. Connected points from surveys 1 and 2

Statement	Agreed to some degree
I am anxious about making friends.	80%
I regret not being more outgoing.	85.6%
I am anxious about communicating with my host family or roommates.	92%
I regret not communicating more with my host family or roommates.	85.6%
I am anxious about not understanding the culture of my host country sufficiently.	64%
I regret not learning more about the culture of my host country.	61.8%
I am anxious about communicating with my classmates.	92%
I regret not communicating more with my classmates.	95.2%
I am anxious I will not be able to speak in class.	92%
I regret not speaking more in class.	95.2%

From examining the table above it would appear that students need assistance in three main areas. Firstly, they need the confidence to meet people and communicate with those around them. Secondly, their English language ability needs to be of a required standard to enable them to communicate with classmates, those they live with, and others they meet. This, of course, is connected to the first point, a higher communicative ability will give the student more confidence. Finally, more knowledge about other cultures would stand them in good stead when going abroad and hopefully inspire them to learn more about their chosen destination before they depart and while they are there.

3.2. The role of VE in improving students' English language ability

Firstly, does VE help improve students' English language ability? A number of studies would suggest this to be the case. Clearly, communicating with others in English in a meaningful way will help improve language ability and the motivation to study (Chen & Yang, 2014). The students who undertake the International VE Project definitely believe this to be true. Hagley and Cotter (2019) surveyed a group of 594 Japanese students and 402 Colombian students, who had completed eight weeks of VE, and found that 81% of the Japanese students thought the exchange was beneficial to learning English, with 90% of the Colombian learners in agreement. In a separate questionnaire completed at the end of an exchange in 2016, Hagley and Harashima (2017) found that 240 out of 272 Japanese students, or 89%, considered the exchange to be beneficial to learning English. In a study conducted in 2017, after surveying 254 Japanese students, who had completed nine weeks of VE, Hagley and Thompson (2017) found that 60% wanted to learn English more because of their experience.

A further point to mention when considering the communication benefits of VE, is that all the students, from all the assorted countries, use English as a lingua franca. The majority of Japanese students who study abroad go into English language programs, generally with other second language learners from across the globe. Each group of second language learners will have their own traits and idiosyncrasies, and it is useful for students to be aware of this, and this knowledge can be gained through VE before a student travels overseas (Guth & Helm, 2012).

3.3. The value of VE in increasing cultural awareness

The second issue to be addressed is if VE raises cultural awareness and the desire to learn more about another country's culture. Guadamillas Gómez (2017) notes that there is a case for this. In her study involving one hundred participants, in equal numbers, from the Faculty of Education at the University of Castilla-La Mancha and the Language Center at Warwick University, she found that students actively participated and highly valued the opportunity to meet and learn from people from a different cultural background. This is backed up by the survey mentioned previously, conducted by Hagley and Cotter (2019), which found that 77% of Japanese respondents and 86% of Colombian students had become more interested in other countries due to VE. Also, Hagley and Thomson (2017) found in their survey that 81% of those questioned wanted to exchange information with students in other countries. VE not only stimulates students to learn more about other cultures but it also creates a desire to share information about their own.

This enhanced wish to learn more about other cultures should lead to students who go abroad spending more time and effort exploring and learning about their host country. This, in turn, will naturally lead to more opportunities to communicate with foreign people, thus improving their knowledge base and language skills. It should also give the students a more fulfilling study abroad experience. During VE, the students talk about their own culture with their partners. This is valuable preparation for when they travel abroad, where they will be asked similar questions, and so will be able to respond in more depth and with greater accuracy. Hopefully, this will lead to their partner replying in kind and so will increase the amount of communication and shared knowledge.

3.4. Building confidence and problem-solving skills with VE

Clearly, the improved language skills and preparation VE would give a student before they travel abroad would improve the student's confidence, and therefore may make him or her more outgoing and communicative. A further advantage of doing VE can be found in the feedback that students gave to Hagley and Harashima in 2017. Students were asked for positive and negative comments about their experiences. Some students reported that their partners sometimes made mistakes and that confusion had been caused by this. Far from being a negative point about VE, this is an overwhelmingly positive point. Firstly, it could reduce the anxiety caused by the possibility of making errors. Students are often held back by the fear of failure. Seeing others make mistakes could help reduce their own unease. Secondly, it will help the students develop toleration for others, and thirdly, and most importantly, it gives the chance for students to build problem-solving skills (Long, 1996). They will have to find strategies to end any confusion that has been caused by the mistake. This is extremely valuable as when they travel overseas there will be many occasions where they are confused or do not understand something.

3.5. The value of VE to assist in cultural acclimatization

When students go overseas, especially for long-term study, almost all suffer from some form of culture shock. There is no real way to define culture shock, as it is different, in terms of symptoms and severity, for each person. After a period of time, the student will generally settle down and become acclimatized to their new surroundings. Hagley and Harashima (2017) suggest that VE gently introduces a new culture to the student, thus avoiding the shock experienced by students who go abroad. Hagley (2016) describes the possibility of students becoming culturally acclimatized by undertaking VE. It is possible that if a student does VE before they travel, thereby opening themselves up to an alien culture and new points of view, the shock they feel when they travel may be reduced. It is highly unlikely that it would be removed altogether, but if the students have started the cultural acclimatization process before they depart for their destination this could help to ease the severity of the experience.

4. Conclusion

Taking the leap to study in a different country is an incredibly brave thing to do. A new culture, a new language, and no familiar faces make it a daunting task. Any assistance students can receive to assuage their fears and help them make the most out of what is generally a wonderful opportunity is very welcome. In VE there is, it appears, a highly effective tool to help the students prepare for their study abroad and give them the skills to thrive in their new environment. Language ability, cultural awareness, and confidence were identified as the areas where students need the most assistance and VE could play a role in all three. The meaningful communication VE provides with those from abroad should motivate students to improve their language skills, and the experience of communicating with other second language learners could prove to be extremely valuable when they travel overseas. Also, the drive it creates to increase cultural sharing not only builds the students' knowledge base but also establishes a genuine reason to communicate. The students' experiences, both positive and negative, during VE provide valuable preparation for their overseas study and mixing with people from other cultures. Traveling overseas to study will never be easy and nothing could completely eradicate the anxiety students feel before they depart, but in VE there is a system which could reduce students' apprehensions and enable them to have a more productive and satisfying study abroad experience.

It would appear that VE could be an extremely useful asset to help students prepare for overseas study, however, in this paper, this is not proven; it is merely a hypothesis. Further study needs to be conducted to assess the validity of this claim. The author is preparing a second study to compare students who have studied abroad without conducting VE in advance to those who have, to try to assess its impact on the study abroad experience. It is hoped that this study will be conducted during 2020-2021 and the results will be available shortly after. In the meantime it is important to remember and understand that anything educators can do to improve the study abroad experience for their students, even if they are unsure of the outcomes, should be done. VE is one method to do this and possibly an extremely valuable one.

5. Acknowledgments

I am very grateful to the students who completed the surveys both before and after their study abroad experience and also to all the scholars and researchers who have built up such a large body of work on VE that I was able to draw upon.

References

Chen, J. J., & Yang, S. C. (2014). Fostering foreign language learning through technology-enhanced intercultural projects. *Language Learning & Technology, 18*(1), 57-75.

Guadamillas Gómez, M. V. (2017). Building global graduates and developing transnational professional skills through a telecollaboration project in foreign language education. In C. Álvarez-Mayo, A. Gallagher-Brett & F. Michel (Eds), *Innovative language teaching and learning at university: enhancing employability* (pp. 49-58). Research-publishing.net. https://doi.org/10.14705/rpnet.2017.innoconf2016.654

Guth, S., & Helm F. (2012) Developing multiliteracies in ELT through telecollaboration. *ELT Journal Volume 66*(1), 42-51. https://doi.org/10.1093/elt/ccr027

Hagley, E. (2016). Making virtual exchange/telecollaboration mainstream – large scale exchanges. In S. Jager, M. Kurek & B. O'Rourke (Eds), *New directions in telecollaborative research and practice: selected papers from the second conference on telecollaboration in higher education* (pp. 225-230). Research-publishing.net. https://doi.org/10.14705/rpnet.2016.telecollab2016.511

Hagley, E., & Cotter, M. (2019). Virtual exchange supporting language and intercultural development: students' perceptions. In F. Meunier, J. Van de Vyver, L. Bradley & S. Thouësny (Eds), *CALL and complexity – short papers from EUROCALL 2019* (pp. 163-168). Research-publishing.net. https://doi.org/10.14705/rpnet.2019.38.1003

Hagley, E., & Harashima, H. (2017). Raising intercultural understanding and skills of EFL students through virtual exchange on Moodle. *Proceedings for the MoodleMoot Japan Annual Conference, 5*, 28-33. http://hdl.handle.net/10258/00009540

Hagley, E., & Thomson, H. (2017). Virtual exchange: providing international communication opportunities for learners of English as a foreign language. *Hokkaido Journal of Language and Culture 15*, 1-10. http://www3.muroran-it.ac.jp/hlc/2017/01.pdf

JASSO. (2019, July 6). *JASSO Outline 2019-2020.* Japan Student Services Organization.

Lee, H. (2018, February 25). *Recent trends in Japanese students studying abroad: welcome news for Canada* [Blog post]. https://www.insidehighered.com/blogs/world-view/recent-trends-japanese-students-studying-abroad-welcome-news-canada

Long, M. (1996). The role of the linguistic environment in second language acquisition. In W. Ritchie & T. Bhatia (Eds), *Handbook of language acquisition, volume 2: second language acquisition.* Academic Press.

MEXT. (2015, September 30). *About Tobitate! (Leap for Tomorrow) Study abroad initiative.* Ministry of Education, Culture, Sports, Science and Technology Japan. https://tobitate.mext.go.jp/about/english.html

9. Improving interactions between teachers and students in virtual exchanges – a case of mentor/learner relationships in MOOCs

Richard Draeger Jr[1] and Steve J. Kulich[2]

Abstract

Shanghai International Studies University has hosted an intercultural Massive Open Online Course (MOOC) course for several years. Course facilitators, mentors, and learners from all over the world are invited to enroll in the class. However, conversations between mentors and learners revealed that most were superficial. Thus, a pilot study was undertaken to improve mentor and learner interactions undertaken. The main focus of the research was to analyze the content of nine sustained conversations in the MOOC. The threads were selected for analysis from the first, third, and final week of the intercultural course. Initial analysis indicated responses made within the same day, and even within the early hours of initial postings, were conducive to sustained conversations. Within the discussion section, several suggestions were given to improve online interactions between mentors and learners. Training and orientation of mentors were suggested. Mentors could be encouraged to use the MOOC's notification system to reply to the learner's comments. With appropriate training, mentors might be able to respond to the learner's comments effectively. In the end, future suggestions for research were given to assess further and improve MOOCs.

---

1. Shanghai International Studies University, School of Economics and Finance, Shanghai, China; dr.draeger79@hotmail.com; https://orcid.org/0000-0002-9241-5335

2. Shanghai International Studies University, Shanghai, China; steve.kulich@gmail.com

How to cite: Draeger, Jr., R., & Kulich, S. J. (2020). Improving interactions between teachers and students in virtual exchanges – a case of mentor/learner relationships in MOOCs. In E. Hagley & Y. Wang (Eds), *Virtual exchange in the Asia-Pacific: research and practice* (pp. 179-199). Research-publishing.net. https://doi.org/10.14705/rpnet.2020.47.1152

Chapter 9

Keywords: intercultural learning, MOOC, mentor, learner, social media.

1. Background

1.1. Introduction to and evolution of online learning

Blackboard, a pioneering online learning platform released in 1997, brought innovations to education (Cole et al., 2017). Historically, instructors used it or other learning management systems to complement traditional in-class lectures (Balula & Moreira, 2014). Sustained interaction between instructors and learners is missing in most online learning platforms. The lack of synchronous communication is also lacking in most MOOCs.

Universities' use of MOOCs has further changed the teaching profession. Instructors can open courses literally to a worldwide audience. MOOCs, however, can have a double personality (e.g. Littlejohn & Hood, 2018). On the one hand, they provide excellent opportunities for intercultural, even global, communication and engagement in virtual learning environments. On the other hand, MOOCs may serve as just another form of social media such as Facebook, WeChat, or LinkedIn. They can claim to attract large enrollments of learners, deliver content to many nations, and provide statistics on numbers of chat comments. But, unless facilitators and mentors are actively engaged, learners may miss out on both perceived and real learning benefits. Intercultural theory – and evidence from an intercultural MOOC – might help assess this issue of what is the role of the mentor in a mentor-learner relationship, and how can interactions and facilitating learning online be improved? This paper provides an analysis of such a case.

1.2. Communication accommodation theory

One of the most widely used intercultural theories has been the transformation of what was first called speech accommodation theory to Communication

Accommodation Theory (CAT) (e.g. Giles, 2016; Giles, Mulac, Bradac, & Johnson, 1987; Zhang, Imamura, & Weng, 2017). Initially, CAT was used to analyze interactions between law enforcement and civilians as well as medical workers and patients (Giles, 2016; Giles et al., 1987). Scholars investigated elements such as word usage and pronunciation between dyads and how those influenced the outcomes of interpersonal interactions. In the case of police officers' and civilians' encounters, conversational patterns were examined to see what led to the use of force, when it happened, and why. Regarding patients and medical workers, exchanges were analyzed to assess the discussion of the treatment of diseases as well as patient satisfaction (Giles, 2016). From these studies, practices and outcomes related to invoking closeness or distance were noted.

Convergence and divergence are the two main tenets of CAT (see Zhang et al., 2017, p. 173). Dyads that seek to close social distance may use inclusive language or questions accompanied with attentive listening skills. Interlocutors who seek to maintain or expand social distance might use rebukes, sarcasm, ridicule, or other disparaging remarks. Within these two dimensions, there are several subcomponents that include accommodation, over accommodation, under accommodation, or no accommodation.

At present, CAT, along with its main tenets and subcomponents, continues to evolve beyond analyzing interlocutors' pronunciation and word usage. An example comes from the first author's dissertation project (Draeger, 2017) that examined foreign experts' teaching beliefs regarding Intercultural Communicative Competence (ICC) and classroom interactions. In that project, CAT was used to analyze how instructors introduced and carried out learning activities during class time. The author specifically assessed whether teachers' classroom interactions supported students' development of ICC. The results indicated that teachers who engaged in creating and delivering learning activities both supported and enhanced students' development of ICC. As a follow up to that study in a different domain, this case study examines the following research question: what is the status of mentor and learner interactions in MOOC courses?

Chapter 9

2. Case study

2.1. Participants

Data collection consisted of retrieving transcripts of conversational threads from an intercultural MOOC course. The class in question has been open to a global audience two times during each academic year since 2015. The fall run is generally from October to November and the spring run begins in March and concludes in April. At the time of writing, transcripts from the fall run of 2019 were available and used for this case study.

The intercultural MOOC run number nine was sponsored by a research university in Shanghai. Faculty, or course leaders, are responsible for creating course content and recruitment of mentors. Postgraduate students and faculty of the research university serve as facilitators, or mentors; both designations are used to reduce redundancy within the report.

2.2. Context for study

People are living more-and-more online in the 21st Century and many are engaging in online learning portals. The challenge though, for instructors and learners in such online courses, is to avoid being inundated with the noise that permeates much of the Internet. The noise of the Internet contains the images and sounds that bombard the average user. Individuals involved with MOOCs who are distracted by the 'noise' of the Internet may lose out on opportunities for learning. In order to improve future runs of the intercultural MOOC, this case study was conducted. The goal of this case study is to analyze a sample of prolonged conversations between facilitators and learners within the selected intercultural MOOC.

Individuals can now access the Internet from a myriad of devices such as laptop computers or smartphones. Most application developers create programs that can be used across most devices. With the touch of a button or swipe of a screen,

Internet users can easily get diverted to some other online offering. In the case of MOOCs, gains from learning can be lost or diluted due to the abundance of information that is available on other sites.

In the case of MOOC participants, courses are also now accessed by a variety of devices. This means that mentors must also deal with challenges inherent in using the Internet. It is then incumbent that instructors' comments be analyzed to determine if their comments encourage and help keep the focus of the learner or seem unengaged and thus distract or hinder intercultural learning within the enrolled MOOC community. Another factor studied is the participant to facilitator ratio; obviously, mentor numbers are outweighed by participants but what is an ideal ratio? If a reasonable ratio is not attained, it could mean that facilitators who even regularly log in to the course may be inundated by comments and not know where to begin.

In a traditional classroom setting, interactions are usually synchronous. Questions are asked and answered in real-time. Likewise, elements of immediacy and class time management are present and influence teacher and student exchanges. In such cases, pressures of class time can negatively influence an instructor's responses with learners and vice versa. When class is concluded, learners' needs for learning new content or clearing up misunderstands may not have been met. This has implications for the teacher and student relationship as well as the learner's perceived benefit and view of the class in question.

2.3. Data collection and analysis

The intercultural MOOC selected for this study ran for five weeks and was offered in the autumn semesters. Each week contains an overall theme and several sub-themes. The module for Week 1 was 'comprehending intercultural communication'; Week 2 is 'contextualizing cultural identities'; Week 3 was 'comparing cultural communication styles'; Week 4 is 'clarifying and contrasting values'; and Week 5 was 'cultivating intercultural adaptation'. The analysis for this study was comprised of three subsequent steps.

The first was the selection of Weeks 1, 3, and 5 for analysis due to beginning, mid, and final sample potential. The second was the selection of conversations where both learners and mentors were involved. The third step was to employ a mixed-method design, on a small scale, to analyze interactions within the MOOC. Quantitatively, time stamps were used to assess the timeliness (promptness) of comments and responses. Qualitatively, the words and ideas expressed were coded and analyzed using CAT for guidance.

2.4. Protection of identities

The primary approach to data collection was convenience sampling within the course. The second author, as a course facilitator, granted permission to the first author, to download discussions from the autumn semester run of the intercultural MOOC (ninth run historically). The next step taken to protect the identities of both facilitators and learners was to remove their online identity and replace them with 'learner' and 'mentor' or 'facilitator' designations.

2.5. Data analysis

This section provides case examples from the sample collected. After the presentation of virtual interactions conducted online, analysis will follow. Mentor and learner comments are kept as they were posted for authenticity (grammar, punctuation, or vocabulary errors are not corrected).

2.5.1. Conversation #1

> "hello, I am from Italy, I a lot to study cultural and social anthropology and languages. I am always been interested at these matters. I think that intercultural communication can be part of the holistic studies of anthropology because I think goes to study cultures but in a globalized way" (Learner, 19 October).

> "Hi _____, welcome here! You have very intuitive hunch and major studies in the IC field did begin from anthropology, notably Edward T.

Hall and his study of non-verbal communication. We look forward to more of your insights!" (Mentor, 19 October).

"thank you" (Learner, 19 October).

This was an exchange based upon intercultural theory, e.g. Edward T. Hall's contributions. The learner shared a bit of her background and awareness in mentioning an academic relationship between intercultural communication and anthropology. The mentor commended the learner for being intuitive while mentioning Hall's name in her reply to add some content to the discussion.

This would be an example of accommodation in several ways. The reply by the facilitator mentioned extremely specific items in the initial comment. Then the instructor referenced a connection between anthropology and intercultural communication. The final is an invitation to the learner to contribute more of her thoughts to the course.

2.5.2. Conversation #2

" افات في العالم كثيرة ومتعددة ومن المهم التواصل والتعارف بين الثقافات "
(Learner, 19 October)

"Hi _____! Though I don't have the literacy to read your language, I know you are saying about the importance of knowing and communicating with other culture. I think express our own identity is important for this learning platform, and your language would make us more diverse and bring some new perspectives. But if you feel doing so, sharing your ideas in English would help more people to understand you and interact with you!" (Mentor, 19 October).

The learner shared a greeting in Arabic. The instructor freely admitted a lack of knowledge concerning the language used, which maintained social distance. However, the learner was greeted by name (username posted with their initial comment) and commended them for contributing a new perspective to

Chapter 9

intercultural communication but also asked if they might use English. This would be an example of accommodation in that new ideas were acknowledged, and a gentle encouragement was made to use the common language of the course.

The mentor was quick to respond on the same day as the initial comment. She also mentions how cultural identities could enrich discussions within the MOOC. The final component of the interaction is an encouragement to the learner to leverage both linguistic and cultural identities so more people could join in the conversations.

2.5.3. Conversation #3

> "Hola! Namasty sabhi ko.i am here to make myself strong in speaking skills.i am very weak in communication orally.and for my dream jobs it is must to communicate and mix up with your coworkers easily and effectively as they can be from different regions.so, i want to make myself more interactive because i am not even expressive with my best friend.so, i just want to improve this and prepare for my dream and want to live that dream. Tips are welcome if any to improve my oral speaking,specially in English. Happy to be here. Thankyou" (Learner, 19 October).

> "Thank you for your sharing about yourself and welcome to the course! It resonates with me and many Chinese students also feel frustrated with their spoken English in part because of their personality. However, I believe that having the willingness to communicate is a good start, right?" (Mentor, 19 October).

> "Yes, thanks" (Learner, 19 October).

The learner mentioned personal linguistic weaknesses and hopes for the course. Specifically, the learner hoped to improve and strengthen general communication skills and to make friends in this course. The facilitator welcomed the learner to the course and established a connection by sharing her own observations of struggles with oral English. The instructor continued her idea in an inclusive way, by including her Chinese classmates. The facilitator commented on the same day as well and concluded with a question to the learner's greeting. Perhaps this is why the learner replied, a couple of days later.

Questions are excellent means of continuing virtual discussions. The content of the response is also rich with inclusive language, especially with the use of 'believe'. The use of 'believe' or 'feel' or 'think' could be used to invite others to virtual conversations. When used effectively, as above, many learners might respond to them.

2.5.4. Conversation #4

> "I have quite an intercultural background but recently I feel I don't really know much about other cultures. I grew up in the US because my mother started working there after she finished her masters, and I met lots of people from Mexico, Spain, Philippines, Japan… I also went to the UK as an exchange student. I have a pen pal in Australia, my sister lives in Italy, and I also have other relatives living all over the world. But recently I met an international exchange student from Turkey, and I found out that I knew nothing about his language or culture. And so, when he told me his language was 'agglutination language' so that it was hard for him to study Chinese, I couldn't really understand him, and I felt so sorry for that. So, I really hope to learn more about other cultures, and most importantly, learn about how to communicate when you meet someone from a culture that you know nothing about. Look forward to the next few weeks of learning!" (Learner 1, 15 October).

> "Hi ＿＿＿! So nice to meet you here! I think your intercultural background will help you better understand this course! And I am sure you can learn something about how to deal with people from a culture you never know" (Mentor, 15 October).

Chapter 9

"Hello, _____ ! I really admire your experiences of different cultures. And I think you have more opportunities than average people to approach various cultures in the world, and it will be amazing to learn something about them from people of those cultures" (Learner 2, 15 October).

"@_____ Yes! I have lots of opportunities to learn about different cultures from people with totally different backgrounds around me, and I feel so lucky about it. Making friends with them allows me to know some differences that we thought would have been the same among different cultures, which actually turned out to be different, and that was something really interesting. But it's strange that every time I meet someone from a new culture, I assume that they would share lots of similarities with countries nearby, even when I know how many differences there are between Chinese and Japanese culture!" (Learner 1, 15 october).

This is a detailed exchange for several reasons. The original Learner 1 talked in-depth about their personal and professional life. Specifically, the learner mentioned his sojourns throughout the world. The learner talked about previous discussions and then ended his comment with hopes for the course.

The comment made by the mentor was brief. The welcome was forthcoming and warm. However, the facilitator's comments on the background of the speaker established no personal or professional connection, compared with previous comments. The comment concluded with a thought concerning one of the course goals, interacting with culturally heterogeneous people (but could be construed as impersonal). What is enlightening is that the quote was made on the same day. What is fascinating about this thread is that an in-depth reply was made by another learner (Learner 2) to the original post. Also, the use of the @ symbol, which is seen in subsequent threads, might be indicative of convergence in virtual conversation (Learner 2 specifically references Learner 1). This is a type of dialogue which could enhance learning in the MOOC as it conveys interpersonal convergence.

2.5.5. Conversation #5

"After finishing the test, a question come to my mind: How can we start a conversation with people from different cultural backgrounds without making them embarrassed or feel offended? Sometimes we often get misunderstood by using improper words. For example, 'have a word with sb' is totally different from 'have words with sb'. It will be rather embarrassing if we use them wrongly. Moreover, we may also make mistakes in using some gestures that have different meanings in different cultures. So, I am eager to know how we can do better to get on well with people from different cultural backgrounds. Yes. Sometimes we may run into a confusion when having an intercultural communication. What we should do is to learn more about different cultures and values so as to avoid embarrassment and misunderstanding" (Learner A, 14 October).

"@_____ I very much agree with you! As someone born and raised in the Chinese culture, even I could sometimes find it hard to read other Chinese people's mind because of differences in our background. Where I come from, a considerable proportion of the population are Hui and Tibetan, and because of decades of inter-ethnic influence, the way I look often makes people mistake me as an ethnic minority – in fact I am Han Chinese. You are right about non-verbal communication – people's outlook, dialect, and body language sometimes communicate more about what others think who they are, but not necessarily who they truly are. This is also why knowledge of intercultural communication is necessary for us to know each other better. :)" (Mentor, 14 October).

The exchange by the learner and mentor is interesting on several levels. The learner largely described hypothetical interactions but made no mention of personal experience. However, the learner used inclusive language in the post (e.g. the use of 'we'). The quote ended with some great ideas suggesting that learning about other cultures could reduce misunderstandings.

The facilitator replies with, "I very much agree with you" which may not be conducive to prolonged conversation in a MOOC course. It is interesting to note that "agree with you..." was seen quite a bit in the following threads. The mentor shared personal background while interacting with the learner. Specifically, she references difficulties in relating to individuals in her own culture. She mentioned that ethnic minorities live in her hometown and that physiologically, she blends in with them but admits that she is Han Chinese. This would be a good example of convergence in that the mentor is using personal experiences to compliment the learner's initial comments. Also, this exchange took place on the same day.

> "@____ [to Learner A above] If I want to start a conversation with foreigners just for chatting with them, I would firstly use the most common greeting words: hi/hello with a big sweet smile to show my friendliness. And then, through his/her reaction to detect whether it is appropriate to start a casual conversation. If it is necessary to inquire them, 'Excuse me?' is quite ok. As for gestures, it is quite complex as different countries have their own set of gestures with different meanings. I do appreciate if this course could have a complete summary of gestures in different countries" (Learner B, 14 October).

This illustrates a great exchange on the same thread. The original comment by Learner A expressed a general sentiment at first. The mentor expanded those ideas through sharing personal experiences. This second Learner B offered some practical advice as this thread was continued. Overall, sustained interactions such as these tend to facilitate engagement and intercultural learning in a MOOC class. The above remark also began with the use of @ and the initial speaker's name. The remark was also made on the same day of the initial thread. Exchanges between multiple individuals are remarkable in that they can provide both personal anecdotes and even practical advice.

2.5.6. Conversation #6

> "I think each one of us is the intersection point of several cultural sets

creating our own 'set', now the objective is to know how to adapt to all those different sets pr packages we will encounter in life, and help others how to do it" (Learner A, 15 October).

"@_____ Good point about our own cultural 'set'! In IC we'd see this set as a box of identities a person holds. Sometimes these identities were very much determined even before we were born, sometimes they are very situational. Learning what identities you want to bring out and how is an on-going process of shaping intercultural communication. Good to see you here too" (Mentor, 15 October).

"@_____ I quite agree with you that our own cultural set is created based on several cultural sets from our family, our schools, the society and many other groups at different levels that we belong to. And sometimes we may not realize how those cultural sets have influenced us. So, I'd like to learn more about how I have become I, and what I might be in the future, influenced by the various cultural sets around me" (Learner B, 15 October).

"I cannot agree with you more. The culture one lives in exerts an invisible influence on one's character, value, and baheviour, etc. On the other hand, one's character and behavior can reveal his or her culture. For example, I am a Hui girl, and my culture has decided that I can not eat pork, and people who know I do not eat pork will naturally think of I am a Hui" (Learner C, 15 October).

Initially, Learner A remarked how overlapping cultural personalities could influence interactions. The mentor concurs and then expounds on it by briefly mentioning intercultural theory. However, the instructor does not introduce any specific theory by name. So, this response might be an example of under accommodation due to that fact. However, Learner B described hypothetical variables which may impact the cultural heritage which people ascribe to. The final comment by Learner C expressed an exact idea concerning Hui identity and the consumption of pork, which is prohibited to practitioners of Islam.

Chapter 9

Within this conversation thread is an acknowledgment of culture's influence on societies and people. Learners and facilitators are sharing multiple ideas about culture as well. Interculturally, this conversation is rich with examples and suggestions both personal and practical.

2.5.7. Conversation #7

> "I grew up in a quite protected environment, not sharing much with people from different status. When I started working at the age of 20, I was surprised with people who had nothing to do with what I've always knew. It was quite shocking. Over the years, fortunately, this has changed, and I've met people from different countries, cultures, and background, both at home and abroad" (Learner B, 15 October).

> "Insightful! Would be great if you could share one of your shocking experiences and how you overcame it so we can discuss further" (Mentor, 15 October).

> "Thank you _____. I grew up in an environment where good manners were highly important and where you had to repect others and give them their space and be helpful in all you could. What I found was people being overfamiliar although they had just met you and knew nothing about you. I think they tried to be friendly, but I felt uncomfortable. They also made differences between new arrivals and people working in the company for many years. So, it was a contradiction. I learned that sometimes people, in work environments, see new colleagues as a threat" (Learner B, 18 October).

This is an example of a prolonged conversation. The learner revealed both personal and professional experiences. The facilitator encouraged the student to share some of those experiences with the MOOC audience. The student replied by sharing personal and professional experiences a couple days later. This could be an example of accommodation on two accounts. The first is that while brief, the mentor invites the learner to share more. The second is that the student reciprocated and shared a few more thoughts, even though several days later (one feature of the course is that when anyone replies, an email is sent noting 'you have received a reply in the course' with an activity link for them to follow up on the comment).

The conversation was revealing on several accounts. The student compared and contrasted work and home cultures, which were in the same geographic region. However, there was not much follow up by the facilitator or other learners.

2.5.8. Conversation #8

"1. Chinese culture is a typical high-context culture. 2. To those who we have good relationship with, we will be higher context, as we have formed our code through long relationship, which means we can easily understand each other without saying directly. But low context culture is when it comes to negotiation. In negotiation, every term, price, time, and other clauses need to be specified and can not be changed so that the contract is biding on both parties. 3. I think we should shift our communication style correspondently when the context changes between private context and public context" (Learner, 31 October).

"I totally agree with you! We need to choose our communication style according to the context we are in" (Mentor, 31 October).

The trend beginning in Week 3 is the brief and delayed responses from mentors. In this conversation thread and continuing, many replied, 'totally agree with you'. To this end, many of the conversations were not sustained. The hosting website provided users with the option to 'like' comments. On the surface, the utterance, "agree with..." or liking a comment may express those emotions. The use of either is good, when backed up with substantial comments or thoughts. With the large number of learners commenting as the course grew, mentors may have been overwhelmed in keeping up and made shorter replies over time.

Chapter 9

2.5.9. Conversation #9

"I've lived in six different countries and traveled to more than 60 so far" (Learner, 18 October).

"Hello, _____! Nice to meet you here, and your experiences are really fantastic. If possible, could you please share your adaptation experiences when you are in these countries? Many thanks!" (Mentor, 11 November).

"@_____ Your life experience is colorful, I think" (Learner 2, 11 November).

There were several examples of divergence in this thread. The learner disclosed how many countries he had been to. The mentor's replies, while interesting, were quite delayed. Also, there does not seem to be any in-depth responses, either objective or subjective, to facilitate prolonged discussion. In previous examples, responses made quickly by the facilitators were likely to receive a response. Another reason for lack of interaction is the nature of the MOOC course as enrollees had access to a course for five weeks and comments and replies were increasingly spread out or spread thin. Either a larger mentor team is needed to sustain support for the course, or more time needs to be devoted to keep up the quality of replies in a timely fashion.

3. Discussion

3.1. Overall summary of this case study

Mentors' initial comments were present in large numbers in the first week and in the early part of the third week. During those times, replies to learners' comments were made on the same day. The theme of Week 1 was comprehending intercultural communication. Students and mentors made introductory comments and extended warm greetings to one another. Self-introductions and greetings made in the first week can be harnessed for conversations in later weeks. The theme of Week 3 was comparing cultural communication styles. Within the module of Week 3, people from North America, Asia, and other continents can share their perspectives and experiences of interpersonal conversational styles where they live. Regrettably, in Week 3, responses by mentors begin to fall off. Week 5's theme is cultivating intercultural adaptation. The content of Week 5 presents learners with an application to practice what they have learned regarding intercultural communication. However, mentors' responses to students' were far fewer in this module than in other modules. Mentors' replies were posted infrequently; some were a day or two delayed. In other cases, responses were posted a month late.

Considering the deficiencies, there are encouraging findings. When learners shared work or private experiences, mentors also shared their personal experiences. Regarding convergence, even intercultural convergence, this is valuable as it permits dyads to compare their respective experiences. When interactants discover similarities and differences, then intercultural learning can begin. Most of the modules included intercultural dimensions that provided students an opportunity to begin conversations. The key issue is how to continue conversations that allow learners and mentors to discover more about their respective cultures. An example would be Conversation 6, where course participants had a healthy discussion about dietary practices and taboos in Islamic culture. Another issue is how to promote in-depth discussions which last throughout the five-week course. The first step might be a modification of the recruitment and training of facilitators.

3.2. Rich intercultural communication

Intercultural MOOCs present many benefits. Firstly, the MOOC which was analyzed was offered free of charge to interested individuals for seven weeks from time of enrollment (adequate time to finish the five weeks of content). Learners could view brief lectures, created by the course leaders, to learn about general intercultural theory and ideas. Students could also do so at a time convenient to them as well in any time zone worldwide (such that comments could appear all over the 24-hour range). Essentially, course leaders and facilitators provided learners an opportunity for intercultural growth.

Learners shared personal, work, and cross-cultural experiences through virtual discussion in the course. The course in question is made available in China, the UK, the United States, and countries throughout the world (there were 2,709 enrollments from over 120 countries and regions in the run examined for this case study). To this end, facilitators, mentors, and learners could communicate internationally.

Considering opportunities for intercultural growth, a question needs to be asked: what is needed to promote and sustain deep online conversation? The best exchanges happened on the same day or relatively close time sequences. There are examples above between learners and facilitators that were occasionally joined in by other students in the same conversation threads; these present an opportunity for virtual convergence, so to speak (in the course, it is designated as social learning: 407 individuals engaged in these multiple learner threads throughout the course=20.7%). Only 72.6% of those who enrolled even started the course (1,967 'learners', which is good for this run as some courses only get 40-50% of those who enroll to start a few steps), and of those only 49.4% engaged with portions of the content (972 'active learners'). In previous runs where mentor activity was notably high, those percentages were increased to 78-80% started and 55-75% active (getting 25-38% engaged in 'social learning').

3.3. Leveraging MOOC technological features

One of the obstacles to intercultural learning and communication is the 'noise' of the Internet. The noise of the Internet contains the images and sounds that bombard the average user. Facebook, Twitter, Tiktok, and others provide notifications in a variety of ways, but users may ignore them. This means that technological innovations are often needed to attract users' attention.

The intercultural MOOC provides learners and mentors with directed notifications. Information provided in these prompts include the name of a course participant who has replied to a specific comment. Mentors who quickly respond to notifications can stimulate continuous virtual interactions with and between learners. However, there are other technological features which may inhibit in-depth cross-cultural exchanges.

Mentors and learners may respond to a message with a 'like' by tapping on the available button. However, it seems that this option has the same effect that 'I agree' has. The overuse of 'like' or 'I agree' may hinder in-depth and critical discussion, which is also needed in virtual cross-cultural communication.

4. Pedagogical principles

4.1. Recruitment and training of mentors

Course leaders' traditional mentor recruitment involved posting invitations to social media group chats to graduate students (MAs and PhDs) who had been trained in the course contents (in this case, intercultural communication majors). Volunteers are then given the opportunity to serve as mentors, but there is minimal training. The primary training tool is a mentoring PowerPoint that compiles some key lessons and experiences from previous online course offerings.

Once the course begins, there is flexibility for both instructors and mentors as to how often they log in, though responsibility for each week is assigned to three to four mentors with encouragement to respond to as many learners as possible. But there are clearly variances in activity and response levels among mentors. Considering this problem, systematic training could be implemented, so mentors can successfully promote intercultural learning.

4.2. Method of training

Course leaders could use offline meetings or Internet applications such as Zoom or Skype to recruit and train volunteers before the MOOC opens (Laverick, 2016). Initial meetings could be devoted to virtual team building endeavors and providing advice to mentors. Veteran facilitators and course leaders could advise new volunteers on how to leverage available technology. Likewise, facilitators could share ideas on how to promote sustained virtual conversations in the MOOC. With the proper training, mentors can promote convergence in virtual conversation within MOOC. Firstly, facilitators can begin by thoughtfully responding to learners' comments as is seen above in the analysis section of this chapter. Secondly, learners who share a bit more of their background might encourage other learners and facilitators to join conversational threads (Conversation 6). Thirdly, when many mentors and learners join in on a virtual thread, there is a possibility for rich intercultural conversation.

5. Conclusion

As this case study has shown, employing principles from CAT, meaningful intercultural interactions can happen in MOOCs. As described above in the introduction, learners from all over the world enrolled in the intercultural MOOC. Convergence happened when people compared their life experiences as well as their cultural identities. Conversations 4 and 6, from the analysis section, are needed so intercultural MOOCs can flourish.

Covid-19 is altering the delivery of instruction all over the world. As a result, individuals are more actively enrolling in MOOCs for educational and social purposes. Because of this, the growing need for mindfulness in recruiting and training of mentors for MOOCs will increase. As course leaders and veterans provide more targeted guidance to novice mentors, the level and quality of engagement of online interaction can keep improving to help fulfill the unique role that MOOCs now play in the educational landscape.

References

Balula, A., & Moreira, A. (2014). *Evaluation of online higher education: learning, interaction, and technology*. Springer Briefs in Education.

Cole, A. W., Anderson, C., Bunton, T. E., Cherney, M. R., Cronin Fisher, V., Draeger Jr., R., Fetherston, M., Motel, L., Nicolini, K. M., Peck, B., & Allen, M. (2017). Student predisposition to instructor feedback and perceptions of teaching presence predict motivation toward online courses. *Online Learning, 21*(4), 245-262. https://doi.org/10.24059/olj.v21i4.966

Draeger, Jr., R. (2017). *Non-native foreign language instructors' teaching expectations concerning intercultural communication competence: communicative practices in the classroom.* PhD Dissertation. University of Wisconsin Milwaukee [ProQuest Dissertations & Thesis Global (10621382)].

Giles, H. (2016). *Communication accommodation theory: negotiating personal relationships and social identities across contexts.* Cambridge University Press. https://doi.org/10.1017/cbo9781316226537

Giles, H., Mulac, A., Bradac, J., & Johnson, P. (1987). Speech accommodation theory: the first decade and beyond. *Annals of the International Communication Association, 10*(1), 13-48. https://doi.org/10.1080/23808985.1987.11678638

Laverick, D. M. (2016). *Mentoring processes in higher education.* Springer Briefs in Education.

Littlejohn, A., & Hood, N. (2018). *Reconceptualising learning in the digital age; the [un]democratizing poteintial of MOOCS.* Open and Distance Education Series/Springer Briefs in Education.

Zhang, Y. B., Imamura, M., & Weng, L. P. (2017). Communication accommodation theory and intercultural communication: interpersonal and intergroup perspectives. In S. J. Kulich & A. S. English (Eds), *China intercultural communication annual* (vol. 2, pp. 168-188). China Social Sciences Publishing House.

10. Project Ibunka – a web-based virtual exchange project

Masahito Watanabe[1]

Abstract

Since 2000, I have been coordinating a web based virtual exchange project, Project Ibunka. Ibunka means different cultures in Japanese. It aims to provide opportunities of authentic interaction among EFL/ESL learners all over the world. The project has been giving English language learners from various countries opportunities to use English for authentic purposes and promote intercultural understanding. Since 2000, more than 6,000 students from 22 countries have joined the project. The long life, the regularly appearing cooperative partner teachers, the diversity of students' cultures, and the high quality of the messages exchanged, are the assets of Project Ibunka. This paper, as a case study of virtual exchange, overviews the background and the project constitution as a whole. It also analyzes the project management and students' written products. The three administrative features, (1) non-unified project goals for partner institutions, (2) selecting and sequencing themes and sub-themes, and (3) moderation by experienced instructors, have contributed to students' quantitative fluency as well as their qualitative improvement.

Keywords: virtual exchange, writing, moderation, bulletin board, theme-setting.

---

1. Yokohama University, Yokohama, Japan; wata33@gmail.com; https://orcid.org/0000-0003-0792-7158

How to cite: Watanabe, M. (2020). Project Ibunka – a web-based virtual exchange project. In E. Hagley & Y. Wang (Eds), *Virtual exchange in the Asia-Pacific: research and practice* (pp. 201-230). Research-publishing.net. https://doi.org/10.14705/rpnet.2020.47.1153

Chapter 10

1. Background

The launch of *Project Ibunka* – a web-based, 12 week long, Virtual Exchange (VE) project among English speaking learners from all over the world – dates back to 2000. Thus, the year 2020 marks its 20th anniversary. *Ibunka* means *different cultures* in Japanese. The project has been giving English language learners from various countries opportunities to use English for authentic purposes and promote intercultural understanding. Since 2000, more than 6,000 students from 22 countries have joined the project.

As a Japanese English language teacher, I have been considering how I can make my English essay writing courses more authentic. In Japan, students' essays are addressed mainly for their teachers, not for readers. *Sharing* is the key to changing English writing learning and teaching styles. If students can share their written messages among themselves, they may start to write more for communication. Even before the popularization of the *Internet*, teachers had strived to make sharing of students' writing in their classes. From the late 1990's, online activities began to transform educational sharing fundamentally. It also started to attract many language teachers.

In 1996, I started to use Local Area Network (LAN) connected computer labs to ensure my students could share their work. The system offered two types of folders for sharing: a *course folder* and a *report box*.

For *course folders*, teachers had [+ write + read] permission, whereas students had [- write + read] permission. In such folders, teachers could save/upload and view/download the documents stored. On the other hand, students could only view/download them. Students could not save/upload anything. For *report boxes*, students had [+ write - read] permission, whereas teachers had [- write + read] permission. Students could only save/upload their reports into this folder, but they could not view/download any reports stored there. On the other hand, teachers could view/download the documents, while they could not save/upload anything. When teachers moved/copied students' reports stored in a *report box* into a *course folder*, they could share their classmates' written products.

In 1997, I compiled a Microsoft Windows application that worked on LAN network drives using Microsoft Visual Basic version 4. This application converted students' text strings into HTML documents and connected them by hyperlinks. Since the local network, i.e. the *intranet* confined the sharing, no one could access the messages from outside of the institution. The *Internet* users around the globe could not read them[2].

In 1998, I opened several free email accounts[3] and shared the user-ids and passwords among university students from Japan and Canada. Based on the suggestions by Warschauer (1995), I posted a call for participation message onto *TESL-L*, an international mailing list for language teachers, and I also found my partner institutions. I organized a group discussion among students. Warschauer (1995) suggested, "instead of pairing each student from your class with just one member of another class, pair each person with three to five partners" (p. 49). "The lack of response issues" (Warschauer, 1995, p. 49) that might often occur in paired interaction could be avoided in this type of group discussion. Students were divided into six groups, and each group had both Japanese and Canadian students. One group shared one email account. Members of the same group checked emails sent to this account by their international peers and wrote their replies in emails. Interactions among students were not confined locally anymore. This was my first experience of VE.

In 1999, I coded a Web Bulletin Board (WBB) system using Microsoft Active Server Pages technology, a server-side scripting language. Students from four countries, Uganda, Israel, Germany, and Japan, joined the project. WBB aimed to convert an *intranet*-based LAN application of 1997 into an *Internet*-based one. The discussion was group-based as in the project of 1998.

Although this four-year period, i.e. 1996-1999, was quite short, Internet technology had transformed an institutionally confined intranet-based sharing system into an internationally opened sharing one. However, the organization

---

2. Refer to Watanabe (1998) for the details of this intranet application.
3. I used Yahoo! Mail, which started in 1997.

of the project during this period was rather primitive. Although the lack of response issue could be avoided using the group-based discussion, just letting students work on the online bulletin boards meant they only focused on casual chatting, paid little attention to instructor's directions, and did not take up more challenging topics. We needed to incorporate the following three additional features to reform this:

- non-unified project goals for partner institutions;
- selecting and sequencing themes and sub-themes; and
- moderation by experienced instructors.

These features have become key in *Project Ibunka* since then.

2. Case study

2.1. Participants

Table 1, Table 2, and Table 3 show overviews of the participation in past projects. For the last 19 years, students from 22 different countries have joined the project. They are Argentina, Australia, Brazil, Burkina Faso, China, Denmark, Finland, Germany, Indonesia, Italy, Japan, Kazakhstan, Mexico, Namibia, Poland, Russia, South Korea, Taiwan, the Netherlands, the US, UAE, and the UK. On average, about 350 students from six countries participate in the project every year. Although most of them are university students studying English as a Foreign Language (EFL), we can also see high school students from both EFL and native English speaking countries. The diversity of students' cultural backgrounds is one of the assets of *Project Ibunka*.

We have a few institutions that join the project almost every year. Students from Indonesia, South Korea, and Taiwan are regular visitors. *Project Ibunka* owes a lot to these regular partner teachers' dedication and enthusiasm. They are another asset of *Project Ibunka* and have contributed to the long life of the project.

Table 1. Countries

Years	Countries
2000	4: Australia, Germany, UK, and Japan
2001	6: China, Germany, Finland, South Korea, Taiwan, and Japan
2002	5: Mexico, South Korea, Taiwan, US, and Japan
2003	5: China, Burkina Faso, South Korea, Taiwan, US, and Japan
2004	7: Burkina Faso, Indonesia, Mexico, Namibia, South Korea, Taiwan, and Japan
2005	9: Brazil, Burkina Faso, Indonesia, Mexico, Namibia, South Korea, Taiwan, UAE, and Japan
2006	9: Burkina Faso, China, Indonesia, Kazakhstan, South Korea, Taiwan, UAE, US, and Japan
2007	8: Argentina, Burkina Faso, Indonesia, Namibia, South Korea, Taiwan, US, and Japan
2008	8: Burkina Faso, Denmark, Indonesia, South Korea, Taiwan, UAE, US, and Japan
2009	7: Burkina Faso, Denmark, Russia, Indonesia, Taiwan, US, and Japan
2010	4: Indonesia, South Korea, Taiwan, and Japan
2011	6: Indonesia, Poland, Russia, South Korea, Taiwan, and Japan
2012	7: Denmark, Indonesia, Poland, Russia, South Korea, Taiwan, and Japan
2013	5: Poland, Russia, Indonesia, Taiwan, and Japan
2014	7: Poland, Russia, Indonesia, Italy, South Korea, Taiwan, and Japan
2015	4: Indonesia, Italy, Taiwan, and Japan
2016	8: Brazil, Indonesia, Italy, the Netherlands, Poland, South Korea, Taiwan, and Japan
2017	5: China, Indonesia, the Netherlands, Taiwan, and Japan
2018	6: Brazil, Germany, Indonesia, South Korea, Taiwan, and Japan

Table 2. Students and postings

Years	Participants	Postings
2000	109	777
2001	240	835
2002	252	1,317
2003	392	1,405
2004	344	1,582
2005	386	1,778
2006	301	1,367
2007	459	2,100
2008	730	3,662
2009	1,058	5,073

Chapter 10

2010	242	1,272
2011	367	1,958
2012	255	1,651
2013	140	906
2014	377	1,970
2015	229	1,200
2016	275	1,333
2017	268	1,042
2018	204	1,283
Total	**6,628**	**32,511**

Table 3. Frequency distribution of partner countries

Countries	Times of participation
Argentina	1
Australia	1
Brazil	3
Burkina Faso	7
China	4
Denmark	3
Finland	1
Germany	3
Indonesia	15
Italy	3
Japan	19
Kazakhstan	1
Mexico	3
Namibia	3
Poland	5
Russia	5
South Korea	14
Taiwan	18
the Netherlands	2
US	6
UAE	3
UK	1

The students' levels of English are from intermediate to higher intermediate, more specifically, Common European Framework of Reference for languages

(CEFR) A2-B2 levels. As we will see later, we provide the following three discussion themes, (1) *school life*, (2) *cultures*, and (3) *social issues/world peace*. Table 4 shows approximate correspondence between these themes and CEFR scales.

Table 4. Discussion themes and CEFR scales (Council of Europe, 2019)

Discussion themes	CEFR Scales
School life	⎤
Cultures	⎬ A2 ⎤
Social issues/world peace	⎦ ⎬ B1 ⎤ B2

2.2. Project description

2.2.1. An overview

Every year, *Project Ibunka* starts by sending out a Project Ibunka Call For Participation message (*Ibunka* CFP, see supplementary material, Appendix A) to several mailing lists and sites for educational collaboration. This document details the (1) project outline, (2) schedule, and (3) student registration directions.

Figure 1, Figure 2, and Figure 3 show the primary interfaces of the current version of WBB. Users see Figure 1 when they are authenticated. This page is a portal to several discussion boards. Figure 2 appears when they choose a discussion board. When they post a comment[4] to a previously posted message, it is shown with some indentation. They can see the relationship between messages posted onto the board. When they click on one of the subject lines, as shown in Figure 2, a message view page (Figure 3) appears.

---
4. Here, a comment means both an additional suggestion, opinion, remark, response, etc. given by a user AND a reply, answer, etc. to an inquiry from others. It should be referred to as a comment/reply.

Chapter 10

Figure 1. Welcome page and theme selection

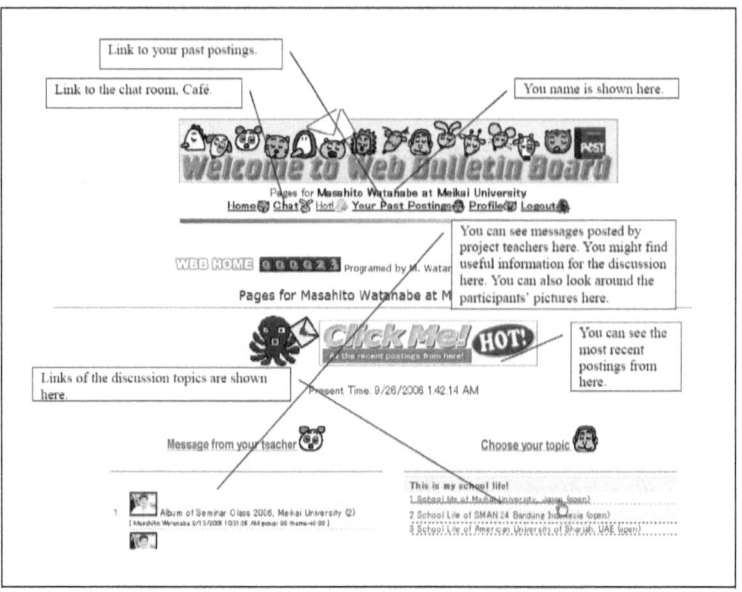

Figure 2. Message tree view

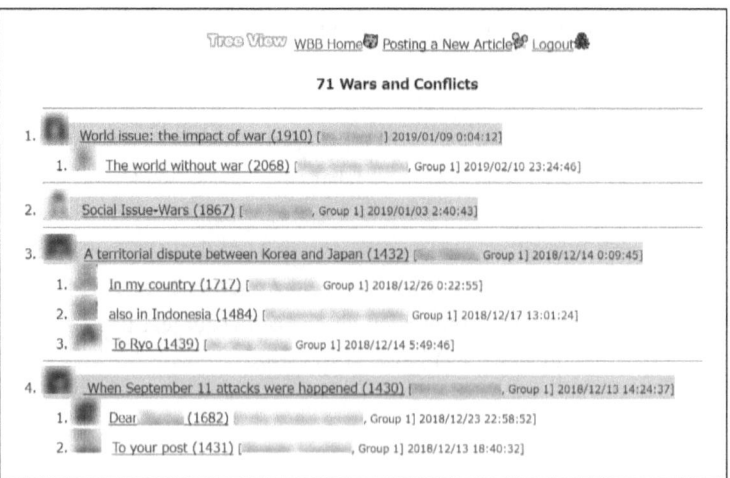

Figure 3. Message view

A few new tools have been added for teachers to retrieve students' postings on WBB since 2000. However, the fundamental phases for the interaction stated in *Ibunka* CFP and project moderation have almost been the same for the last 19 years.

Chapter 10

2.2.2. Features

The following three sub-sections explain the three unique features of Project Ibunka: (1) non-unified project goals for partner institutions; (2) selecting and sequencing themes and sub-themes; and (3) moderation by experienced instructors.

Non-unified project goals for partner institutions

Although I started the project with the goal of improving students' English writing, this is not the sole goal of the project. Every institution can set up its own goals. Most of the partner teachers evaluate students based on their contributions to the project activities. However, this is not required at all. In fact, some teachers use Project Ibunka for self-learning opportunities for their students, and do not use students' contributions for course evaluation. Students also can post almost any messages they like irrespective of regulatory standards listed in the Project Ibunka CFP message. Both teachers and students can enjoy considerable leeway in the project. Figure 4 displays this graphically (Watanabe, 2006).

Figure 4. Goals of Project Ibunka

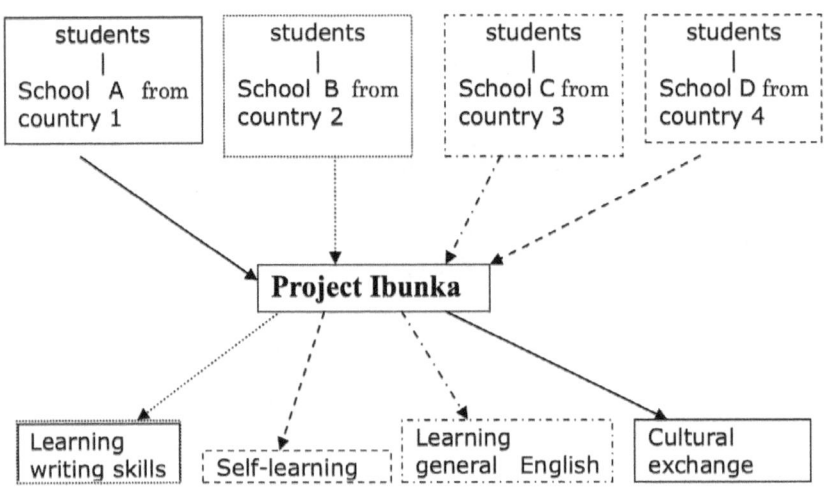

Compare Figure 4 to Figure 5, which depicts online team-teaching projects. In team-teaching, not only students but also teachers collaborate for a few unified goals of the project. Teachers are responsible for the development of students from other institutions too.

Figure 5. Goals of online team-teaching[5]

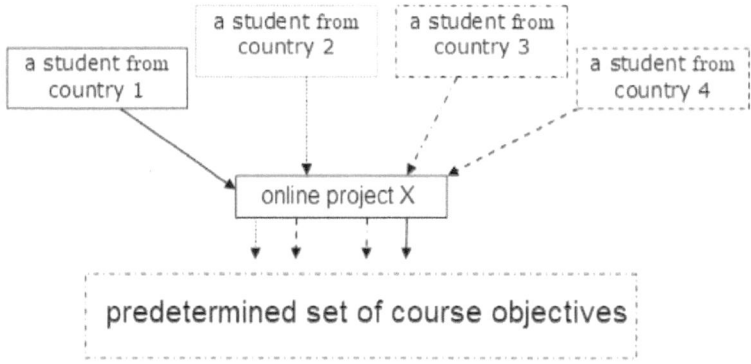

Project Ibunka does not specify any common educational goals for partner schools. Instead, it provides only the opportunities for VE among students. Thus, partner teachers should carefully design their courses so that students might achieve desirable outcomes through participation in the project. However, they do not have any responsibility for the goals set up by other partner teachers. It guarantees educational flexibility for teachers. They do not have to negotiate among partner teachers about the core concepts of the project, nor do they have to make any fundamental revisions in their course syllabus. This also has contributed to facilitating project participation.

Selecting and sequencing themes and sub-themes

As is stated in the Project Ibunka CFP message, the project has three themes for discussion, i.e. (1) *school life*, (2) *cultures*, and (3) *social issues/world peace*.

---
5. The original idea of this figure comes from Watanabe (2006, p. 36).

They are sequentially arranged, and each lasts for four weeks. These themes are roughly in line with CEFR scales (see Table 4). Students start from the topics of so-called, *big C* cultures and move to *little c* cultures (Erasmus+, 2017). *School life* requires students to write a message with 200 or more words; *cultures*, 300 or more; and *social issues/world peace*, 400 or more. Students have to write longer and more challenging essays as the themes proceed. Thus, the themes are arranged by the degree of language and cognitive skills required.

Each theme has several sub-themes. As for the theme, *School life*, a series of sub-themes, such as (1) *School Life of [...] - Indonesia*, (2) *School Life of [...] - Indonesia*, (3) *School Life of [...] - Indonesia*, (4) *School Life of [...] - Taiwan*, and the others are listed in Figure 6 (institution names are masked).

Figure 6. School life sub-themes

School life (Sept. 24 - Oct. 21)
1 School Life of ▓▓▓▓ - Indonesia (open)
2 School Life of ▓▓▓▓ - Indonesia (open)
3 School Life of ▓▓▓▓ - Indonesia (open)
4 School Life of ▓▓▓▓ Taiwan (open)
5 School Life of ▓▓▓▓ - South Korea (open)
6 School Life of ▓▓▓▓ Taiwan (open)
7 School Life of ▓▓▓▓ - Germany (open)
8 School Life of ▓▓▓▓ - Brazil (open)
9 School Life of Yokohama National University - Japan (open)
10 School Life of ▓▓▓▓ - Indonesia (open)

For this theme, *School life*, students play two roles: a *host* and a *guest*. First, host students (i.e. students from the same institution) post messages about their school life onto the board with their institution name. Then, when guest students (i.e. students from different institutions) make a comment or an inquiry to the hosts, the host students then reply to them. This is a type of group discussion and promotes ice-breaking among partner students.

The themes, *cultures,* and *social issues/world peace* are not group-oriented. They are open to all participants. They each have the following sub-themes.

Events and places of interest
- Festivals in My Country/Town/School
- Annual/Seasonal Events of My Country/Town/School
- Tourist Spots and Theme Parks of My Country/Town
- Christmas of My Country/Town/School
- Birthday Party
- Dating and St. Valentine's Day

Food
- Fast Food, Snacks, and Sweets of My Country/Town
- Breakfast, Lunch, and Dinner of My Country/Town/School

Entertainment
- My Favorite TV Programs, Films, Animations, and Comics
- My Favorite Music
- My Favorite Sports Activities
- My Favorite Fashion
- My Favorite Novels/Literary Works
- My Extracurricular/Club/Volunteer Activities
- Internet and Mobile Phone Uses
- 56 Traditional Arts of My Country/Town

Family
- How Parents Raise their Children in My Country
- Young People of My Country/Town
- The Aged of My Country/Town

Education
- Elementary School Education
- High School Education
- University Education

Chapter 10

- This is How I have Learned English
- Students' Job Hunting

Humanistic Activities
- This is What I Believe and Think, My Religion and Philosophy
- This is my Language
- Other Topics

Social issues/world peace
- Wars and Conflicts
- Crime
- Educational Issues
- Family and Human Issues
- Economic and Political Issues
- Health and Disease
- Environmental Issues
- Other topics

The diversity of the sub-themes, especially that of *cultures*, is to ensure learner-centered voluntary participation in the project. All students are free to follow any topics they like, and they do not have to take the topics a teacher or a group had determined in advance. Compared to the *cultures* theme, the *social issues/ world peace* theme has less sub-themes. The sub-themes are broader in nature. This topic brings students with similar interests together, and facilitates more concentrated and critical discussion.

Moderation by experienced instructors

Intercultural exchanges, especially when they are organized online as a VE, require an experienced *moderator*, whose role Carlson (1989) defined as follows:

> "[moderators] help people get started, give them feedback, summarize, weave the contributions of different folks together, get it unstuck when necessary, deal with individuals who are disruptive, or get off the track,

bring in new material to freshen it up periodically, and get feedback from the group on how things are going and what might happen from the group on how things are going and what might happen next... [Further, the facilitator needs to] communicate with the group as a whole, sub-groups, and individuals to encourage participation" (pp. 6.11).

Teachers' moderation is significant in *Project Ibunka*. Teachers have to give students various types of information, reply promptly to the inquiries posted, achieve a sense of unity, reduce the risk associated with VE, and guide them to better learning cooperation. The weekly-published project newsletters mainly undertake the role of this. They are published 12 times by the end of the project. They provide information about (1) current tasks for students, (2) the operational procedures of WBB, (3) the partner schools, students and teachers, (4) the compositional skills, (5) common online asynchronous communication skills, (6) several excellent postings of the week, (7) a few reading materials for critical thinking, and others (see supplementary material, Appendix B).

Recognition of outstanding contributors to the project is another valuable means of moderation. WBB has a unique system of classifying and counting students' postings. Every student has an area, *Your Past Posting* (see Figure 7), where all the postings that have some relevance to him/her are listed. On this page, those postings that the student himself/herself wrote are shown without any indentation. They are called *outbound messages*, meaning that the message has gone from him/her to other participants. On the other hand, if their messages can get comments from others, those incoming messages are shown with some indentation. They are called *inbound messages*, meaning they have come from others and arrived to him/her.

At the end of the *Your Past Posting* page, you can find a table that shows the number of both outbound and inbound messages for each of the three themes. *Points* at the right end of the table shows the total number of both outbound and inbound messages. This number, called *the contribution point*, can be taken as a measure of a student's effort in the project. Every year, on the sixth and twelfth issues of the newsletter, the following contributor ranking is published (Figure 8).

Chapter 10

Figure 7. Your Past Postings page

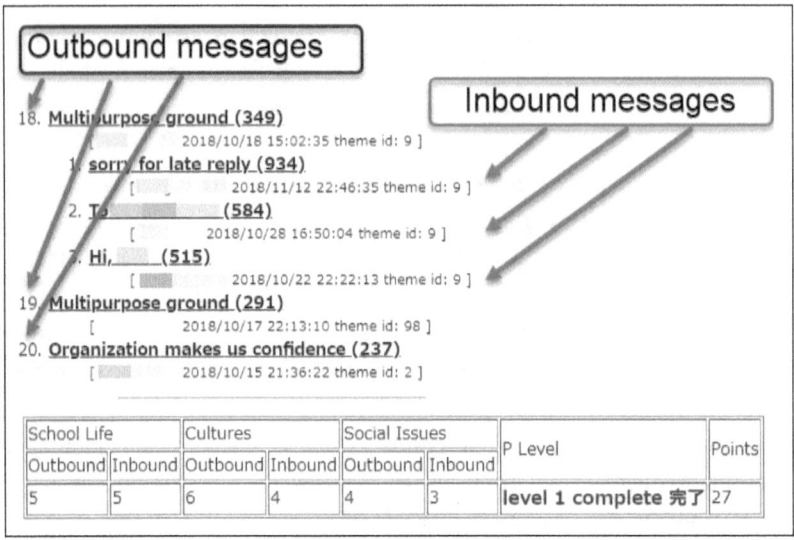

Figure 8. Contributor ranking (Project Ibunka2018, Newsletter No 12, p. 5)

rank	name	Outbound Total	Inbound Total	Total	school
1		66	30	96	Indonesia
2		49	17	66	Indonesia
3		27	16	43	Indonesia
4		32	8	40	- Germany
5		23	15	38	Indonesia
5		24	14	38	- Germany
7		24	11	35	- Germany
8		15	17	32	- South Korea
8		24	8	32	- Germany
10		20	11	31	- Germany
10		17	14	31	- Germany

The ranking acknowledges students' efforts in the project and gives them motivation for further work. Note that to get higher points, students should post their messages considering their readers as much as possible. Otherwise, their postings cannot induce readers to make their comments. *The contributor points* offered in *Project Ibunka* promote writing for communication.

Two types of certificates can be attained after the project is completed. They are given to students who have fulfilled the following requirements for a Level 2 participation certificate:

- have written at least one post for each of the three themes, i.e. (1) *school life*, (2) *cultures*, and (3) *social issues/world peace*. Each contained at least 200, 300 and 400 words, respectively; and

- have made at least three comments to the postings of other partner students for each of the three themes. Each of the participants' comments contained at least 100 words.

They are also given to students for a Level 1 participation certificate, in addition to the two requirements for Level 2 participation, one should at least recieve two comments from other partner students for each of the three themes.

In my writing courses, the fulfillment of Level 2 participation is one of the requirements of the course. If students do not achieve this level, they will fail. The level ensures students at least 12 points in total[6]. Points over 12 are, of course, evaluated. In order to achieve better marks, they have to work on both outbound and inbound messages. This evaluation policy copes with the lack of purpose, one of the two issues[7] that occurred in online pen-pal exchanges, as identified by Warschauer (1995, p. 49). Writing by computer to people in other parts of the world can be a very exciting experience, especially in the beginning, but for many students, the initial excitement can wear off. Experience

---

6. 12=4x3, i.e. four outbound points for each of the three themes.

7. The first issue pointed out in Warschauer (1995, p. 49) is lack of response. This often occurs in one-to-one exchange of pen-pal. However, it rarely occurs in one-to-many exchange of online bulletin-board.

has proven that international email exchanges can become lackluster if they are not somehow integrated into the curriculum of the course.

2.3. Data collection and analysis

In this paper, a quantitative analysis is conducted with all data collected from *Project Ibunka 2018*. The research data mainly come from two database tables: *user profile* and *forum*. A *user profile* table is created by a database administrator and stores information relevant to all of the users, such as user-ids, passwords, personal names, schools, and others. It is not accessible by standard users. It gives us an overview of registered users' participation. A *forum* table stores information relevant to all the messages posted by users, such as posters' user-ids, message subject lines, message bodies, posting times, theme-ids, and others. A record of every user's access to this table is created once a user posts his/her message to the online forms. It provides an overview of the nature of interactions among users.

I set up two essential features in the analysis of students' interactions, i.e. *thread-initiating* and *influential*. If a message posted is not a response to any previous messages, it is [+ thread-initiating], meaning the message starts a discussion anew. If it is a response to a message posted, it is [- thread-initiating], meaning the message is a comment to a previously posted one and does not start a new thread. If a message induces other students to post a comment to it, it is [+ influential], meaning it influences readers. If not, it is [- influential], meaning it does not invite others to comment.

With these two features, postings are classified into four types. In Type 1 postings, [+ thread-initiating] and [+ influential], the author started a new topic, and other students made one or more comments. In Type 2 postings, [- thread-initiating] and [+ influential], the author commented on a message previously posted, and this comment inspired others to reply. In Type 3 postings, [- thread-initiating] and [- influential], the author made a comment, but it was not commented on by anyone. In Type 4 postings, [+ thread-initiating] and [- influential], the author started a new topic, but no one commented. Table 5 summarizes this.

Table 5. Four types of interaction

	Thread-initiating	Influential
Type 1	+	+
Type 2	-	+
Type 3	-	-
Type 4	+	-

3. Results

Of the 204 participants of *Project Ibunka 2018*, 12 are teachers and 192 are students. The number of postings by each student varies significantly from 0, minimum, to 66, maximum. The following is a frequency distribution table of students' postings. Table 6 shows the number of postings (bins), the number of students (frequency), the Cumulative Frequency (CF), and the Cumulative Frequency Ratio (CFR), followed with a histogram, as in Figure 9.

Table 6. Frequency distribution of students' postings

Postings (Bins)	Students (Frequency)	CF	CFR
0	32	32	16.7%
1-2	49	81	42.2%
3-4	17	98	51.0%
5-6	17	115	59.9%
7-8	17	132	68.8%
9-10	17	149	77.6%
11-12	11	160	83.3%
13-14	9	169	88.0%
15-16	8	177	92.2%
17-18	3	180	93.8%
19-20	3	183	95.3%
21-22	1	184	95.8%
22-24	4	188	97.9%
25-26	0	188	97.9%
27-28	1	189	98.4%
29-30	0	189	98.4%
31-32	1	190	99.0%
33-34	0	190	99.0%

35-36	0	190	99.0%
37-38	0	190	99.0%
39-40	0	190	99.0%
41-42	0	190	99.0%
43-44	0	190	99.0%
45-46	0	190	99.0%
47-48	0	190	99.0%
49-50	1	191	99.5%
51-52	0	191	99.5%
53-54	0	191	99.5%
55-56	0	191	99.5%
57-58	0	191	99.5%
59-60	0	191	99.5%
61-62	0	191	99.5%
63-64	0	191	99.5%
65-66	1	192	100.0%
Total	**192**		

Figure 9. Histogram of students' postings

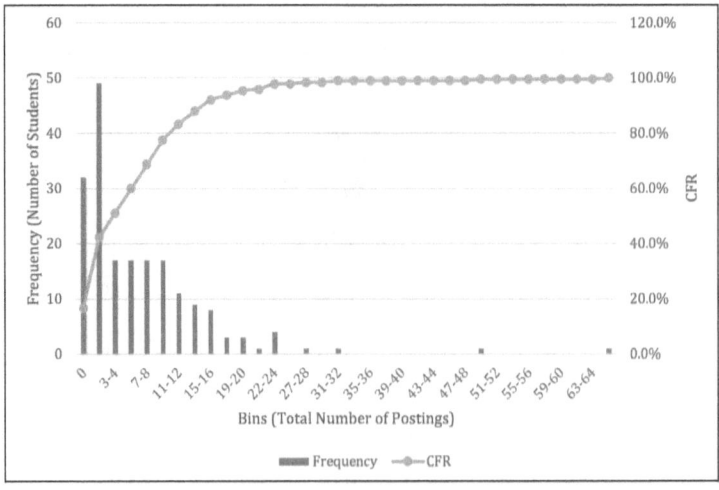

Table 8 shows, of all the students, 42.2% posted less than three messages during the project period. Considering 6.65, the average number of postings, the overall shape of the Figure 9 bar chart is far from that of a normal distribution.

The following table shows the frequency distribution of the different themes. Students' theme selection patterns are classified into eight types, i – viii in Table 7. On this table, note Type i students, who did not participate in any themes at all, amount to 16.7%. We have three types for those who took only one theme, Type ii, iii, and iv. Among these three, Type ii (18.8%), who only took Theme 1 and finished, outnumbers the other two. Thus, coupled with Type i, 35.5%[8] finished participation by the end of Theme 1.

Similarly, of the three two-theme-taking types, Type v (21.9%), who took Theme 1 and 2 and finished, outnumbers the other two, Type vi and vii. Again, coupled with Type i and ii, 57.4%[9] ended by the end of Theme 2. Of all the students, 41.7% participated in all three themes. It means that 58.3% did not participate in all three themes. In short, nearly 60% of participants did not complete all three themes.

Table 7. Frequency distribution of themes taken by students

Themes taken	Type	Theme 1	Theme 2	Theme 3	Students	Ratio
0	i	NA	NA	NA	32	16.7%
1	ii	√	NA	NA	36	18.8%
	iii	NA	√	NA	1	0.5%
	iv	NA	NA	√	0	0.0%
2	v	√	√	NA	42	21.9%
	vi	NA	√	√	1	0.5%
	vii	√	NA	√	0	0.0%
3	viii	√	√	√	80	41.7%
				Total	192	100.0%

Table 8 below shows the number of students classified by their countries, schools, and classes. It also shows the number of students who posted less than three messages and the ratio by country, school, and class.

---

8. Type i (16.7%) and Type ii (18.8%) make 35.5%.

9. Type i (16.7%), Type ii (18.8%), and Type v (21.9%) make 57.4%.

Table 8. Frequency distribution of the students who posted less than three messages

Countries/schools/classes	Students	Less than 3	Ratio
Brazil	**10**	**9**	**90.0%**
A University - Brazil	10	9	90.0%
Germany	**16**	**0**	**0.0%**
B University - Germany	16	0	0.0%
Indonesia	**65**	**40**	**61.5%**
C High School - Indonesia	10	4	40.0%
D High School - Indonesia	10	9	90.0%
E University - Indonesia	45	7	15.6%
Class E-1, E University - Indonesia	23	3	13.0%
Class E-2, E University - Indonesia	22	4	18.2%
Japan	**23**	**2**	**8.7%**
Yokohama National University - Japan	23	2	8.7%
South Korea	**12**	**6**	**50.0%**
F University - South Korea	12	6	50.0%
Taiwan	**66**	**44**	**66.7%**
G University - Taiwan	66	44	66.7%
Class G-1, G University - Taiwan	26	15	57.7%
Class G-2, G University - Taiwan	40	29	72.5%
Total	**192**	**81**	**42.2%**

In some of the institutions, only a few participated in the project. For these institutions, participation was rather voluntary. It did not constitute a required factor for course evaluation. On the other hand, some institutions regarded it as a crucial requirement for the course. Their participation rate was quite high.

These tables confirm the fact that *Project Ibunka* does not have any rigid educational goals, as we saw above. Every partner teacher is free to decide how he/she can use *Project Ibunka* for his/her course and set up his/her course objectives.

However, the low student participation rate does not undermine the value of the project. Compare Table 8 to Table 9, which shows the number of students' postings classified by students' countries, schools, and classes, and the ratio to all postings, i.e. 1,283. Table 8 shows 61.5% of Indonesian students posted less than three messages. On the other hand, Table 9 shows their contribution amounts to 44.0% of all of the messages posted:

Table 9. Frequency distribution of students' postings by countries, schools, and classes

Countries/schools/classes	Postings	Ratio
Brazil	**17**	**1.3%**
A University - Brazil	17	1.3%
Germany	**287**	**22.4%**
B University - Germany	287	22.4%
Indonesia	**565**	**44.0%**
C High School - Indonesia	39	3.0%
D High School - Indonesia	14	1.1%
E University - Indonesia	512	39.9%
Class E-1, E University - Indonesia	217	16.9%
Class E-2, E University - Indonesia	295	23.0%
Japan	**190**	**14.8%**
Yokohama National University - Japan	190	14.8%
South Korea	**47**	**3.7%**
F University - South Korea	47	3.7%
Taiwan	**177**	**13.8%**
G University - Taiwan	177	13.8%
Class G-1, G University - Taiwan	78	6.1%
Class G-2, G University - Taiwan	99	7.7%
Total	**1,283**	**100.0%**

Thus, students' motives for the project can differ significantly even among the students of the same institution.

Table 10 Shows the type of interaction[10], their frequencies, and the average number of words contained in the messages.

---

10. Refer to Table 5 for the details of interaction types.

Table 10. Frequency distribution of students' postings by types of interactions

Interactions	Postings	Ratio	Average words
Type 1	302	23.5%	322.1
Type 2	231	18.0%	156.6
Type 3	641	50.0%	153.3
Type 4	109	8.5%	341.1
Total	1,283	100.0%	209.6

Since Types 1 to 3 are somehow connected with messages posted by other participants, 91.5 %[11] of all messages are *interactive*, meaning they have achieved communication. This reflects message sharing on the WBB. Writing courses hosted in traditional classrooms where sharing is problematic cannot achieve such interactions.

The numbers listed under the row of *average words* differ among types. Types 1 and 4 messages are both [+ thread-initiating]. They are posted to start a new discussion. The values, 322.1 (Type 1) and 344.1 (Type 4), are double the value of 155.6 (Type 2) and 153.3 (Type 3), which are both [- thread-initiating] and posted to comment on an existing message. It is a natural move in communication since we need more explanation about a topic when we start a discussion anew than when we comment.

Table 11 explores students' interactions in more detail than Table 10. It shows the number of postings in each of the three themes and the interaction types. It also shows the corresponding average number of words. Here, it is important to see the values of the same interaction types differ across the three themes (see also Figure 10 and Figure 11). It gives you an idea of how the nature of interaction differs depending on the themes. For example, compare (1) Type 1, *school life* values, i.e. 22.0% (ratio) and 271.6 (average words), (2) Type 1, *cultures* values, i.e. 22.6% (ratio) and 313.4 (average words), and (3) Type 1, *social issues/world peace* values, i.e. 29.7% (ratio) and 433.6 (average words).

---

11. Type 1 (23.5%), Type 2 (18.0%), and Type 3 (50.8%) make 91.5%.

The values with two asterisks (**) show the largest one, while those with one asterisk (*) show the least one, among the interactions of the same type[12]. The following graphs visualize this table.

Table 11. Frequency distribution of students' postings by themes and types of interactions

Themes/interactions	Postings	Ratio	Average words
1. School life	**563**	**100.0%**	**176.6**
Type 1	124	22.0%*	271.6*
Type 2	123	21.8%**	144.6*
Type 3	279	49.6%	138.7*
Type 4	37	6.6%*	249.8*
2. Cultures	**501**	**100.0%**	**210.3**
Type 1	113	22.6%	313.4
Type 2	90	18.0%	165.3
Type 3	247	49.3%	154.4
Type 4	51	10.2%**	332.3
3. Social issues/world peace	**219**	**100.0%**	**292.8**
Type 1	65	29.7%**	433.6**
Type 2	18	8.2%*	195.4**
Type 3	115	52.5%**	186.4**
Type 4	21	9.6%	523.3**
Total	**1,283**		**209.6**

In Theme 1, *school life*, Type 4 interactions ([+ thread-initiating, - influential]), where messages are left uncommented, shows the least ratio, 6.6%. It means as many as 93.4% postings are *interactive*. Type 2 interactions ([- thread-initiating, + influential]), where one participant's comment to the previous message induces others to reply, shows the largest, 21.8%. Even the comments addressed to others are commented in return with high probability. A friendly and casual atmosphere is rich on Theme 1 boards.

---

12. For example, (1) the ratio of Type 1 interaction of Theme 1, 22.0%, with one asterisk, is less than the other two Type 1 ratios, 22.6% (Type 1, Theme 2) and 29.7% (Type 1, Theme 3), and (2) The average words of Type 4, Theme 3, 523.3, with two asterisks, outnumbers both that of Type 4, Theme 1, 249.8 and that of Type 4, Theme 2, 332.3.

Figure 10. The ratio of discussion types by themes and types

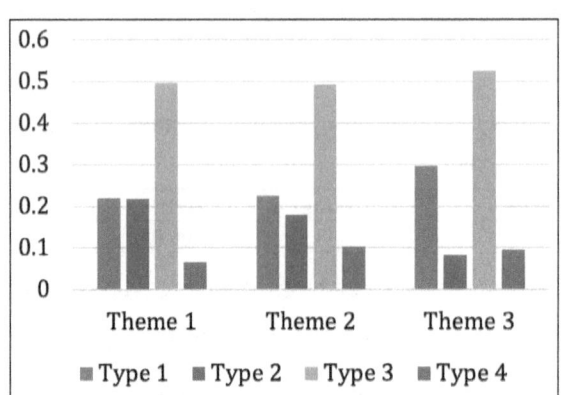

Figure 11. The average number of words by themes and types

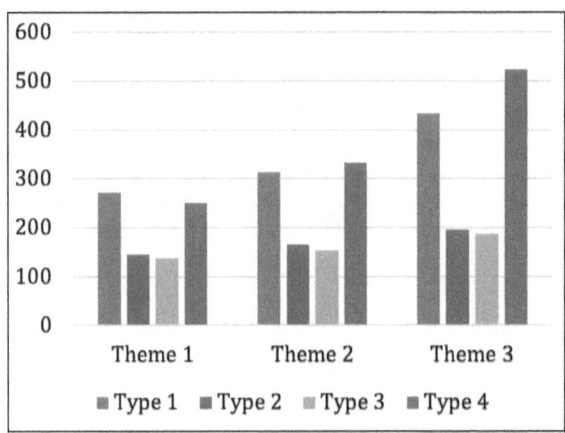

On the other hand, in Theme 3, *social issues/world peace*, first note that values listed under the row of *average words* are all given with two asterisks, i.e. the largest ones. Even in [- thread-initiating] Type 2 and Type 3 interactions, students write more words than in other themes. It is generally the case that the more challenging topics become, the more words we should write to conclude. The ratio of Type 3, 52.5%, is the largest. Since Type 3 is [- thread-initiating, - influential], the challenging topics posed might be too formal to attract comments. We can also infer that students might have lost their enthusiasm for writing in this theme since they had already written a great deal before they started Theme 3.

The largest number might reflect the fact that students are asked to write more words in Theme 3 at the beginning of the project. However, they are completely free to write and post any messages in this theme. Partner teachers rarely prevent their students from posting when their essays do not contain the number of words required. In fact, *Ibunka* CFP stipulates 100 words or more for a comment to a previously posted message irrespective of the three themes. However, non-thread initiating postings, i.e. Type 2 and Type 3 messages, gradually increase the word count as the themes proceed.

Between Themes 1 and 3, Theme 2, *cultures*, shows some intermediate characteristics on interactions. Except for the ratio of Type 4, 10.2%, all the values of ratio and average words are given without any asterisks. They come between light and feasible Theme 1, and formal and challenging Theme 3. The largest ratio of Type 4 might arise from the fact that we offer as many as 27 discussion boards for this theme, and some messages are more likely to be unattended.

We can conclude from the analysis above that each of the three themes maintains distinct aspects of interaction, and they are arranged on a scale of learner manageability. If students can go through three themes, they can start from light chatting and gradually end in a formal intercultural discussion.

4. Pedagogical principles

Project Ibunka started with the aim of making English writing activities more communicative through the Internet in 2000. Seppo Tella (1991, 1992a, 1992b) of the University of Helsinki, who organized a series of studies on educational aspects of international Information and Communication Technology (ICT) exchange, pointed out the following three benefits of ICT writing, saying it:

- gives a more learner-centered working environment; students can choose their themes and topics for writing;

- brings quantitative change in writing; students enjoy the intercultural communication and write more than in regular classes; and

- brings qualitative change in writing; to get comments from partners, students have to respect the flow of on-going discussion and often have to adjust the content to make it suitable for their readers.

Although it depends heavily on the nature of each student, if he/she is well-motivated, the three benefits have been realized in *Project Ibunka*. It provides students with many choices of theme and sub-theme. We can find students who post a lot of messages moved by their own will to respond. Students who go through the three themes gradually increase the average number of words contained in a message as stated in the *Ibunka* CFP. They change their writing styles depending on the themes and the interaction types.

5. Conclusion

It is true that more detailed qualitative analysis of changes in students' intercultural awareness is required. However, we can say that Project Ibunka offers many opportunities to experience cultural differences. For example, compared to many partner students in other countries, Japanese students do not have many opportunities to use English for communication in the classroom and on campus as well as in their daily life after school. Their English is accurate but lacks fluency. As we see from Figure 8, *contributor ranking* of partner students, no Japanese students rank in the top 20. However, when a Japanese student posts a message about his/her school life, a few Indonesian students more than likely write comments to him/her. It gives them the confidence that their English is sufficient to communicate with English learners from foreign countries. During the phase of the Theme 3 discussion, we can find articles about religions in Germany, Taiwanese music, a finger cutting tradition in Indonesia, the Chuseok festival of South Korea, Independence Day celebrations in Indonesia, *Eragon*, a fantasy story by C. Paolini, family life in Germany, a traditional torch parade in Cianjur, a city in West Java, a sweet 17 birthday party in Indonesia, *How to Get Away with Murder*, an American TV drama, and several others. These topics cannot be bypassed without stimulating students' intellectual curiosity.

In this article we saw the three core administrative features of *Project Ibunka*, which are repeated below:

- non-unified project goals for partner institutions;

- selecting and sequencing themes and sub-themes; and

- moderation by experienced instructors.

Due to these VE features, and in addition to the three benefits of ICT writing courses outlined above, *Project Ibunka* also provides three major educational benefits:

- experiencing cultural diversity by reading messages of foreign students;

- learning intercultural strategies and skills by interacting among participants with different cultural backgrounds; and

- improving gradually their quality of writing by undertaking tasks that become more challenging in the course of the project.

Although the low participation rate of partner students might be considered an issue of the project, if teachers and students are well-motivated to participate in the three themes of the project, they are sure to achieve the desirable educational goals that each partner school would have.

Chapter 10

6. Supplementary materials

https://research-publishing.box.com/s/1jjczwki7mibh2ah1fhd1mb62s045ecy

References

Carlson, L. (1989). Effective moderation of computer conferences: hints for moderators. In M.G. Brochet (Ed.), *Moderating conferences* (pp. 6.10-6.13). Universtiy of Guelph

Council of Europe. (2019). *Global scale - table 1 (CEFR 3.3): common reference levels.* https://www.coe.int/en/web/common-european-framework-reference-languages/table-1-cefr-3.3-common-reference-levels-global-scale

Erasmus+. (2017, May 19). *"Big C" culture, "little c" culture.* Erasmus+ KA2 Project Co-funded by the European. https://erasmusmyway.wordpress.com/2017/05/19/big-c-culture-little-c-culture/

Tella, S. (1991). *Introducing international communication networks and elecronic mail into foreign language classrooms (Research report no. 95).* University of Helsinki, Department of Teacher Education.

Tella, S. (1992a). *Boys, girls and e-mail: a case study in Finnish senior secondary schools (Research report no. 110).* University of Ehlsinki, Department of Teacher Education.

Tella, S. (1992b). *Talking shop via e-mail: a thematic and linguistic analysis of electronic mail communication (Research report no. 99).* University of Helsinki, Department of Teacher Education.

Warschauer, M. (1995). *E-Mail for English teaching.* TESOL.

Watanabe, M. (1998). Using Meikai University's newly created Web Bulletin Board to teach writing in LAN-connected computer labs. *JABAET Journal, 2,* 73-84.

Watanabe, M. (2006). Better e-moderation for OET and Project Ibunka. *Meikai Journal, Faculty of Languages and Cultures, 6,* 33-66.

11. Musings on virtual exchange in the Asia-Pacific and beyond

Eric Hagley[1]

Abstract

As Virtual Exchanges (VEs) become more common in foreign language classrooms around the world, teachers are rightly asking 'what will my students be getting from this'? If their students are advanced, they can enter into in-depth interactions thus attaining broader and deeper intercultural knowledge as a minimum, from participation in VE. However, for beginner students, VE also has much to offer. Whether they are simple intercultural interactions that have a profound effect on students who have never interacted with people from other countries and cultures or advanced interactions, VEs have the potential to improve the lives of all who participate in them. The question then is 'why are there not more of them'? This chapter will reflect on the situation in the Asia-Pacific region noting some of the problems associated with incorporating VEs there. It will also try to show the importance of a more international approach for the incorporation of VE into education systems.

Keywords: virtual exchange, intercultural understanding, ICC.

1. Introduction

The chapters preceding this one have, along with much other research elsewhere, made the case that VE is important, particularly in the fields of

---

1. Hosei University, Tokyo Japan; iveprojectorg@gmail.com; https://orcid.org/0000-0002-4795-8043

How to cite: Hagley, E. (2020). Musings on virtual exchange in the Asia-Pacific and beyond. In E. Hagley & Y. Wang (Eds), *Virtual exchange in the Asia-Pacific: research and practice* (pp. 231-240). Research-publishing.net. https://doi.org/10.14705/rpnet.2020.47.1154

language and culture education. There remains many issues that need to be overcome to ensure it becomes a standard part of classes in these fields. O'Dowd and Lewis (2016) give in-depth coverage of what has already been written on the history of VE. There is not much that can be added to their detailed history. What their work shows, however, is that the terminology used throughout the history, and the present, of VE is varied, and because of that, can be confusing. Computer Mediated Communication (CMC), eTandem, Collaborative Online International Learning (COIL), telecollaboration, online intercultural exchange, and many more terms have been used to label VE. Later in this chapter I hope to address this. The confusion caused by the disparate terminology is one area that holds back the adoption of VE particularly in Asia. If the field cannot agree on basic terminology, how can the core ideas be disseminated and taken up?

Another area that can be problematic when VE is incorporated into classes is assessment. As in other parts of the world assessment is important, but for educators in Asia a numerical grade is often crucial. VE is generally not seen to lend itself to numerical grading, however, with modern assessment methods, this should not be a problem that cannot be overcome. Integrating valid and reliable grading into VE is essential for it to become standard in language classrooms everywhere. Some ideas on this aspect will also be offered later in this chapter.

More than anything else, better collaboration between education departments at the institution and government level in Asia is essential to foster VE in the region. Students and educators see VE as an incredible means of building bridges, connecting societies, and developing better understanding between individuals and across cultures. Research shows the benefit of VE to language learning (Ware & O'Dowd, 2008) and intercultural understanding (Chen & Yang, 2014; Thorne & Black, 2007), yet in the Asia-Pacific region, as with many other regions around the world, there are few inter-government projects that are promoting this incredibly powerful educational practice. A discussion needs to be started on how best to systematically incorporate VE into curricula throughout the region and the world.

2. Terminology

The early days of online communication saw Turoff and Hiltz (1978) use the term CMC and thereafter many language teachers also used the term (Chun, 1994; Warshauer, 1996). This was fine until other devices became available. Now not only computers are used – modes of communication have changed dramatically as too the different kinds of exchange. We now see single language exchanges (English as Lingua Franca (ELF), Spanish as lingua franca), dual-language exchanges (presently called eTandem, twinning, and others), and multi-lingual exchanges. Some exchanges are synchronous while others are asynchronous or combinations thereof. There are text only, voice only, and video only exchanges and combinations thereof too. There have been exchanges that were email-based, Learning Management System (LMS)-based, Voice Over Internet Protocol (VOIP)-based, and combinations thereof too. Some exchanges have been simple language-based ones, others have been cultural. Some have involved collaboration and been task-based, while others were just exchanges of information for language learning. Many others have involved academic fields outside of language learning. Rather than give individual references to each of these, the reader should look at the recently created VE research database at the UniCollaboration's site[2]. Here you will find all the examples listed above and more.

Therefore, it is a challenge to find a single term to cover this variety of activities. Recently the Steven's Initiative (2020) has created a useful typology to try and clarify many of the terms used. The document states "this effort represents an important and necessary first step towards improving discourse around virtual exchange and making progress toward a mature field" (Steven's Initiative, 2020, p. 16). It is a very major 'first step' that goes a long way to creating a better understanding of the field. However it is still not particularly clear and it is suggested here that all exchange types should come under the umbrella term VE. How might this look?

---

2. https://www.zotero.org/groups/2434739/virtual_exchange_and_telecollaboration

Chapter 11

At the moment eTandem is a commonly used term in this field but this could become 'Dual Language Virtual Exchange' (DLVE). The word 'tandem' implies a tight unity in direction and movement. Tandem diving, a tandem bicycle, tandem kayaks – these all have people doing the same thing, going in the same direction and speed. This is not always the case with DLVE as students can be, and often are, at different levels of language attainment. When participating in DLVE, the things students do and the speed they do them at can also be different yet the relationship can still be very beneficial. The DLVE model is more like dual carriageways where different vehicles are going in different directions and at different speeds but still using the same carriageway. "eTandem" is an often used model within the VE field and should therefore not have a different name but instead be one type of VE. Multi-lingual VE would be the obvious title given to VEs with more than two languages being used. The semantics is essential as people who hear the term know more clearly what it is referring to.

Telecollaboration is another term used, often interchangeably, in the VE context. After a particularly fruitful conference at her institution in Barcelona, I was talking at the post-conference function with Melinda Dooley, one of the prominent people who has moved the field forward through incredibly hard work, enthusiasm, and total belief in its benefits. She was passionate when talking about the difference between VE and telecollaboration. I agreed at the time that indeed there is a difference, but also believe that if collaboration is the main objective of a particular VE then 'Collaborative VE' (CVE) would be a better term than telecollaboration as it encapsulates the collaborative side of 'telecollaboration' while maintaining the crucial VE terminology. This same logic applies to COIL.

The disparate terminology is holding back VE particularly in Asia due to the confusion it creates. Without more consistent terminology there is a greater chance of misunderstanding. Once the term VE is settled on it can be properly expounded and its application in various fields developed. The US government and European groups have settled on the term and it would now be wise for educators and researchers to also ensure that we use it in all future research.

The UniCollaboration group named its journal the *Journal of Virtual Exchange* and there are other areas where the push for standard terminology is gaining momentum. It is crucial that it continues and the terminology becomes standard across the field. Once that happens, those wanting to support VE development and promote it in Asia can do so with more confidence.

3. Assessment

Another major issue VE has in Asia is assessment. Most of the skills that students use in VE are soft skills. These are usually more difficult to assess numerically compared to other basic skills, and it is much more difficult to separate students by one percentage point or less when assessing their soft skills. This, unfortunately, is often required by educators in Asia who also need specific reasons as to why there is a difference between particular students' grades. Byram (1997, 2008) and others have made great strides in outlining what is needed to assess Intercultural Communicative Competence (ICC) which has resulted in excellent materials being published recently such as Lázár et al.'s (2020) work. However, as noted in the methods of assessment section of the ICCinTE project[3], "there will always be some subjectivity in assessing ICC" (n.p.). It is unfortunate indeed that this statement alone will often preclude VE from being incorporated in some Asian contexts at present. All education systems need to trust their educators to assess students' work impartially even if there is some subjectivity. Still, ICC assessment also needs to continue to develop even better tools that ensure assessment can be both formative and summative.

Training is an essential part of the process. Over the period 2015 to 2020, the EU-sponsored Erasmus+ project included Asia, though only 15% of the mobility budget was aimed there. Part of this project was the RICH-Ed program in China which has provided many excellent opportunities for educators to develop better understanding of interculturality and many resources have been made available through that program. However, unlike the EU, there is yet to be a concerted push

---

3. http://archive.ecml.at/mtp2/Iccinte/results/en/assessing-competence.htm

from Asian governments' education departments to coordinate the development of intercultural programs for intercultural training and VE implementation in an Asian context. Several language and culture associations such as GLoCALL, AsiaCALL, and APVEA work to improve this situation but more needs to be done at a government level. At present the development of VE is being led by European educators but there is much that educators and researchers in Asia can offer. Indeed, the cultural influences of Europe on who is and who is not interculturally competent according to CEFR[4] ratings, and therefore receiving a higher grade, need to be investigated by researchers and educators from Asia and other regions as they may well hold different beliefs. Japan has developed their own CEFR-based descriptors but these do not touch on ICC. Much more needs to be done throughout the region.

In the meantime, educators need to make use of the descriptors and rubrics that are available and that have been tested for validity and reliability such as those developed for the CEFR (2018) companion model and outlined in the sections 'facilitating pluricultural space' and 'sociolinguistic appropriateness'. Also there is Bennett's (2008) intercultural knowledge competency rubric. These and others can be adapted to our students' classroom environments and be used to assess how students' ICC develops.

4. Internationalization of VE

VE is an exceptional way of allowing your students to access an international audience and be interculturally acclimatized in a safe and secure environment. However, many of the larger VEs that are in the international sphere at the moment are not truly neutral. Nowadays it is almost impossible to find a truly 'neutral' project as funding for these is usually tied to a specific outcome. The goals of the Soliya project[5] for example, while noble, are not linked to a truly free exchange of ideas. The purpose of the project is specific and participants are also limited

---

4. Common European Framework of Reference for languages

5. https://www.soliya.net/

to particular cultures. There is no doubt that it is an incredible project and the results speak for themselves but there are power and culture imbalances within it. The project exists due to the wealth of the participating Western institutions and their ability to fund it. This is the reality even though it is a non-profit, and while the institutions deserve kudos for their efforts, wouldn't it be better to make the exchanges more global in both makeup and application? There would be obvious hurdles to overcome but being more inclusive of non-Islamic Asia, South and Central America, as well as other parts of Africa, to name just a few regions, would bring deeper insights that should enable a broader view of the world for participants.

Initiatives sponsored by the UniCollaboration group share similar problems. Funding for many of these is supplied by the EU so obviously the projects should have a benefit for EU-based countries and institutions. This is understandable but there needs to be a truly international exchange with "no strings attached". The International VE Project (IVE Project) attempts to be that yet its funding from the Japanese Kaken program means it is not fully neutral, even though students from any culture can join it freely. If that model could become self-funded it would be a big step toward becoming more neutral. The world is a big place so the logistics of creating a truly international, yet neutral, exchange are complicated but that should not stop people attempting to create one.

There are probably many more students involved in individual teacher-organized class-to-class exchanges than in all the major VEs put together. These smaller-scale VEs usually involve just two or maybe three cultures. The teachers involved have probably met at conferences or in some other way and decided to pair their classes. There is more freedom to do what you want in these types of VE and much of the research on VE to date has come from them. At present there is no way to know the actual numbers involved in such exchanges. To boost the standing of VE within research and education circles, a database of all such VE would be very beneficial. The Steven's Initiative is, at the time of writing, trying to make one for VE where US classes/institutions are involved but this is clearly not enough. To truly appreciate the variety and depth of VE around the world an international organization would also be beneficial.

5. VE for future language classes

For those teachers who want their students to interact with others from around the world, but do not have the time or know-how to make that happen, the large-scale VEs outlined above are an option. UniCollaboration also has VE partnering fairs and there are other options available as outlined on the Steven's Initiative website. Sister school partnerships are another option. Asian governments, however need to do more to promote VE throughout Asia and could learn much from the UniCollaboration and Steven's Initiative projects. Many countries within Asia face numerous problems and there is a lot of misunderstanding between the cultures therein; thus, it is of paramount importance that better mutual understanding between the many cultures and people of this region occurs. VE is an excellent way to do this and there are a number of arenas in which VE could take place. One of the best would have to be the language classroom.

It has become clear that VE should be at least one part of all second and other foreign language courses. As language classes are included in most degrees at universities throughout Asia, and as culture is intrinsically tied to language, it would seem obvious to include VE in language classes. The question then, is how best to enable this to happen? The extra work required of language teachers to ensure a platform is maintained, interactions take place, and everyone is on the same page, is too much to ask of already over-worked educators. Though many teachers might already have their students in VE, it is often difficult to maintain the VE long-term as funding is not guaranteed and partner teachers may move on. The need for ready-made VEs that can be incorporated into language courses is obvious. The IVE Project mentioned above is one such method where both ELF exchanges and dual-language exchanges take place, and research in this book and elsewhere (Hagley, 2020; Qu & Hagley, forthcoming) shows the benefits of participating therein. However the scale required for all language learners to be a part of a VE is such that no single VE could possibly handle the millions of students studying English in the region, not to mention the many other second languages that are being studied. For this reason, more effort needs to be made at the government and institution level to develop platforms and resources for VE to be carried out.

6. Conclusion

VE has quickly grown to be an integral part of many education programs in the EU and the US. Collaboration is taking place online between many researchers in numerous fields throughout other parts of the world as well but it is rarely systematically or firmly established in the curricula of institutions in the Asia-Pacific region. This situation needs to be rectified particularly in the fields of language learning and intercultural studies. Of course, there are obstacles in the way, but some of these can be overcome quite easily. Certainly, the VE terminology in the language field will be easier to understand if all the terms come under the VE umbrella. More problematic is the issue of assessment of student participation in VE. This has to be refined such that teachers and students can feel confident in knowing what it is they are being assessed on, and how they are being assessed. The CEFR scale is a good starting point but does not truly capture the online aspect of VE; hence more work needs to be done particularly in the Asia-Pacific region. Better appreciation of the soft skills required to be proficient in ICC is also necessary and an understanding that a grade between one and a hundred will never be able to tell you whether you are proficient. To ensure all this happens and that VE can be carried out easily throughout the region, national education departments need to work more closely together to develop platforms and systems where VE can flourish further. To improve understanding between people and cultures, and for the betterment of international relations in the region, the development of superior language and intercultural competence among students is an important step. VE needs to be systematically incorporated into education systems for this to happen. This book has hopefully gone some way to helping, however, as has been noted, much still needs to be done to make this happen.

References

Bennett, J. M. (2008). Transformative training: designing programs for culture learning. In M. A. Moodia (Ed.), *Contemporary leadership and intercultural competence: understanding and utilizing cultural diversity to build successful organizations* (pp. 95-110). Sage. https://doi.org/10.4135/9781452274942.n8

Byram, M. (1997). *Teaching and assessing intercultural communicative competence.* Multilingual Matters.

Byram, M. (2008). *From foreign language education to education for intercultural citizenship.* Multilingual Matters.

CEFR. (2018). *Common European framework of reference for languages: learning, teaching, assessment companion volume with new descriptors.* https://rm.coe.int/cefr-companion-volume-with-new-descriptors-2018/1680787989

Chen, J. J., & Yang, S. C. (2014). Fostering foreign language learning through technology-enhanced intercultural projects. *Language Learning & Technology, 18*(1), 57-75. http://llt.msu.edu/issues/february2014/chenyang.pdf

Chun, D. M. (1994). Using computer networking to facilitate the acquisition of interactive competence. *System, 22*(1), 17-31. https://doi.org/10.1016/0346-251x(94)90037-x

Hagley, E. (2020). Effects of virtual exchange in the EFL classroom on students' cultural and intercultural sensitivity. *CALLEJ, 21*(3), 74-87.

Lázár, I., Huber-Kriegler, M., Lussier, D., Matei, G., Peck, C., Busch, B., & De la Maya Retamar, G. (2020). *A guide for language teachers and teacher educators: developing and assessing intercultural communicative competence.* Council of Europe.

O'Dowd, R., & Lewis, T. (2016). Introduction to online intercultural exchange and this volume. In R. O'Dowd & T. Lewis (Eds), *Online intercultural exchange: policy, pedagogy, practice* (pp. 3-20). Routledge. https://doi.org/10.4324/9781315678931

Qu, M., & Hagley, E. (forthcoming). *Effectiveness of Moodle-enabled blended learning in a Japanese university's Chinese language program.*

Steven's Initiative. (2020). *Virtual exchange typology.* https://www.stevensinitiative.org/wp-content/uploads/2020/04/Stevens-Initiative-Virtual-Exchange-Typology.pdf

Thorne, S. L., & Black, R. W. (2007). Language and literacy development in computer-mediated contexts and communities. *Annual Review of Applied Linguistics, 27*, 133-160. https://doi.org/10.1017/s0267190508070074

Turoff, M., & Hiltz, S. R. (1978). *The network nation.* Reading.

Ware, P., & O'Dowd, R. (2008). Peer feedback on language form in telecollaboration. *Language Learning & Technology, 12*(1), 43-63. http://llt.msu.edu/vol12num1/wareodowd/default.html

Warshauer, M. (1996). Comparing face-to-face and electronic discussion in the second language classroom. *CALICO Journal, 13*(2&3), 7-25. https://journals.equinoxpub.com/index.php/CALICO/article/view/23397/19402

Author index

D
Deardorff, Darla K. v, xiii
Draeger Jr, Richard viii, 6, 179

H
Hagley, Eric v, ix, xi, 1, 6, 231
Healy, Sandra vii, 4, 125

K
Kaufmann, Thomas viii, 5, 145
Kennedy, Olivia vii, 4, 125
Kulich, Steve J. viii, 6, 179

L
Liu, Ran vii, 3, 77

M
Matsui, Hisae vii, 4, 105
Miao, Liyang vi, 2, 11

R
Ryan, Andrew viii, 5, 165

V
Van Maele, Jan vi, 3, 37

W
Wang, Yi'an v, vi, vii, xi, 1, 2, 3, 11, 77
Watanabe, Masahito vi, ix, 3, 6, 61, 201

www.ingramcontent.com/pod-product-compliance
Lightning Source LLC
Chambersburg PA
CBHW021838220426
43663CB00005B/302